MOVING IMAGE

Legenda/Moving Image publishes cutting-edge work on any aspect of film or screen media from Europe and Latin America. Studies of European-language cinemas from other continents, and diasporic and intercultural cinemas (with some relation to Europe or its languages), are also encompassed. The series seeks to reflect a diversity of theoretical, historical, and interdisciplinary approaches to the moving image, and includes projects comparing screen media with other art forms. Research monographs and collected volumes will be considered, but not studies of a single film. As innovation is a priority for the series, volumes should predominantly consist of previously unpublished material.

Proposals should be sent with one or two sample chapters to the Editor, Professor Emma Wilson, Corpus Christi College, Cambridge CB2 1RH, UK.

APPEARING IN THIS SERIES

1. *Spanish Practices: Literature, Cinema, Television*, by Paul Julian Smith
2. *Cinema and Contact: The Withdrawal of Touch in Nancy, Bresson, Duras and Denis*, by Laura McMahon
3. *Cinema's Inter-Sensory Encounters: Krzysztof Kieślowski and Claire Denis*, by Georgina Evans
4. *Holocaust Intersections: Genocide and Visual Culture at the New Millennium*, edited by Axel Bangert, Robert S. C. Gordon and Libby Saxton
5. *Africa's Lost Classics: New Histories of African Cinema*, edited by Lizelle Bisschoff and David Murphy
6. *Agnès Varda Unlimited: Image, Music, Media*, edited by Marie-Claire Barnet
7. *Thinking Cinema with Proust*, by Patrick ffrench
8. *Blanchot and the Moving Image: Fascination and Spectatorship*, by Calum Watt

Managing Editor
Dr Graham Nelson, 41 Wellington Square, Oxford OX1 2JF, UK

www.legendabooks.com

Agnès Varda Unlimited

Image, Music, Media

Edited by Marie-Claire Barnet

LEGENDA

Moving Image 6
Modern Humanities Research Association
2016

Published by Legenda
an imprint of the Modern Humanities Research Association
Salisbury House, Station Road, Cambridge CB1 2LA

ISBN 978-1-909662-31-5 (HB)
ISBN 978-1-78188-315-0 (PB)

Printed in Great Britain

Copy-Editor: Dr Anna Davies

CONTENTS

Acknowledgements ix

Preface 1

1 Cléo and Dorothée 11
EMMA WILSON

2 Agnès Varda's *Cléo de 5 à 7*: A Triptych of the Textile 27
FRANCESCA MINNIE HARDY

3 *L'Une chante, l'autre pas*: Music, Movement and the Utopian Community 45
PHIL POWRIE

4 *Lara Croft dans un champ de patates*: A Ludomusicological Approach to Agnès Varda 65
HANNAH MOWAT

5 Re-viewing Varda's *Le Bonheur* (1964): Accident? Suicide? Or the Natural Order? That is the Question 87
MARK LEE

6 *Mise en abyme*, Irony and Visual Cliché in Agnès Varda's *Le Bonheur* (1964) 97
CATHERINE DOUSTEYSSIER-KHOZE

7 Ways of Seeing in Agnès Varda's *Les Dites Cariatides* (1984) 109
ISABELLE MCNEILL

8 La mer, la mer, toujours recommencée: A Centrifugal Reading of the Beach in the Work of Agnès Varda 127
FIONA HANDYSIDE

9 Still Varda: Photographs and Photography in Agnès Varda's Late Work 143
SHIRLEY JORDAN

10 Les Cabanes d'Agnès 157
GILL PERRY

11 Out of sites: Art Matters, Contemporary Activism, and Public Encounters with Agnès Varda 171
MARIE-CLAIRE BARNET

Appendix:
1 Cléo's 50th Birthday: Questions-Answers 197
CORINNE MARCHAND
2 Agnès Varda's Interview: Verbal Ping-Pong and Matching Points 203
AGNÈS VARDA

Index 210

ACKNOWLEDGEMENTS

Most grateful thanks are due to different institutions and individuals who have helped throughout this project to celebrate Varda as the 'artiste tout court', with extra special thanks to Durham University, The French Embassy (London), Ciné-Tamaris (Fanny Lautissier, Cecilia Rose and Stéphanie Scanvic), The Tyneside Cinema (Jonny Tull and his team) and its captivated/captivating audience when given back their voices in the dark room, Emma Wilson and Graham Nelson for their unconditional support at Legenda, Phil Powrie for his stellar chairing of the Q&A, Hannah Mowat and Kelle Truby for the unexpected gifts of breaking (artistic) news and endless virtual treasure troves of photos, and Isabelle McNeill for the magician's box of 'boni'. I am indebted just as much to all the contributors for all their shared thoughts and the generous gift of written words, Catherine Dousteyssier-Khoze, Fiona Handyside, Francesca Hardy, Shirley Jordan, Mark Lee, Gill Perry, and many more who had kept their kind but eagle eyes on virtual 'Vardian' links, Christopher Da-Silva, Adrián Francisco-J. Hernández, Santi Fouz-Hernández, and Thérèse de Raedt. For their brilliance, and joyful, faithful support, 4 grateful bows to Abir Hamdar, Lucille Cairns, Vasanti Piette, and Tom Wynn. I could not have gone very far without the accompanying footsteps and guiding spirit offered by Thomas and Margaux Lequeu, in bustling galleries, mazes of cemeteries, or the end of the very long rue Daguerre, or Valérie Mréjen for all her inspiring 'secrets de fabrique' on artistic practices. Marie Dupas most kindly offered detailed information about the passage Pommeraye in Nantes. Anouk, Marine and Nigel Saint appear constantly cast behind the scenes but are always right at the front, in many doorways, I thank them for being my fabulous first aid trio and immediate family, and above all for the cheerful Cherbourg-style umbrellas always ready at the right moment, and the most precious space of free time. Lastly, I owe more than sunflowers and rainy days roses (the kind to be found in *Le Bonheur* and *Peau d'Âne*) to 3 people without whom this whole project would not have even started, the legendary, star crossed or rather (re)united couple of actors of *Cléo de 5 à 7*, Corinne Marchand and Antoine Bourseiller; and Agnès Varda herself, on top of her artistic visions, for the refreshing surprise of a melon, the much needed energy from rare Noirmoutier potatoes, the 8th March 2015 message, and all the words of reluctant wisdom and festive freedom. This volume is dedicated to all of you, with a final mention of the enduring power of artistic creation: this work has been accompanied by a trio, or quatuor, of (firmer than) fictive characters, who can blend so seamlessly into our lives, touching us, beyond words, in 'that ideal Braquean silence', as Julian Barnes reminds us of the enduring and vital presence of paintings. I cannot therefore not mention my own 'femmes puissantes', or the mighty muses in mind for this project, for all seasons and all situations: Demy's radiant duo of singsongy (singing as speaking, blunt and beautiful) 'demoiselles de Rochefort', Delphine and Solange, and Varda's ravishingly rebellious anti-heroines, her dashingly dark and luminous Cléo, and the defeated *and* defying, immortal Mona.*

M.-C. B., Durham, February 2016

* See Julian Barnes, 'Hodgkin: Words for H.H.', in *Keeping an Eye Open: Essays on Art* (London: Jonathan Cape, 2015), pp. 259–71 (p. 271).

PREFACE

Écrire un commentaire de plus... Comment taire?
[Can you comment one more time...? How can one not?][1]

A simple first statement by Agnès Varda is a reminder that one would not be so well advised to cast or label her complex work in the past (tense): 'This film (*The Gleaners*) is not really about memory. I think *now* is so interesting: now as a society, my own life, situations I see, the rotten politics everywhere.'[2] She has underlined repeatedly and most adamantly that she is looking decidedly forward, and also sideways, not quite backwards in a simply linear or nostalgic way: 'Why would one want to get rid of the past? As Jacques Prévert put it, "sometimes, it can jump back right in your face and scratch you". Sometimes, it runs like a river too, and disappears from view quite naturally. I don't work on lasting memories or with the weight of the past on my mind'.[3]

It may be equally unwise to underestimate the obvious and undeniable fact that her massive body of multimedia artistic work keeps on growing, in many directions. This volume originated in the further conversations all the contributors wanted to pursue after the joyful celebration of the fiftieth anniversary of the release of *Cléo de 5 à 7* (shot in 1961, released and nominated for the Cannes Festival Palme d'or in 1962), as part of the film festival in her honour held at the Tyneside Cinema, Newcastle, in November 2012, to coincide with the international conference I organised in the presence of Agnès Varda (rarely seen in the UK), 'Agnès, Cléo and Co: Varda's Cinema at the Tyneside'. How to see such an iconic film again and 'now', and differently? To be surrounded by a most attentive and warmly dedicated audience, bursting with enthusiastic and richly varied questions, was a very promising start. Antoine Bourseiller, who had lost and found my questions to him on postcards earlier that same year — and who sadly died the following spring — remains the unforgettably tender and teasingly poetic soldier roaming the streets with a panic-stricken Cléo, about to go back to Algeria and his own war troubles. While he emitted self-deprecating doubts about his vanishing memory, he kindly sent me a 1973 Avignon Festival postcard of Carolyn Carlson in his own production of *Onirocri*, 'to salute the lucky viewers who would discover *Cléo* for the very first time', a film he had loved for 'the filming adventure and the overall message', and 'a testimony of its times!'. Corinne Marchand, Varda's immortalized Cléo, had already, and most graciously, answered in writing a few questions about her star role, and her precious replies — as well as Varda's answers to the Tyneside Q&A — are included in this volume, illuminating again and slightly differently many of her many different feature films and arguably lesser-known short films. It was also quite revealing to hear that Agnès Varda, curiously enough perhaps, did not expect to be known or acknowledged for the more recent art installations she has been doing over the past decade. What's not to note or not to like in her astonishing output: from the prestigious 50th Venice Biennale (*Patatutopia*, Utopia Station, 2003), to the first national audiovisual commission at the Panthéon to commemorate *Les Justes de France* ('Hommage de la Nation aux Justes de France' [National Homage to the Righteous Among Nations], on 18 January 2007, with former president Jacques Chirac and Simone Veil), or the recreation of her beloved Noirmoutier island in Paris at the Cartier Foundation (*L'Île et Elle*, Fondation Cartier pour l'Art Contemporain, 2006).

In *Agnès Varda: le cinéma et au-delà*, under the editorial team of Antony Fiant, Roxane Hamery and Eric Thouvenel, several critics had indicated that it was high time to revisit Varda's expanded corpus in its many genres and (dis)guises.[4] Despite Varda's relative or surprising doubts about her recognition as a visual artist, it seems again timely and fruitful to highlight, at the very least, how hugely impressive Agnès Varda's creations are — not merely in their longevity but also in their staggering hybridity. These are creations of an artist who now in her late 80s continues to gain accolades: Carrosse d'or, Cannes film festival 2010; Pardo d'Onore Swisscom [Honorary Leopard], Locarno, summer 2014; Palme d'Honneur, Cannes film festival 2015; and reaching more international audiences since her striking self-portrait, *The Beaches of Agnès* (2008), which was awarded the César Award in 2009, the same year she was made *Commandeur de la Légion d'Honneur.*

For a wider audience of classic 'New Wave' French film buffs, just as for new generations who discover her recent installation work, it could be forgotten that Varda has also been taking photographs since the 1950s, notably recording the Avignon festival, trips to Cuba or China (revisited in *Plages et pages chinoises* [*Chinese Beaches and Pages*], Beijing, 2012), political unrest or hippie ideals in 60s California (revamped in the Winter and Spring 2013–14 show, *Agnès Varda in Californialand*, Los Angeles County Museum of Arts, 3 November 2013–22 June 2014) or documenting her film shootings and her husband Jacques Demy's colourful film sets. However, if we can stress the present tense, she seems to have been making much more installation and multi-media art work since the 2003 Venice Biennale, and is becoming increasingly visible on social media, as Ciné-Tamaris (formerly Tamaris Films, 1954) has a Twitter following and a Facebook presence, and has joined the KissKissBankBank public funding site for wider support, making a 'general' or independent appeal, as launched in 2013 to fund the digitalization and 'to save *Les Parapluies de Cherbourg*'. Updates on these websites show that since 2002, Varda has been endlessly working on 'active' transfer and archiving on the latest DVD format, involved in Demy's and her own films' restoration and distribution, tirelessly 'on the road' and extremely busy meeting various publics, or collaborating on ongoing projects, as lately publicized with the visual artist, JR, 'AV et JR deux artistes en goguette' [in high spirits, and gone on a jolly trip, my translation of the double meaning] in the South of France, in order to meet more people, and produce 'new' films and photos in the summer of 2015. Copies of the photos will be given to their subjects as well as the contributors and supporters of the KissKissBankBank appeal.

Over the past few years, and since the resonant popularity and box office success of *Les Glaneurs et la glaneuse* [*The Gleaners and I*] (2000), I would suggest that it has become increasingly acknowledged by different audiences that all her work is still as vibrantly innovative and 'on the move' as ever. Her activities may have been taking new directions, with her involvement in diverse solo or collective exhibitions, such as that dedicated to Jacques Demy (*Le Monde en*chanté *de Jacques Demy* [*The Enchanted/Singing World of Jacques Demy*] at La Cinémathèque française, in collaboration with Ciné-Tamaris, curated by Matthieu Orléan with Rosalie Varda-Demy, 10 April-4 August 2013), which signalled a lifetime of independent production, as well as archiving and restoration. And the the very same year, as mentioned above, *Agnès Varda in Californialand* saw a new reconfiguration and a fresh (re)focusing on her own work, i.e., her 'Californian period', with revamped echoes of her films *Black Panthers* (1968), *Lions Love (... and Lies)* (1969), or *Mur Murs*, and *Documenteur* (1981), without forgetting the remixing and installing of her trademark Fondation Cartier 'cinema hut'. With *Tout(e)/All Varda* (one notes the pun and extra emphasis on the feminine 'e'), her latest DVD collection, appearing in 2012 — a monumental box-set of her 'complete' films produced by ARTE Editions and announced (quite dramatically) in Newcastle as her 'last film opus' — Varda's artistic activity carries on blooming.

Hence the title to this volume, *Varda Unlimited*, with a renewed accent on her interdisciplinary creativity: when will she stop filming? How could that be possible, one might wonder, even, after such a 'final' announcement? One cannot quite imagine why and how she could put a stop to such a seemingly endless flow of creativity. Could it be that chance, her much trusted and chosen force of creativity, was not to be so favoured any more? This type of tricky question has no definitive answer either, as Varda herself underlined regarding her exhibitions: 'I often said that chance was my first assistant but that's not enough. Other key elements are the time and timing of the filming and the places of exhibitions. The installations I prepare are almost all readymade in my mind according to the location where they will end up, at least for the first show; so it's not chance but circumstances which will alter them, or sometimes make them even better.'[5]

'Time doesn't pass but I pass, it's very simple, makes sense, no?', mused Varda on her so-called 'light thinking' and reflecting, however, how 'work flows in (her) mind' ceaselessly , though one may not quite agree this is quite 'light' metaphysics.[6] Let's imagine longevity, length, the duration: there was a special weekend, 30 November to 2 December 2013, at the restored 'Nouveau Latina' cinema, or *ciné des cinéphiles* in the Marais, held to pay a non-stop homage to the 32 films of *Tout(e)/All Varda* [which could also be translated also as 'Typical of Varda]. The three-day meeting may indeed have been experienced as an unfolding *triptyque atypique* [Atypical Triptych] of Agnès Varda herself with the public. Time never stops (except when captured by a camera?): on 8 December 2013, the very first 'Salle Agnès Varda' officially opened at the Louis Daquin Cinema in Blanc-Mesnil. It was all renovated with three rooms in total: the Salle Agnès Varda with 245 seats, the surprisingly smaller Salle Orson Welles with 125 seats, and the intimate Salle Jean Eustache with only 77 seats. The Louis Daquin cinema may arguably be far less well-known but could it now become a household name in Seine-Saint-Denis? *Extra muros* and in the Parisian suburbs, it seems quite fitting that Varda has gained a new (cinematic) 'room of her own' in the middle of our (ageing) *villes nouvelles*, and not that far from Le Bourget and Drancy — two symbolic *lieux de mémoire* (Nora, 1984–87) with highly different travels and transits in mind[7]. Furthermore, lest we forget — an element that is most appropriate when linked with a 'visual artist'[8] whose linguistic puns and literary connexions are legendary — it is to be noted that this 'cultural space' is not that far from the Théâtre and Cinéma Jacques Prévert (Aulnay-sous-Bois) or the Centre Culturel André Malraux (Le Bourget again, with renewed cultural destinations). Their very names strike a resonant echo with the similar artistic hybridity and commitment to a far and wide 'democratisation' of 'culture' so vitally present at the very heart of Varda's multidimensional work. The inaugural programme chosen and presented by Varda includes a revealing documentary series ('*téléfilms*' with a difference), commissioned by Arte, *Agnès de ci de là Varda* [*Agnès From Here From There Varda*, 2011], which maps out Varda's recent encounters with some of her favourite artists around the world. Perhaps it is another nod to her appeal to a much wider audience, addressed via smaller screens, but one cannot miss her highly defined agenda to track down the intricate paths and unpredictable ways of international contemporary artists, and the very clear focus of her travelling camera on all different manifestations of 'art' via the people she likes best, admiration, affection and connection being the defining criteria for her visits, frankly acknowledged in her own introduction to her series.

All the contributors to this multi-voiced series of essays also establish new dialogues, as we could not believe in an end or establish limitations to such an active and creative spirit. Therefore we propose to glean among her various outputs in order to review, reread, re-examine Varda's vastly rich productions in and beyond film in their many thematic affinities and other striking correspondences that appear to constitute her ongoing 'puzzle' or collage of multimedia art productions. Delphine Bénezet's most original, erudite, and passionately thorough take and survey on a hard-to-classify filmic *oeuvre* illuminates why 'resistance and ethics' are key stakes for Varda, 'always the outsider', and keys to open up aspects of her multifaceted work. But she further observes that the political agenda also seems inextricably woven into 'rêveries' or 'magic moments' (as Phil Powrie has already noted) that are produced as well as triggered as responses to her visual creations, when one looks again at this 'experimental filmmaker and technological innovator' who, for decades, has resisted the diktats of representation.[9] Perhaps one could also suggest that rather than considering, or unwillingly constraining, her installations to be 'eclectic and unorthodox' (Bénezet, 5), one could think again of an alternative view that might just as well see a coherent *fil rouge* [red thread] that can tie up all her different multimedia creations and installations, with common themes and issues emerging, as well as strong echoes to be heard between apparently different pieces, whatever their scales might be, and whether they appear deadly serious and monumental (honouring *Les Justes de France* at the Panthéon, as analysed in this volume by Shirley Jordan), or seriously playful (*les cabanes*, beach huts or open-air cinema reinvented, along all our so-called domestic(ated) homes, not so sweet homes, as revisited also by Gill Perry).

That this red thread, the vivid and unfading colour of Varda's passion for her 'art' and political commitment, can also be thought of as an 'eclectic', at times odd (beach?) ball of wool (surrealist connections can be visible), with different strands and colours, I would fully agree with. However, over the years, I would also argue that the re-creation of different installations, with their re-cycling and quasi organic re-inventing of her own collections — and Jacques Demy's archives — could encourage us to reconsider a strong and singular 'Vardian' vision, that may seemingly go in many directions, but simultaneously follows her paradoxically linear, constant, vibrant dedication to a multiplicity of formats, voices, points of views. Alison Smith's masterly volume on Varda's films points out that her work is indeed 'an unusually coherent whole', and rereading her written self-portrait, *Varda par Agnès* (currently being updated) 'is to realise to what extent the issues which preoccupied her at the time of her earliest adventures still interest her.'[10] As Smith rightly highlights, there is no rejection of some of her films; nor, one may add, is there either a simple wistful backwards glance or an anti-nostalgia *tabula rasa* effect, as amply demonstrated in the art of gleaning she adopted and adapted. We need to bear in mind too that she notoriously likes to play with 'meaningful surprises and revelations', the flux and frictions between documentary and fiction, the chiselled structure and duration in films, and so-called 'time effects' in the ornate frames or the very split structure of 'new' video and 'old' photography used for the recent triptychs she produced: 'it's what I call marking the passage of time within time.'[11]

Inside and beyond the many, old and new, waves, and the still-to-be-deciphered black boxes of *cinéma d'auteur*, where does one situate such an artist? For one could predict that labels can never be attached that definitely to the fluidity and freedom of the Vardian *opus magnus*.[12] What might seem to trigger Varda's filmic and artistic creation is not only (self-) doubt, curiosity, chance, but also a need for and an acute sense of sought-after 'public' participation, and a subtle sense of fully acknowledged risk, as 'participatory art' is notoriously hard to pinpoint and define.[13] When asked if in doing exhibitions she wants to let 'people take part, have happenings', her open-ended answer leaves room for interpretation and invites us to reconsider what kind of 'risky' business art encounters can prove to be: 'In my films, I always leave some room, some space for interpretation. The audience had to be witness and part of the film. In the installations, the artist is more at risk.'[14] One may recall what Christian Boltanski, a fellow 'free' spirit and creator interviewed in her *Agnès de ci de là Varda*, had to offer as the beginning of an answer to these uneasy issues of (self-) recognition; how the focus of the author and the multiplicity of the viewers are both required; and moreover, how 'unfocused' a piece of art can ultimately be: 'A good work of art can never be read in one way. My work is full of contradictions. An artwork is open — it is the spectators looking at the work who make the piece, using their own background. A lamp in my work might make you think of a police interrogation, but it's also religious, like a candle. At the same time it alludes to a precious painting, with a single light shining on it. There are many ways of looking at the work. It has to be 'unfocused' somehow so that everyone can recognize something of their own self when viewing it.'[15]

Artistic influences are also a strong component of the creative process, acknowledged but deconstructed by Varda as 'pleasures' when she referred to the 'images copiées-décalées' [recut and pasted] in her films from her adaptation or *décalage* of Braque for *La Pointe courte* onwards.[16] Recognizing Renoir, Manet and Berthe Morisot as obvious sources of inspiration for *Le Bonheur*, in which she had to compose with fast wilting flowers literally sprayed with paint, Varda furthermore refers to Picasso's stylistic inventions and his Vollard series of drawings, or Viva, Warhol's muse, and their influence for *Lions Love (... and Lies)*, Titian, Goya, Dalí for *Jane B by Agnès B*, just as she can recall with a skip in her heartbeat Boltanski's illuminated rusty boxes with children's pictures, Bacon's triptychs, a face captured by Fautrier: 'With all these artists, it's not so much that they influence me; they nourish me, they inspire me'.[17]

Agnès Varda may claim that she as a photographer, a filmmaker and an artist has (had) 3 'lives (re)united into one neat package'. Yet one may not be quite certain if this self-portrait as an 'autobio-triptych' will be the last, or does not promise, rather than hide, even much more.[18] How can Varda's continuing and expanding body of artistic work, as 'a testimony to her/our times', to quote Bourseiller, resonate for/in us, today and in the years to come? By precisely reconfiguring how and what this organic and live artistic work is still achieving, our volume wants to offer new stepping stones along this open-ended line of enquiry. We chose and criss-crossed some resonant examples of her many adventures in mixed media, music, moving and so-called 'fixed' images, in a back and forth non-chronological order, as a fitting echo of the ebb and flow of her favourites seascapes, in order to leave interpretations, lasting impressions, further inquiries, and other engagements with her *oeuvres* and well as with a wide audience ideally open-ended, subject and actively open to change.

Emma Wilson (University of Cambridge), with the inspiring and inspired muses of 'Cléo & Dorothée' in mind, offers a convex and complex mirror to Francesca Minnie Hardy (University of Aberdeen): '*Agnès Varda's Cléo de 5 à 7*: A Triptych of the Textile'. Her homage to Dorothée Blanck is particularly moving and timely. Catherine Dousteyssier-Khoze (Durham University): 'Mise en abyme, Irony and Visual cliché in Agnès Varda's *Le Bonheur* (1964)' is also in a direct dialogue with Mark Lee (Mount Allison University): 'Re-viewing Varda's *Le Bonheur* (1964): Accident? Suicide? Or the Natural Order? That is the Question.' Music, motion, 'movement' as women's lib mottoes, with a plethora of other turns and tunes, roaming further afield, including synaesthetic encounters, or rebel shots and virtual footsteps, all entwined and twisted thematic lines of thought are reprised differently by Phil Powrie (University of Surrey) in '*L'Une chante, l'autre pas*: Music, Movement and the Utopian Community', by Hannah Mowat (University of Cambridge) in '*Lara Croft dans un champ de patates*: A Ludomusicological Approach to Agnès Varda', and by Isabelle McNeill (University of Cambridge) in 'Ways of Seeing in Agnès Varda's *Les Dites Cariatides* (1984)'. Images taken, or shaken and stirred again, mobile on the beach, in and out of galleries, on and 'off the walls', are reviewed under the various angles adopted by Fiona Handyside (University of Exeter): '*La mer, la mer, toujours recommencée*: A Centrifugal Reading of the Beach in the Work of Agnès Varda', Shirley Jordan (Queen Mary, University of London): 'Still Varda: Photographs and Photography in Agnès Varda's Late Work', Gill Perry (Open University): 'Les Cabanes d'Agnès'; and Marie-Claire Barnet (Durham University): 'Out of sites: Art Matters, Contemporary Activism, & Public Encounters with Agnès Varda'.

Echoes of Nina Ricci's 'Deci-Delà' perfume (1994) and variations of poetry and songs may be heard in *Agnès de ci de là Varda,* but I note that the distinction from Verlaine's ill winds of 'Chanson d'Automne' (1866), blowing '*deçà* delà', can also suggest that not only is rhyming involved in Varda's work — titles and travels included — but a myriad of much more complex and puzzling tempos, as perceptible in Charles Trénet, Georges Brassens, or Léo Ferré's alternately swing, moody, or jazzy versions, perhaps more like the latest to date Benjamin Biolay's ambiguously upbeat take on the legendary tune of last farewells (2015). As a final twist to a traditional questionnaire as found in *The Guardian* weekend supplement, asking notable or famous people who would play them on the screen, in case we might wonder who would Varda have liked to play herself for a change behind the camera as a character or an actress, here is her multifaceted reply: 'If I could have acted as a character in my own films, I would have liked to play, young or old, Mona in *Sans toit ni loi* [*Vagabond*]. If I had been a character in a film by someone else, I'd have liked the plutonium factory worker played by Meryl Streep in *Le Mystère Silkwood* [*Silkwood*]... or Yolande Moreau as herself in *Quand la mer monte* [*When the Sea Rises*].'

Bis repetita placent. Let us highlight some key turning-points when the conception and production of this volume triggered a series of synchronicities and synergies, echoing the collective nature our criss-crossing chapters try to capture, when face to face with Agnès Varda's long-lasting, inspiring and always surprising visual inventions. When Agnès Varda went back to LA in the autumn of 2013 for a major retrospective of her restored 'American' films, alongside rarely exhibited photos, and the creation of a revamped beach shack (which we can see Agnès touring herself on our own volume cover, thanks to Graham), she wanted to repeat the clear statement about the shifting state of her practice, 'I have been a filmmaker, I am a visual artist now'. However, one could always read beyond this apparent division, or simplification of time, with a third potential for creativity expressed in the making of the magazine (*Zoetrope: All-Story*, Fall 2013, 17, 3, pp. 1–2). 'Sea you later!', the message on the back cover of the magazine, can also be the perfect nod to the future, in a photograph with these words added, stacked up vertically, drawing our attention and focusing the mind in this beach scene, like a cheerful pun posted on a vacated billboard. 'Sea you later!' appeared in the centre of a seemingly 'empty' frame, though a void simultaneously filled to the brim by the 3 horizontal fat and thin slices of grey sky, grey sea and greyish sand. In *Zoetrope*, Varda produces a disorderly alphabet, with 'C' for *Cléo*, and for her key question, 'Can we narrate the passage of time?'

Has the passage of time changed our own changing perceptions and receptions of Varda's multi-faceted work? This overall collection, as stated in our many chapters, clearly intends to revisit, as well as create, perspectives about cinema, and

Agnès Varda celebrating *Cléo* at the Tyneside Cinema, Newcastle, 2012
(courtesy of Tyneside Cinema)

art in general, produced by women 'today', and the volume stands precisely in synchronicity with one of the key (and odd) queries that still concerns cinema, art, and gendered identity. Where are women in 'a world (almost) without women'? asked Aurélie Godet in a special issue of *Cahiers du cinéma* (September 2012, 687, 6)? It is therefore appropriate to return to another screen star who has sadly and recently left us, Chantal Akerman, who was, paradoxically, more than disappointed, in fact completely disheartened, to be nominated in 2012 as the only woman film maker among the top 100 best films listed every ten years as a benchmark in *Sight and Sound*, without any mention of 'Agnès or Marguerite (Duras)' (*Cahiers du cinéma*, 687, 33, 78).

The latest exhibition, *Varda/Cuba*, at the Beaubourg Centre in Paris (11 November 2015-1 February 2016), establishes a clear dialogue between both the original photos and an 'animated' short film of the prints, *Salut les Cubains* (1963). The beginning of the short film captures the very spectacle of gallery-viewing seen by a detached observer 'with a smiling distance, never irony'.[19] I had never paid attention to that sequence before seeing it performed 'live' in the room at the Pompidou Centre. What permeates the film, meanwhile, is an obsessive refrain of gratitude, 'Hi, Hello, or Hail to the Cuban people'. To all the anonymous and ill-designated public, the ultimate nod goes to you: *Salut les Vardiens!*

Notes to the Preface

1. Agnès Varda, 'Préambule en bulles', in *Album d'Agnès V.: images et notes latérales*, in *Tout(e) Varda* box-set (ARTE Éditions, 2012), 3 [my translation].
2. A. Varda interviewed by Melissa Anderson (2001), in T. Jefferson Kline (ed.), *Agnès Varda Interviews* (Jackson: University of Mississippi Press, 2014), 181.
3. A. Varda, correspondence with the author, 18 July 2014 (my translation).
4. A. Fiant, R. Hamery, and E. Thouvenel, eds, *Agnès Varda: le cinéma et au-delà* (Rennes: Presse Universitaires de Rennes, 2009).
5. A. Varda, correspondence with the author, 18 July 2014 (my translation).
6. A. Varda interviewed by Julie Rigg (2005), in T. Jefferson Kline (ed.), 188.
7. See Pierre Nora, ed., *Les Lieux de mémoire* (Paris: Gallimard), including *La République* (1984), *La Nation* (1987), *Les France* (1992).
8. See A. Varda for Nathalie Obadia's press release; she favours the English terminology visual artist or 'artiste tout court' <www.cine-tamaris.com/IMG/pdf/cp_agnes_varda_-_uk.pdf> [accessed 25 September 2015]
9. Delphine Bénezet, *The Cinema of Agnes Varda: Resistance and Eclecticism* (New York: Wallflower Press, CUP), 2014, pp. 3–5.
10. See A. Varda, *Varda par Agnès* (Paris: Cahiers du cinéma, 1994); Alison Smith, Agnès Varda (Manchester: Manchester University Press, 1998), 198.
11. A. Varda, interview in *Lisières*, 13 (19 October 2000) 5–28 (p. 20). Varda on her latest to date dual types of triptychs: 'C'est ce que j'appelle mettre le temps dans le temps', Conversation with the author, Paris, 16 May 2014.
12. See the meticulously produced catalogue of Ciné-Tamaris, with full 'Index des films' for both Varda's and Demy's films, further thematic 'suggestions de programmation', and the cover quoting Varda's warm homage to film distributors who still support 'Le cinéma d'auteur' (23 pages, n.d.)
13. See Claire Bishop, *Installation Art* (London: Tate, 2005), pp. 6, 8. See my chapter in this volume for further discussion.
14. A. Varda, 'Interview with Chris Darke', London, Ciné Lumière, 28 October 2006.
15. Christian Boltanski, 'Tamar Garb in conversation with Christian Boltanski', in *Christian Boltanski* (London: Phaidon Press, 1997), p. 24.
16. A. Varda, interview in *Lisières*, 13; see 11 and 13 [my translation]. See the Acknowledgements above for the intertextual echo in Julian Barnes's meditations on art.
17. Ibid., p. 13.
18. See A. Varda interviewed by Olivier De Bruyn, 'Dans ce coffret, il y a mes trois vies créatrices en une' [In this box set, my three creative lives are all united in one], *Le Point*, 29 November 2012. <http://www.evene.fr/user/login> [accessed 23 September 2015].
19. A. Varda, interview with Karolina Ziebinsk-Lewandowska, 'Socialisme et cha-cha-cha: Cuba 1963 vue par Agnès Varda', *Varda/Cuba*, Paris, Éditions du Centre Pompidou, 2015, 10.

CHAPTER 1

Cléo and Dorothée

Emma Wilson

> 'Chloe liked Olivia', I read. And then it struck me how immense a change was there. Chloe liked Olivia perhaps for the first time in literature.
>
> VIRGINIA WOOLF, *A Room of One's Own*

(i)

In her volume *Varda par Agnès*, Varda explains her casting of actress Dorothée Blanck as Cléo's model friend in *Cléo de 5 à 7* (1962):

> Pour L'AMIE DE CLÉO qui pose nue, j'ai tout de suite pensé à Dorothée Blanck que j'avais filmée, nue aussi, dans *L'Opéra-mouffe* et photographiée pour des essais. Les journaux avaient parlé de cette jeune sourde-muette rééduquée jusqu'à faire l'actrice. Moi j'aimais sa modestie absolue. Elle avait un corps qui faisait rêver des peintres et des photographes, comme on a un don pour faire la tarte Tatin ou un don de clairvoyance. On aimait qu'elle existe, simple et sensible. (Varda 1994: 53)
>
> [For CLÉO'S FRIEND who poses naked, I immediately thought of Dorothée Blanck who I'd filmed before, also naked, in *L'Opéra-Mouffe* and who I'd photographed for casting shots. The papers had talked about this young deaf-mute girl who had been rehabilitated to become an actress. I liked her absolute modesty. She had a body that inspired painters and photographers, just as people have a gift for making tarte Tatin or have second sight. It was a joy that she just existed, sensitive and unaffected.]

Varda's words speak of the particular qualities of Dorothée Blanck's body, her sensuous existence.[1] Posing naked, and her gift for this, are associated with simplicity, sensitivity, an absolutely unexplained, nourishing presence and aura. Varda acknowledges here the contact, the thrill, between living bodies and artists, models and photographers. This is conjured not only as response to physical loveliness, but as a further warm skin and flesh appeal, naked and unassuming all at once. Varda explores this in her filmmaking practice, opening relations between the traditions of Western painting and her own art practice, and imagining new ways in which a woman artist approaches her model or muse.

In *Ways of Seeing*, John Berger singles out 'a few exceptional nudes' that are 'paintings of loved women, more or less naked' (1972: 57). He writes: 'the painter's personal vision of the particular women he is painting is so strong that it makes no allowance for the spectator' (1972: 57). Berger's beautiful accounting for that enhanced intimacy, that affect and relationality, beyond exposure, in certain examples in the tradition of the nude — he offers Rembrandt as his particular illustration at this instance — binds the tradition of Western art to a heterosexual narrative and binary of power relations. The paintings show the woman's appeal to the artist, his love of her, the intimacy that arises, affectively, between them. Berger argues too, looking at Rembrandt's *Danäe* (in the Hermitage), that 'the way the painter has painted her includes her will and her intentions in the very structure of the image, in the very expression of her body and her face' (1972: 58). He reaches towards a form of mutuality arising in love. Yet, as cited above, he sees this making no allowance for the spectator.

Varda's account of Dorothée Blanck's appeal is interesting in comparison in the ways in which it offers a similar sense of alchemy, radiance, intimacy, yet does not bind this into a love relation between artist and model. I find striking the ways Varda's words intimate affect, the love, tenderness and energy that are held about Dorothée's body, yet names this a possession of the actress herself, an inner gift. And, in speaking of love directly, Varda finds a far more open economy than Berger; her explanation is *tout court*: 'On aimait qu'elle existe, simple et sensible.' The impersonal pronoun opens out multi-directional possibilities in love, as it opens possibilities too for an affective charge for the spectator as much as for the painter, or photographer. This chapter emerges, indeed, from my own sense of being opened by Dorothée's existence, her bodily presence, as it is glimpsed in differing degrees of intimacy in the early films of Agnès Varda. The chapter's aim is to look at ways in which Varda opens and transforms that relation between body and viewer so that it is open to desire and undoing, and allows for movement in both artistic and affective relations.

In discussion of Varda's imaging of a naked Jane Birkin in *Jane B. par Agnès V.*, Sarah Cooper writes:

> [Varda] blocks an overview of Birkin as nude. She suggests that the female film-maker's approach to her muse breaks with her presentation within a western tradition, and thereby also questions gendered knowledge of the female body according to the codes of spectatorship. The conventional visually-informed and male gendered knowing gaze is refused. This establishes a bond between Varda and her model that de-eroticises the latter in order to love her differently, in her own way (2006: 83)

Cooper's argument is important in drawing attention to Varda's engagement with thought about the western tradition of painting, about knowledge of the female body and about codes of spectatorship. In questioning power, Cooper sees Varda undermining the apparent hierarchy of male/artist and female/muse relations and looking instead towards a 'bond', consensuality, complicity. Cooper speaks of Varda loving Birkin 'differently'. She configures the relation between artist and model, Varda and Birkin, as close, particular, intense, founded on excluding the male gaze. For her that 'bond' explicitly 'de-eroticises' the model.

Cooper speaks of Varda blocking an 'overview' of Birkin nude. Considering this I see it as telling that Varda's camera *moves* over Birkin's body, apprehending it rather than fixing it pictorially, in a strategy Varda uses too in her filming of her male lover Jacques Demy. These moving images of Birkin revel in her sensuous loveliness. As they pass over her surface they are pearly, limpid, ecstatic in their sensing of her skin, her nipples, her smile. This is not about the desire of the filmmaker. Varda works rather, I think, to transform perspectives on sensuality, viewing and intimacy. Varda can release Birkin's loveliness in the image and see it and imagine it and not fix it. This is done in the camera's moves, in its following of the line of her body, the stretch of her skin, the close-up images of her nipple in all its impressionability. The lability of the images and their bodily stretch I see as part of the opening of conventions of representation, the sensing of new feeling about the reclining nude. The sequence rests finally on Birkin's lucid gaze that reveals at the end of the series of shots that she is present in the image, responsive, calm, looking back. As hinted in my epigraph from Woolf, I argue that Varda's filmmaking opens an economy where women look at each other, like each other, where rivalry is not the response to radiance and limpid beauty, where that liking is unsettling even in its opening of intimacy.[2] It is this aspect of Varda's broader reshaping of relations between self and other, between life and art, that I focus on here.

In speaking about her casting by Varda in *L'Opéra-Mouffe* [*Diary of a Pregnant Woman*] (1958), Dorothée Blanck writes:

> elle avait demandé à des peintres, c'est comme ça que je l'ai connue, s'il y avait 'un nu froid' dans Paris; alors ils ont dit 'Il n'y en a qu'un seul, c'est Dorothée!' Elle ne voulait pas un nu érotique, elle ne voulait pas en faire une strip-teaseuse.[3]
>
> [she had asked some painters if there was an 'icy nude' in Paris, and that's how I got to know her; so they said 'There's only one, Dorothée!' She didn't want an erotic nude, she didn't want to make her into a stripper]

Her words reveal Varda's intention to re-view images of the female body, to strip away the conventions of erotic display. She looks to find in Dorothée Blanck a different image of nudity. In her filming of her, as I will argue, she presents her as a living, vivid, sensual other. Varda's role as female artist representing a female model, her take on this and response to it, are used to open sensuality in the image, to reimagine eroticism perhaps, whilst also redirecting how desire saturates the relation of artist to muse or of model to spectator. Varda's images of naked women are sensually lovely, at least to some viewers, and this appeal, this lustre, is only enhanced, I think, by the openness of their modes of address.

Varda allows the women she films, Dorothée Blanck, Jane Birkin, to be a living, electrifying, moving presence in her corpus of work. This living presence brings with it alterity, challenge, opening, undoing, all the effects and sensations of intimacy and encounter.[4] This reimagining, with the erotic, with the sensory, is one of the feminist interventions of Varda's art.[5] In the sections that follow I explore Varda's filming of Dorothée Blanck in *L'Opéra-Mouffe* and in *Cléo de 5 à 7*. I suggest that Varda's attention to Dorothée Blanck's body, and in particular her arrangement of a series of images of contact and closeness, and her attention to Dorothée as moving, wriggling, changing, open a reimagining of nudity, eroticism, and undoing.[6] In collaboration with Dorothée Blanck, Varda as a young woman filmmaker invents new possibilities for critical, and passionate, engagement with a pictorial and erotic tradition of Western painting and sculpture. These are issues that will be pursued throughout her career.[7] Varda reimagines the relation of artist to model, opening it differently so it is more consensual, variously gendered, in all less fixed.

(ii)

In *Undoing Gender* Butler writes:

> Let's face it. We're undone by each other. And if we're not, we're missing something. If this seems so clearly the case with grief, it is only because it was already the case with desire. One does not always stay intact. It may be that one wants to, or does, but it may also be that despite one's best efforts, one is undone, in the face of the other, by the touch, by the scent, by the feel, by the prospect of the touch, by the memory of the feel (2004: 19)

The form of relation Butler speaks of here opens the self to the other, where affect — grief, desire — unsettle self-possession, leaving self opened to other, ecstatically perhaps yet also at moments involuntarily, unwillingly. Butler opens here specifically to contact, to the self in the face of the other, and to bodily closeness, the sensory as well as the erotic, the touch, the scent. Not only the physical acts themselves, touching and being touched, but anticipation and memory, and we might add anxiety and longing, open the self to the other. Butler's words speak of undoing where I speak of opening. I take her language of undoing, and coming undone, as positively inflected — 'if we're not [undone] we're missing something' — in intimacy, and psychically. Undoing opens to movement as well as risk. The self is no longer intact or fixed. This is the ethos I suggest Varda too explores in her imaging of relation, including, as explored here, the relation of artist to model, and of women to one another.

Varda explores questions of opening in her early films, in particular in her attention to the female body and its flesh. *L'Opéra-Mouffe*, the diary of a pregnant woman, holds near its start an image of a woman's pregnant torso, the full arc of her belly almost touching the skin of her thighs, her breasts swollen and her nipples distended. The footage shows the woman breathing. Her living flesh, and its small moves, are the focus of the camera. This move of breath is repeated in a following closer shot where the camera focuses just on the orb of her belly and her navel, the frame almost filled by the tight, real skin. In a third framing we see the woman on her side, her body laid out, sinuous. She is, in unlikely manner, a pregnant odalisque (looking forward to the future reclining shots of Jane Birkin and Jacques Demy).[8] Each shot opens and varies the images of female nakedness through this approach to pregnancy. The last image is the loveliest with its shadows and curves, yet it is also unsettling, awkward, as the woman's breath changes the shape of her belly — we see it moving — accentuating the weight and physical challenge of bearing a child.

The three sequences are rendered intimate and unreal at once by a sheer black background so that they recall Surrealist photography yet make it gravid, living, drawing us to feel as well as look. These are thoughts and feelings of embodied experience, a filmic stream of consciousness. There is a cut that suddenly reframes the previous images as the belly is replaced by, and aligned with, a pumpkin. The formal continuity between the shots is maintained in the return of a curve and shading, but the move from flesh to fruit is brutal, and more so when the greengrocer turns the pumpkin on its side, bisects it with a knife, and lays bare the seeds and pulp inside. A closer shot of this interior offers an image of soft, nestling, fecund, unfixed fruit flesh. It is scooped out, clasped by the grocer, his fingers deep in the pulp, intimately hollowing a fruit womb.

I see this prologue matching Butler's words about undoing, offering a fleshy variation, a specific poetic opening about pregnancy that yet connects to other modes of opening and finds in these connections a mode of embracing a failure to stay intact. Butler and Varda come together in their specific attention to the body and the ways it is lived and imagined. For Butler: 'The body implies mortality, vulnerability, agency: the skin and the flesh expose us to the gaze of others but also to touch and to violence' (2004: 21). Butler espouses an ethos of vulnerability, where our exposure to others leads to undoing, opening, and to a heightened engagement, with others and ourselves, as at once feeling, intimate and unknowing. And Varda reminds us, as she explores images of nakedness, of the skin and flesh exposed to the gaze of others, that the female body is not just a beautiful object, its skin a smooth surface, but a living, moving, desiring, fearing organism, exposed to violence and also to touch, exquisite sensation.

In *L'Opéra-Mouffe* Varda moves on from exploring undoing through the pregnant images at the start to looking more directly at the amorous body in sequences with Dorothée Blanck. Again here she reimagines the reclining nude. The major sequence is entitled 'Des Amoureux' and runs from 3.10 to 4.55. In this she pursues her exploration of exposure in two modes, in the filming of acts of love, and in reflections on the art historical tradition of the representation of women. And, as I have suggested, contact and movement are key in the sequence.

(iii)

The female lover (Dorothée Blanck) appears first in her nightgown, looking out of the window. Her lover, his torso bare, approaches her from behind and puts his hand on her shoulder. She is yielding, smiling, illuminated as she turns in his arms and he pulls off her nightgown. She is laid bare here in an image of joy, of mutuality, of modern love. (Later in the film, we see the words 'La Moderne' on the side of the sewing machine in the lovers' apartment.) In a disconcerting cut, Varda moves us to see the lovers close to, face to face. Movement in the frame is crucial here, the blink of the man's eyes, the brush of his eyelashes. Then there is a cut again to a differently-scaled image as the woman emerges naked into the court outside the apartment.[9] In a further rehearsal or shuffling of scale and modes of attention, we see the lovers in bed with antiquated, flowered wallpaper behind them. The female lover is laughing. They turn in one another's arms. Her openness, her receptivity, her well-being render the shots serene. Her lover stretches with happiness. The film cuts to close-up body images as we see their further touching, the camera following the line of her torso (as it does Birkin's later).

The film cuts then to its most composed *tableau vivant*, its most direct address to the pictorial tradition and to the relation of artist to model and muse. It is as if the line of the torso, the curve of her body, has conjured this reflection on art historical tradition, in the way that the film works as stream of consciousness, as evolving, moving and associative in its forms and images. In the *tableau vivant*, Dorothée Blanck lies out on a daybed, stretched like Velazquez's *Rokeby Venus* (1647–51). She holds a mirror in her hand and in this her face can be glimpsed. The shot is beautifully imagined with her fragility and suppleness on view in the delicate choreographing of her body, with the lines of shadow on her body picked up in a crossing network of leafless, linear trees and branches.

Yet what is most remarkable in this *tableau*, as in the earlier pregnancy shots, is the life and movement within the frame, arising from the living felt presence of the actress, of her moves and gestures filmed by Varda.[10] Dorothée Blanck angles the mirror in different directions as if she is playing with her image. Then she puts it down. Her body is never entirely still, but she wriggles, moves it naturally, stretching, unselfconscious with her back to us, so we see her body in its lived dimensions even as she is framed in the pictorial setting. The felt, lived, move of flesh and skin is part of the odalisque image.[11] She never settles into a fixed ideal so we see her as living, as more lovely because she moves, feels, is.

Varda cuts again to the lovers in close-up and a closer apprehension of this woman's flank, her back, her buttocks, so close they seem warm, so close we feel them through the skin of the lover's face, smiling as he rests his cheek against her side. This relay of sensations is pursued as he strokes and holds a cat, its fur in his arms. Varda shakes up the images of the lovers again as we see Dorothée move to clasp his feet against her cheek, her back displayed again differently, foreshortened from this angle as she was stretched out before. We see her hand holding his foot and then he turns her way and clasps her again and they are enwrapped in each other. A cut shows her eye in close-up (as with Birkin later), and then they are turning again and curling into each other beneath the sheet, and glimpsed asleep, mirroring each other, her hands on his torso. The sequence comes to a close.

The lovers are glimpsed again closer to the end of the film, meeting in the marketplace on the rue Mouffetard, viewed by a male observer (Antoine Bourseiller). Here Dorothée Blanck's smile is glimpsed as she clasps her lover. They are in outdoor clothes but the earlier sequences have lined the images with intimacy. Varda returns us then to the interior love-making, as we see them, back in their apartment, glimpsed in reflection in a mirror, then after love, the woman's head resting on the man's torso.

Dorothée Blanck comments on these lovemaking scenes in an interview with Vincent Jourdan for the radio programme 'Bande à part':

> il y avait des tas de plans où l'on ne savait plus si c'était le genou, si c'était l'épaule, ou des entremêlements; d'ailleurs, j'ai eu le sentiment quand j'ai vu 'Hiroshima', notamment la scène d'amour 'Tu me fais du mal, tu me fais du bien!', que Resnais avait repris cette idée de corps entremêlés sans qu'on puisse distinguer si c'est une cuisse...[12]
>
> [there were lots of shots where you no longer knew if it was a knee, if it was a

> shoulder, or limbs entangled; and so, when I saw 'Hiroshima', particularly the love scene 'You hurt me, you give me pleasure!', I had the feeling that Resnais had borrowed this idea of bodies entangled so you can't say what's a thigh...]

She points to the novelty and influence of the scenes and specifically the involvement of the bodies and reimagining of love.

I see the sequence with the lovers supplementing the ways of thinking about undoing and opening in *L'Opéra-Mouffe*, allowing desire, contact, movement, the most tender forming and reforming in love, pictured visually, to be one of the modes through which Varda, like Butler, explores how we are enmeshed with each other. The lovers shown offer a tender pre-history of the pregnant woman, a sensing, a feeling of passion in the film. They offer an image of involvement and enmeshing of self and other. This theme is considered far more broadly in *L'Opéra-Mouffe* as Varda opens the film to a human stretch of themes, looking at precarious living on the streets of Paris. In this film the scenes between the lovers might seem like an interlude. I argue rather that these scenes too offer images of involvement, of the self undone by the other. In her embrace and entwining of the intimate with the political, as throughout her career, Varda observes her lovers with grace, showing them with affection and wonderment, showing their novelty and freshness, their ingenuousness and freedom. The film embraces their ease of involvement, illustrated in Dorothée Blanck's simplicity, her sensitivity. Her shifting, touching, receiving, giving, assuage or at least co-exist with the anxiety and grief of the film, as it explores all the ways we are undone by one another.[13]

Attention to Dorothée Blanck, herself a model and actress, who plays a female lover, who carries her own unspoken loveliness, allows the involvement as well of a lived reality and an artistic tradition, as early in her career Varda thinks through, feels, reimagines possibilities for filming, apprehending, exposing the living other in screen. This involves her contact with and movement on from the images of women we have known. In exploring undoing and opening, Varda opens this mode to new scrutiny, to new feeling. This happens in the reimagining of the *tableau vivant* and also more lavishly through the whole naked sequence. The opening to feeling, to the unexpected, is expressed visually in the form of the collage of turning shots from different perspectives, in different scales, newly imagining and inventing, unsettling the love relation. Varda explores here a specific privilege of cinematic montage and pushes it to new extremes of opening and undoing in the relay of shots.[14] Supporting this, opening Varda's filmmaking beyond itself, is the appeal of Dorothée Blanck, her call to body and heart. This quality of Dorothée Blanck and involvement in Varda's art in newly felt and imagined shots, is explored further in *Cléo de 5 à 7*.

(iv)

Cléo de 5 à 7 is a film about a woman (played by Corinne Marchand) who is looked at, who objectifies herself and adores the gaze of others, and who undergoes a sea-change, opening up, being touched by others. In her short film, *Cléo de 5 à 7: Souvenirs et anecdotes* (2005) Varda evokes 'une démarche féministe' in the film, saying of Cléo that 'elle va se redéfinir elle-même'. This moment is illustrated in re-editing of extracts from *Cléo de 5 à 7* where we see Cléo suddenly divesting herself of her blonde wig and shaking out the hair. This moment of metamorphosis is at the centre of the film and announces its second act where Cléo walks through the streets of Paris alone, visits the model Dorothée (Dorothée Blanck), and finally encounters Antoine (Antoine Bourseiller), the soldier who is about to return to Algeria.

Cléo de 5 à 7 is in this sense a film which traces a turn, a tropistic move in its protagonist, from thoughts of mortality to emergent, tender, immediate life. Cléo's encounter with Antoine and the film's concomitant embrace of its political moment, of the terror and contingency of the Algerian War, are the film's vital force.[15] Yet the film espouses, like *L'Opéra-Mouffe*, an ethos of connectivity, of association, of refusal of separation of intimate and public. In this regard, attention to Dorothée and to her role in Cléo's metamorphosis, and awareness of the film's binding of the intimate politics of the body, exposure, flesh, nakedness, to a broader questioning of agency, risk and vulnerability, are also vital to the film's ethical and feminist project. As Varda writes in the screenplay at this point: 'Apparition du thème de la nudité. (Dorothée le représente, formellement; plus loin, Antoine l'exprimera spirituellement.)' (1962: 67) ['Appearance of the theme of nudity. (Dorothée represents it formally; further on, Antoine will represent it spiritually)'].

This opening to the other in the second half of the film belies indeed an opening of the imagination in Varda's approach to film art, its affective and ethical relations. If the film fairly unequivocally, and with a due existentialist drive, embraces Cléo's project to assume her identity and not to be fixed as an other, through the character of Dorothée (as she is played by Dorothée Blanck), Varda again opens up different possibilities for thinking about the female body unfixed, de-objectified in representation and for re-thinking the relation of the artist (and filmmaker) to his or her living models.

These relational and ethical issues of the use of the other in making art are developed further in the narrative form of *Cléo de 5 à 7* where Dorothée's perspectives on nakedness and modeling are formative not only in her assumption of her professional role but also, crossing from the public to the intimate sphere, in her friendship with Cléo. If Cléo learns to look rather than to be looked at, Dorothée also shows that there are different ways of apprehending visual attention, of loving, living and being. *Cléo de 5 à 7* shimmers with its different mirroring reflections on women loved and living, and this plurality, this opening to different unsettled narratives, is also part of its ethos, its initiatory reflections on life and art.

Dorothée's sequence in the film begins in a sculpture studio.[16] The sequence opens up as a type of studio installation, a series of sculptural rooms, at the centre of the feature film.[17] Varda offers here a reflection on the kinship between sculpture as art form and her use of cinema as medium that attempts to hold dimensional, vulnerable bodily forms, the impress and imprint of the material world. If Varda is interested in showing sensory navigation of the external spaces of Paris in both *L'Opéra-Mouffe* and *Cléo de 5 à 7*, she is also interested in the matter and texture in the artist's studio. In this sculpture studio she offers a new imagining of the role, the scope, the agency of the artist's model.[18] As Frances Borzello writes, principally of models working in the nineteenth-century in England and France: 'The fact that they are paid means models become objects to be used as the buyer desires' (2010: 7).[19] Key to the presentation of Dorothée by contrast is her remarkable freedom. Ungar comments on the ways in which this freedom is expressed in her very bodily gestures and comportment: 'Dorothée's ease with her body and her lack of affectation are in direct contrast to Cléo's distress' (2008: 71).[20] As Varda writes in the screenplay: 'Dorothée, le modèle, est sans prétention ; sa présence, son comportement, sont l'image du simple bonheur de vivre' (1962: 67) ['Dorothée, the model, is without pretention; her presence, her behaviour, are the image of simple joy in living'].

In her first appearance in *Cléo de 5 à 7*, Dorothée is glimpsed after a series of Cléo's subjective shots. A mobile camera takes us past the plaster forms, the film attentive to the textures, tactile, clotted, of this sculpted matter, the contrast of different densities of pliable, sensuous material. The screenplay tells us: 'Dans une salle très claire, de grandes sculptures couchées, des ébauches' (1962: 65) ['In a very bright room there are large sculptures, reclining, unfinished works']. At this point the sculptures have no point of reference, no model to which they refer, and the unfinished plaster shapes create a series of near abstract forms on the screen. As in *L'Opéra-Mouffe*, Varda is interested in shots which open our viewing in new ways.

Through the doorway in the far wall we catch a glimpse of the first of a series of variations on a sculpture of a naked woman. We see her face on and we see her smaller effigy from the side. As the camera moves into the room she appears again, larger still, screen right. The figure of a woman is seen in the angles of the various effigies from the front, from the side, from the back, as she turns. Within the moving frame the statues appear as a series of motion studies, looking back to the protocinematic capture of movement in still photography. Amidst the series of statues, their massed, unfinished forms, we see sculptors at work.

After a cut to Cléo, establishing her as the subject of the point of view shots, we cut back to the studio and see Dorothée posing. She stands with her back to the camera and to the sculptors, beautifully poised, her hands clasped at the small of her back. Showing her modelling here, standing up, her back on show, Varda creates a different variation on her image as reclining nude in *L'Opéra-Mouffe*. She writes in the screenplay: 'une vingtaine de jeunes gens en blouse blanche tentent de recréer, en plâtre sur armature, une femme mince coiffée d'un chignon qui pose nue' (1962: 65) ['twenty or so young people in overalls attempt to recreate in plaster on an armature a slim young woman posing naked with her hair up']. Her words point to the ways in which the sculpture studio is the space where artists attempt to capture life in art. She continues: 'le corps du modèle apparaît et disparaît derrière les sculptures la représentant' (1962: 66) ['the model's body appears and disappears behind the sculptures representing her']. Shots show parts of Dorothée's flesh glimpsed in between the sculpted forms, bringing the difference in materials into vivid contrast. Dorothée's body here is still but holds an almost velvety life, shadow, tactility. The statues resemble her and yet their forms are still far remote in their fixity from Dorothée's living aura. Her body, filmed by Varda, is angular with a bone showing at her elbow, her spine and scapulae visible through the skin, yet softer and curved too where we see the top of her thighs, the greater density of flesh, entirely different in texture from the sculpted matter. Varda shows the play of presence and absence, through juxtaposed images in a single shot. So she reflects formally on an interrelation between art and life, sculpture and model, both on view in her frame.

Dorothée, her living flesh, elastic, tactile in its appeal to our eyes, is a radiant presence in the sculpture studio. She is the focus of attention of the sculptors in the studio, and the viewers of the film. As the scene evolves, Varda pays particular attention to the friendship between Dorothée and Cléo which is viewed as an autonomous, unselfconscious connection. Varda writes in the screenplay: 'Cléo fait le tour de l'atelier. Dorothée l'aperçoit enfin et lui sourit' (1962: 66) ['Cléo goes round the studio. Dorothée catches sight of her at last and smiles at her']. In a sudden move Dorothée turns, abandoning her pose. The film cuts to its next chapter heading 'Dorothée de 17h.52 à 18h.' Against this title Dorothée is seen crossing her eyes, and blowing out her cheeks, wriggling her face, before she breaks into an angelic smile. If this playfulness makes her resemble a performer such as Josephine Baker, the gesture illustrates too the elasticity of her skin and organs, how she wriggles and moves and laughs.[21] We see her on her makeshift plinth, her hair softly pinned, her arms draped. But then we see her get down, we see her get dressed, with Cléo's help, and we see her get paid for her labour. Dorothée and Cléo leave the studio, this space of art, and we follow them outside into the yard, a further space of the correlation of sculpted and living forms.[22]

The screenplay offers Dorothée's inner monologue — 'Tiens, Cléo qui vient ici. Ce qu'elle est gentille; ce qu'elle est belle' (1962: 67–68) ['Look, it's Cléo coming. How sweet she is, and how beautiful'] — and we have a sense that her appreciation of Cléo is part of the calm and ease she creates around her. In the conversation that ensues as they leave the studio, we sense that this passage through a scenario of modelling, of nakedness and art, has allowed Cléo different reflections on the body. She says to Dorothée: 'Ils sont si calmes, si attentifs. Vraiment, ça ne te gêne pas de poser?' (1962: 69) ['They are so calm and attentive. Doesn't it bother you posing for them?]. Dorothée replies, with simplicity, 'Mais non, pourquoi?' (1962: 69) ['Not at all, why?']. Cléo is lucid about her own fear of exposure which we rapidly see linked to her vanity: 'Il me semble qu'on est encore plus nue que nue devant plusieurs personnes. J'aurais peur qu'on me trouve un défaut' (1962: 69) ['I feel that one is even more than naked with lots of people there. I would be afraid they'd find a fault in me']. Dorothée's reply reflects all the qualities Varda found in the actress as she cast her:

> Quelle idée! C'est rien ça. Moi je suis heureuse de mon corps, pas orgueilleuse. Quand ils me regardent, je sais bien qu'ils recherchent autre chose que moi, une forme, une idée, je ne sais pas... Alors, c'est comme si je m'absentais, comme si je dormais... Et puis on me paie pour ça, tu vois (1962: 69)
>
> [What an idea! That's nonsense. I'm happy in my body, not proud of it. When they look at me, I know they're looking for something else other than me, a form, an idea, I don't know... So, it's as if I was leaving myself, as if I was sleeping... And then, you see, they pay me for it].

Dorothée and Cléo are in the frame together here through this dialogue and Dorothée speaks disarmingly, lightly, her features always animated. Dorothée and Cléo engage in dialogue, a sharing of intimacy. As she speaks of her own security in her body, her opening to its exposure, Dorothée offers a narrative for Cléo to which she may aspire but which she has not yet been able to own. Through their involvement, their sharing, Dorothée offers a different lived experience of the flesh, a new simplicity and tangibility. She offers an alternative to Cléo's taut, tortured apprehension of her own body. As the screenplay relates: 'Elle est, avec Cléo, amicale et calme, puis émue' (1962: 67) ['She is friendly and calm with Cléo, and then moved'].

Dorothée takes Cléo's arm her in a rush of affection. Her smile is open here as she engages Cléo with humour, lightness, limpidity. Her black velvet band seems to nestle in her hair. Her dress, silky cotton, fits and forms her body perfectly, its neckline echoing the shape of her neckbones. She is responsive, playful, rapid, tactile, arm in arm with Cléo. Her hand seems tender on Cléo's forearm. The frame is filled with the rush of Dorothée's hair, its flow and thickness, its movement creating something fluid, an area of *flou*, of something living, almost animal, in the image, as Dorothée moves and responds to Cléo.

Beyond the sculpture studio the ensuing scenes with Dorothée open a space of comedy in the film where Dorothée drives her friend haphazardly around Montparnasse, whisks her into a cinema to watch a silent film, and then disappears at the end, running up a flight of stairs. At the end of the sequence we watch her as she runs, her lightness accentuated by the moves of her arms, the flow of her dress and hair. She moves faster than the other city dwellers around her, creating fluidity in the frame. She turns to wave as she runs up the stairs. It feels as if she has disorganized the fixity, the sobriety of the city. She is like a fleeting Surrealist Muse, yet smiling, *désinvolte*. These shots of Dorothée might be compared to shots of a woman running in slow motion that are included in *L'Opéra-Mouffe*. In *Cléo de 5 à 7*, Varda allows such stream of consciousness elements to unfold even in the more realist diegesis, so these shots of Dorothée running open a space for thinking about Cléo's new claiming of life, of vividness, of liberty, all she apprehends through her friend.

In her account of the film in *Varda par Agnès*, Varda writes of Cléo at this point: 'Elle se met à voir les choses et les gens d'une façon plus simple' (1994: 48) ['She begins to see things and people in a simpler way']. She shows Cléo's response to seeing 'Dorothée, son amie modèle qui pose, transparente et innocente' (1994: 48) ['Dorothée, her model friend who poses, open and innocent']. Varda's words indicate her sense of the role of Dorothée in Cléo's story and the presence she holds for her. This encounter with Dorothée, a living muse, a vivid other, shows Cléo moving over from opacity to exposure, receptivity, a new understanding.

Varda plays with these concerns in an artistic context, allowing her to bind together questions about art and questions about how to live. In *Varda par Agnès* she speaks of the inspiration afforded to *Cléo de 5 à 7* by images of Death and the Maiden by Baldung Grien. She writes: 'Tout ce que je sentais de la tension intérieure de cette femme douce pendant les quatre-vingt-dix minutes du film (de 5 heures à 6 heures 30), tout cela est inspiré par ces femmes et ces squelettes de Baldung Grien' (1994: 48) ['Everything I could feel of this gentle woman's inner tension through the ninety minutes of the film (from 5pm to 6.30), was inspired by Baldung Grien's women and skeletons'].[23] She speaks about how '[u]ne petite reproduction d'un de ses tableaux était souvent punaisée au mur, là où nous tournions' (1994: 48) ['a little reproduction of one of his paintings was often pinned up on the wall where we were filming']. She goes on to intimate the influence and role of painting in her cinematic career: 'C'est la force de la peinture de proposer des oeuvres qui peuvent devenir inspiration et rêverie continue' (1994: 48) ['Painting has the power to offer works which can become a source of prolonged inspiration and musing']. If Baldung Grien's maiden, a standing nude, pale, her hands clasped, her face contorted with grief, saturates and inspires Varda's realisation of Cléo, it seems the more significant that Varda redraws this image of the standing female nude, and shifts our sense of her affect and sensuality, in her realisation of the sequence in the sculpture studio, in the peace and loveliness of Dorothée's body.

(v)

In *L'Opéra-Mouffe*, we move from the image of the pregnant woman reclining, and her associative images of cutting and hollowing, to the freed-up images of Dorothée Blanck, a sentient and lively odalisque. In *Cléo de 5 à 7* we move from the maiden in the grip of death, Cléo fearful of abnormality and fault, to the unselfconscious ease and play of Dorothée on her plinth. In both films Varda traces a move in the female psyche, an apprehension of opening and undoing, of living and breathing, an embrace of threat and a movement on. She plots this through visual narratives, a collage of shots of lovers and a *tableau vivant*, a navigation of a sculpture studio, that address moments in the tradition of Western art, and that reimagine these representations. I have traced two tropes Varda introduces into this reimagining, contact and movement, figured extensively and in different ways in the two films. The filmmaker uses the actress and model Dorothée Blanck, her physical ease and loveliness, to open out these new images of female nakedness, of a living model animating art.

In her relation to her model, and muse, Varda opens meanings about art, about love, about opening and undoing. The model here is a living other, loved and unowned, who unfixes the image on screen. In her attention to this shift in the artist/model relation, her own to the actress Dorothée Blanck, and the different relations explored in the diegesis of both films, Varda shows how her art undoes and unsettles traditions in representation. She looks beyond the intimacy of Berger's imagining of loved women, finding different modes of attention to other living women. Rather than contrast the fixity of art to the vividness of life, Varda makes cinematic art that opens to contact and to movement, which allows art to show the animate, the affective, to show how we may be moved, changed, undone by one another.

Bibliography

Borzello, Frances, 'Introduction' to Lidia Guibert Ferrara, *Reclining Nude* (London: Thames and Hudson, 2002), pp. 6–7

Borzello, Frances, *The Artist's Model* (London: Faber and Faber, 2010 [1982])

Boubat, Edouard, *Lella* (Paris: Contrejour, 1987)

Butler, Judith, *Undoing Gender* (New York and London: Routledge, 2004)

Guibert Ferrara, Lidia, with an introduction by Frances Borzello, *Reclining Nude* (London: Thames and Hudson, 2002)

Ungar, Steven, *Cléo de 5 à 7* (London: BFI/Palgrave Macmillan, 2008).

Varda, Agnès, *Varda par Agnès* (Paris: Editions Cahiers du Cinéma et Ciné-Tamaris, 1994)

Wilson, Emma, 'Mortal Flesh: Agnès Varda de ci de là', *Forum for Modern Language Studies*, 50:1 (2014), 57–68

Woolf, Virginia, *A Room of One's Own* (London: Chatto & Windus/The Hogarth Press, 1984 [1929])

Filmography

Agnès Varda de ci de là (Agnès Varda 2011)
Cléo de 5 à 7 (Agnès Varda 1962)
Cléo de 5 à 7: souvenirs et anecdotes (Agnès Varda 2005)
Les Dites Cariatides [*The So-called Caryatids*] (Agnès Varda 1984)
Documenteur (Agnès Varda 1981)
Du Côté de la côte (Agnès Varda 1958)
French Cancan (Jean Renoir 1954)
Hiroshima mon amour (Alain Resnais 1959)
Jane B. par Agnès V. [*Jane B. for Agnès V.*] (Agnès Varda 1988)
Lola (Jacques Demy 1961)
Mur murs (Agnès Varda 1981)
Ô saisons, ô châteaux (Agnès Varda 1958)
L'Opéra-Mouffe [*Diary of a Pregnant Woman*] (Agnès Varda 1958)
Les Plages d'Agnès [*The Beaches of Agnès*] (Agnès Varda 2008)
La Pointe Courte (Agnès Varda 1955)
L'Une chante, l'autre pas [*One Sings, the Other Doesn't*] (Agnès Varda 1977)

Notes to Chapter 1

1. The actress's surname is given variously: in the credits to *L'Opéra-Mouffe* it is given as Blanks; in the credits to *Cléo de 5 à 7* as Blanck; and in the volume *Varda par Agnès* as Blank (but it will be Blanck in the new edition). For further details on Dorothée Blanck and her career see the excellent website: <http://mapage.noos.fr/dorotheeblanck> (accessed 18 September 2015). Dorothée Blanck also has a blog: <http://blanckdorothee.blogspot.co.uk/> (accessed 18 September 2015).
2. In *Varda par Agnès*, Varda references Woolf writing that 'l'intériorité de Woolf ne semblai[...]t pas avoir d'équivalent dans les quelques films dont j'entendais parler' (1994: 38) ['Woolf's interiority didn't seem to have an equivalent in the films I was hearing about'].
3. See <http://mapage.noos.fr/dorotheeblanck/unentretienavec.html> (accessed 18 September 2015). Dorothée Blanck appeared first (uncredited) as a dancer in Renoir's *French Cancan* (1954). She worked as a model in the art world, as her words indicate, and was then recommended to Varda for *L'Opéra-Mouffe*. She later acted in Jacques Demy's *Lola* (1961), again playing the role of

a dancer, with Corinne Marchand, before being recruited by Varda again to play Cléo's model friend in *Cléo de 5 à 7*.

4. My work here is subtended by reference to Judith Butler in *Undoing Gender* as also with relation to Varda in my article (Wilson 2014), 'Mortal flesh: Agnès Varda de ci de là'.
5. Another story can be told of male corporeality in Varda's filmmaking, but my concern here, separately, is with the specific possibilities of a woman artist's filming of women. See Isabelle McNeill's discussion of the male nude in her chapter 'Ways of Seeing in Agnès Varda's *Les Dites Cariatides* (1984)'. McNeill's account brilliantly underlines the different valence of the naked man and naked women in the street, showing how Varda is thinking through and challenging gender difference all at once.
6. Her relation to this world is represented in the sequences about her artistic apprenticeship in *Les Plages d'Agnès* (2008).
7. This theme is pursued notably in films such as *Jane B. par Agnès V.* already cited and in different ways, with relation to flesh, in the recent ARTE TV series *Agnès Varda de ci de là* (2011).
8. In her introduction to Lidia Guibert Ferrara's volume, *Reclining Nude*, Frances Borzello writes about the ways in which the tradition was initiated by Giorgione in his *Sleeping Venus* (1510). She continues: 'Although there are not painted predecessors for Giorgione's nude, there are hundreds of successors who fall into line behind her. In no way are these reclining nudes homogeneous. They are fine art's version of music's variations on a theme. They display the front of their body, the back of their body. They look at the spectator, they ignore the spectator, they sleep oblivious to the spectator's gaze. They are voluptuous, they are slim. Sometimes they lie in a landscape, their hummocks and hollows echoing nature itself, and sometimes they rest indoors, as luxuriously displayed as the costly fabrics on which they lie. Very few are completely naked. They wear a necklace, a bracelet, a hat. And they have hair. Not pubic hair but hair on their head, curling, flowing and as wayward and beautiful as the feminine ideal itself' (2002: 7). These variations are pursued still further by Varda imagining a nude who reclines pregnant.
9. In its dilapidation, and with its rows of hanging washing, the court resembles a space from an Atget photograph now estranged by the presence of naked lovers.
10. As Borzello says, by contrast, of the tradition in painting: 'The reclining nude is never a picture of reality. It is an artistic genre in which the live model is transformed into a carrier of meanings: she becomes nature, or vice, or a figure from mythology' (2002: 7).
11. Varda returns to the odalisque at different stages in her career, using it notably in her images of male and female reclining nudes in *Documenteur* (1981), in reconstruction of Titian's *Venus of Urbino* (1538) in *Jane B. par Agnès V.* and in her images of seaside reclining nudes in her installation at the Fondation Cartier, *L'Île et Elle*. See Fiona Handyside's brilliant discussion of this element of the installation, *Grande Carte Postale ou Souvenir de Noirmoutier*, in her chapter in this volume. Handyside draws attention to the ways in which Varda adds, precisely, intimacy and depth to the seaside reclining nude.
12. See <http://mapage.noos.fr/dorotheeblanck/unentretienavec.html> (accessed 18 September 2015).
13. It is apt indeed that Blanck shows Resnais using similar close-up images to Varda at the moment in Duras's screenplay of *Hiroshima mon amour* where we hear the words: 'Tu me tues. Tu me fais du bien' ['You kill me. You give me pleasure'], opening the same stretch of emotion.
14. Comparable strategies of re-viewing and re-framing from different angles are used in her first feature, *La Pointe Courte* (1955).
15. Graffiti calling for peace in Algeria are glimpsed in the latter parts of *L'Opéra-Mouffe* showing the ways in which Varda opens questions of this particular political situation and its spectral presence in Paris in the earlier film as well.
16. The film offers in this regard a reflection on the Left Bank art world of which Varda was herself a part, studying art history at the Ecole du Louvre, while Jacques Demy studied at the Ecole des Beaux-Arts in Nantes before moving to the Ecole nationale de photographie et de cinématographie in Paris. The images of Dorothée in the studio and on the streets of Paris are reminiscent too of the photographs of Edouard Boubat, collected in his volume *Lella* (1987), with his evanescent images of young girls, his models and friends who were also themselves students of drawing in Paris.

17. Varda herself moved on later in her career to work as an installation artist. Already in her feature films there is an interest in the accumulation of meanings in a designed space that can be navigated by the senses. In *Cléo de 5 à 7*, the separate spaces of the film are so many locations in which Cléo comes to perform her identity differently.
18. Varda reflected on images of fashion models in her early short *Ô saisons, ô châteaux* (1958) and she explores the role of models for photographers in the opening parts of *L'Une chante, l'autre pas* [*One Sings, the Other Doesn't*] (1977).
19. Borzello explains the conventional role of the artist's model more broadly: 'The fantasies about models divide into two: the model as the artist's sexual partner and the model as the artist's inspiration. More often than not the sexual and inspirational roles are entwined. Fantasies focusing on the model's sexual aspect deal with her beauty, her sexual generosity towards the artist and her scorn of conventional morality' (2010: 5).
20. Ungar goes on to suggest that Dorothée's way of being reflects how Cléo herself may once have been. I think rather that Dorothée represents all that Cléo may become.
21. I'm grateful to Isabelle McNeill for commenting on this to me.
22. See Phil Powrie's inspiring reading of the sculpture class as a sequence about tension between human flesh and animate material, static sculptures and fluid movement in his chapter in this volume.
23. See, for example, Hans Baldung Grien, *Death and the Maiden* (1517) and *Death and Woman* (1518–1520).

CHAPTER 2

Agnès Varda's *Cléo de 5 à 7*: A Triptych of the Textile

Francesca Minnie Hardy

> I am able to see texture. My sense of sight is pervaded by my sense of touch. Smell is cooperative with taste and taste with sight. [...] My sense of sight, then is a modality of perception that is commutable to my other senses, and vice-versa. My sight is never only sight — it sees what my ear can hear, my hand can touch, my nose can smell, and my tongue can taste. My entire bodily existence is implicated in my vision.[1]

Cléo de 5 à 7 recounts a peculiar double life of film: documenting, in narrative form, ninety minutes in a young woman's life, whilst ethnographically documenting 1960s Paris.[2] As both an artwork and an archive, that is, a document of our world and of another imaginary one, the film traces the 'tenuous line between art and "reality"',[3] as if the one might spill over into the other. This twofold vitality has bred a tripartite vision of the film which plots Cléo, the woman seen; Paris, the city seen; and Cléo, the woman seeing. Collectively, this threefold existence views the film as a lesson in looking which charts the 'perambulatory odyssey'[4] of the eponymous female lead — new starlet Cléo 'Florence' Victoire — as she journeys through Paris on a voyage of self-discovery and towards a look of her own. Cléo's wanderings thus form a city symphony-cum-Bildungsroman hybrid, her self-discovery mediating a spectator's contemporaneous discovery of Paris.

This article, in teasing out what is but a small part of the textile richness embedded in *Cléo de 5 à 7* (hereafter *Cléo*), will make a claim for this tenuous line between art and reality, artwork and archive, being most emphatically staged by the colour black — a tenuous claim perhaps for a film shot predominantly in black and white. There is, of course, an exception to *Cléo*'s monochromatic palette: the brilliant colour of the film's prologue, wherein Cléo visits Madame Irma, a fortune-teller, our leading lady's impatient pessimism apparently preferring the immediacy of the mystic's forecast to the doctor's deferred prognosis, with the occult here festively hued by the kaleidoscopic carpet upon which the tarot cards are laid out. At the film's start, then, the tenuous line between art, what we might think of as otherworldly, and reality, what we might consider worldly, is colourfully bolstered. For the cosmic, 'astrological time'[5] of the tarot is decidedly unmoored from the 'real-time' of *Cléo*'s runtime and its total 'topographical coherence'[6] firmly rooted

FIG. 2.1. Colourful fantasy and black-and-white reality

in the reality of 21 June 1961 by an Europe 1 radio broadcast from that very date.[7] Indeed, as Valerie Orpen highlights, Varda herself 'sees the cards as an "illustration" of life' which is 'not to be confused with black and white "reality"',[8] making my appeals for black staging the tenuous line between art and reality appear ever more tenuous. Through its mise-en-scène, then, *Cléo* here tacitly yet vividly brackets off imagination, fantasy and play, anchoring them to the supposed frivolity of colour and estranging them from the esteemed cleanliness, and quotidian quality, of black (and white) lines. Yet as the only colour spoken out loud by the film, mentioned on three occasions, black enjoys an undoubted privilege in *Cléo de 5 à 7*. With this privilege in mind, in what follows I will first offer an appraisal of colour within the film, paying particular attention to how black has already captured the imagination of existing critical accounts. I shall then propose a reading of *Cléo* that radically repositions the tripartite yet what I will come to identify as resolutely monologic portrayal of the film that existing interventions purvey, my aim being to explore the black textile triptych that is threaded through its material surrounds, this black, textile triptych itself reconfiguring the tenuous line between art and reality by becoming this very line.

Through a glass darkly

Following *Cléo*'s opening chapter scant mention of colour is made. Yet colour, both concretely and abstractly, constitutes a decisive structuring principle across the film, not least through its episodic designs, each of which, according to Varda, '*color* the story, or rather the angle in which the portrait of Cléo is painted'.[9] Our vision is effectively inflected with a set of contours peculiar to particular protagonists. Such colour concern is further illuminated by Cléo's blondeness. Constitutive of her 'iconography of femininity',[10] and a key feature that distinguishes her from the ordinariness of the city, Orpen astutely observes that Cléo's blondeness makes her 'an exception' amongst New Wave models of femininity, for her blondeness 'represent[s] a clichéd and outdated form of stardom that belonged to the *cinéma de papa*'.[11] This signifier of stardom is most emphatically and famously 'demolished' by Jean-Luc Godard in *Le Mépris* (1963) 'by covering [Brigitte Bardot's] ostentatious mane with a wig'.[12] Cléo's blondeness, however, is non-parodically boosted by a wig which, during her watershed moment, she rips from her head, shedding this 'iconic' ornament to reveal a shorter (still blonde) bob beneath it. In *Le Mépris*,

Godard essentially adorns his leading lady with this black follicle prosthesis in order to render her (momentarily) anonymous, and it is the anonymity which is implicitly accomplished by cloaking oneself in black that existing critical accounts dedicated to *Cléo* chorus — a critical harmony which chimes with the figures of both shedding and disguise. Essential to how the current canon perceives black to be operating within the film is thus its ability, exploited by Godard a year after *Cléo*'s release, to offer Cléo a serenely self-assuring and unproblematic anonymity that is responsible for the accord between her inner and outer selves, which precipitates as the film progresses. Variously, but harmoniously, commentaries on the film predicate Cléo's transformation upon what Steven Ungar calls her 'newfound invisibility' within the cityscape, obtained and enjoyed once she has shed the signifiers of her stardom.[13] Orpen echoes the transformative properties of Cléo's more sober sheath, noting: 'Indeed, in the black dress, Cléo does become anonymous and is thus better able to observe others and leave aside her former "fake" identity.' Yet this assessment quickly negates the affirmative characteristics of Cléo's "more real" attire by positing it as 'her final "camouflage" outfit', that is ultimately 'a costume, a masquerade to protect her from the reality of the outside world'.[14] Roy Jay Nelson touches upon a similar proposition when considering the 'little film-within-the-film' Cléo watches alongside Dorothée, an old friend, and Raoul, Dorothée's boyfriend. In this short, the lead protagonist, who is famously played by Jean-Luc Godard,

> commits a grotesque error because he is wearing dark glasses [which] provides a first lesson: the costumes we don to protect ourselves from exterior harm change our own perception of the outside world. If Cléo has been dressing in order to influence others (and she once wears sun glasses in a ridiculously unnecessary effort to remain incognito), it is partly because she is too self-centered.[15]

Steven Ungar ventriloquizes this thinking on protection and perception, noting how 'The film-within-a-film can be read in tandem with Cléo's personal transformation. When the protagonist [...] realises that he was seeing everything darkly (*en noir*) because of his sunglasses, he takes them off before reuniting with his love, Anna'.[16] In effect, through his dark glasses, Godard's worldview is filtered through an unreal lens, with everything he sees *en noir* becoming otherworldly, for when he removes them, reality is restored. Significantly, too, Sandy Flitterman-Lewis aggregates each of these tropes at length:

> The anonymity she craves — the better to observe others around her — is facilitated when she puts on dark glasses. Here the dark glasses become the instrument of vision, of insight: By becoming anonymous Cléo thus sees, and in seeing others, she begins to understand herself. Because in this sequence [Le Dôme] the camera coincides so often with Cléo's point of view, the spectator now takes Cléo's position as subject rather than object of vision.[17]

This subjectivizing shift confers 'a productive vision [...] on both spectator and character alike'[18] — from object to subject of vision — and Flitterman-Lewis likewise ties this change in outlook to an image change akin to Godard's character in the silent short:

> She then tears off the traditional attributes of stereotypical feminine beauty — blonde wig and feathered satin peignoir — and thereby activates her transformation from object to subject through a change in image. In order to leave the world of those who have defined her as a cliché [...] she now puts on ordinary-looking clothing (a black dress, simple jewelry) and with a violent sweep of a black curtain [...] she emerges, *changed.*[19]

Even syntactically here, Flitterman-Lewis hints at the interrelation between a change in Cléo's perception, prompted by a change in her image, hinged on a change of (colour and) dress. Nestled within, yet evidently distinct from, the film proper, it is perhaps to be expected that reflection on this playful, silent short reverberates across many writings on the film because it depicts a matryoshka-esque exploration of looking that acts as what Claudia Gorbman, in her much celebrated essay on the film, has described 'as a metaphor for Cléo's dilemma of perception'.[20] By further consolidating the interrelation between disguise, disrobing and black, *Les Fiancés du Pont Macdonald* thus bears resonances with the way(s) of seeing which Flitterman-Lewis et al. believe *Cléo* 'confers' upon its lead protagonist, and its audience, as each (supposedly) 'assumes the power of vision, a subjective vision of her own'.[21]

Anonymity, achieved by donning dark glasses and dark dresses, invests *Cléo* with an intriguing tension by establishing a close proximity between discussions of subjectivity and masquerade. In fact, I would argue that this contiguity risks undoing any claims made for a more harmonized, truer sense of selfhood through their sustained recourse to role-playing in the cultivation of the self — especially with regards to the respective theses' focus on a concurrent sense of insulation that Cléo's continued masquerade facilitates, and which, moreover, reminds a spectator of the isolation from others she endeavours to overcome. Most significantly, though, and despite the extant tripartite vision of the film, implying multiplicity, the above-mentioned monochromatic machinations render *Cléo* ultimately monologic, that is, too centred on what Nelson has prescribed as the film's 'fundamental subject': 'Cléo's self-image'.[22] Otherwise put, these monochromatic machinations tie our engagement with the film too intimately to the figure of Cléo and her vision in their attempts to bestow what they consider a more productive, subjective vision onto the spectator. Yet just as donning her dark disguise insulates Cléo from others, as she becomes less alienated from herself, essentially we too become insulated from the film, through our own look being subjected to Cléo's expressionistic vision, rather than acquiring a look of our own. Indeed, the film's documentary credentials are even undermined by Cléo's colouring 'elements of [its] realist décor that mark[...] time and place' with 'strong affect — linked to [...] death [...] that charges them with special meanings'[23] — for example, the masks she sees during her taxi ride from the Rue de Rivoli to the Rue Huyghens. As we celebrate fifty years of *Cléo de 5 à 7*, then, it is thus high time that we revise its 'fundamental subject' by tracing what I conceive as the film's textile trajectory, rather than Cléo's through the city. As such, we can recast the lesson-in-looking that the film relays in terms of a spectator's encounter with the filmic image, rather than with Cléo's self-image, whereby we can shift critical attention from Cléo's own perambulatory odyssey through Paris to the textile odyssey through the film that a spectator undertakes and which this black, textile triptych articulates. I will do so by recalibrating the two principal concerns of existing interventions — the anonymity and everydayness that black permits — and examining the direct encounter with a spectator such revisions enact so that the lesson in looking which *Cléo de 5 à 7* offers is co-incident with, but independent of, Cléo's. These changes are twofold. One set mobilises the senses of imagination, fantasy and play which the existing critical canon unwittingly embellishes with black (but overlooks), through its frequent allusions to costume, disguise and masquerade — effectively unbracketing these properties from the film's vivid prologue. Indeed, the film itself sounds out these otherworldly qualities of black on the three occasions that it is spoken by the film's protagonists (as we will see below). The other set rejects outright the anonymizing properties of black by treating this textile triptych as the tenuous line between art and reality, where the precariousness between the two is exposed through its inviting a spectator to body forth before *Cléo*'s imagery, rather than remaining passively and disinterestedly before it, so that as Cléo discovers the contours of her own body, we too discover our own corporeality.

Through a body fully

Significantly, this co-incident but independent spectatorial lesson in looking does not judge looking as an ocularcentric exercise, which in a cinematic context has promoted three metaphors that 'have dominated film theory': 'the *picture frame*, the *window*, and the *mirror*'[24] and their respective 'transparent', 'opaque' or 'refractive' and 'reflective' characteristics.[25] In these terms, *Cléo de 5 à 7* offers us a window onto Cléo's world that monologically insists upon her self-image and worldview, which, at first sight, might appear to function as a 'conduit'[26] for a spectator's subjective vision, that is, where she experiences a sense of intersubjectivity by looking with, and not only at, Cléo.[27] Such seeing, in remaining anchored to Cléo and her self-image, is largely a lure. Film theory's recent *bodily* turn, however, admits a fruitful way out of this ocular dead-end, emblematic of 'the sensory hierarchy that subtends Western philosophy, in which only the distance senses are vehicles of knowledge, and [...] of beauty'.[28] The *bodily* turn thus redresses '[t]he neglect of touch, smell, and taste (and to some extent, hearing)', as well as 'the tendency to dismiss the proximal senses as inferior that underpin [...] Western thought'.[29] It does so by no longer witnessing cinema as though through a frame, window, or mirror, and instead pursuing an economy of looking and subsequent model of spectatorship wherein 'the viewer shares and performs cinematic space dialogically'.[30] She is able to do so through 'embodied perception' which, as Vivian Sobchack determines, 'is not *lived* theoretically', but rather as 'actual embodied praxis'.[31] Importantly, Sobchack asserts 'such generalization' should *not* be 'regarded as constituting a theory'; instead 'it must be regarded paradoxically as a theory of the moment when there is no theory, when theory is both unthought and incomplete in its momentum as *praxis*'.[32] This (non-)theory of the moment, this praxis, therefore seeks to (re-) embody the eye by underlining its being 'part of the whole body',[33] whilst dehierarchizing the sensorium. For, as Sobchack summarizes:

> although the eyes are the body's access to a particular form of information, the body's other modes of access to its world always also inform vision — providing alternative sense and significance to it.[34]

Arguably, then, one sensory modality *colours* another, and as this article's epigraph states, 'My sense of sight [...] is a modality of perception that is commutable to my other senses, and vice-versa'[35] and through which I not only see texture, but feel it too, thanks to the synaesthetic configurations our bodies are capable of through such sensory co-option. This commutability is expressly experienced via Laura Marks's (non-)theory of haptic visuality where 'the eyes themselves function like organs of touch'[36] in order to collapse the distance, the 'separation between the viewing subject and the object'.[37] Drawing us in close to the object of our perception, 'haptic looking tends to move over [its] surface [...] rather than plunge into illusionistic depth, not to distinguish form so much as to discern texture. It is more inclined to move than to focus, more inclined to graze than to gaze'.[38] A haptic look, then, does not concern itself with the signification of fixed forms, instead preferring the unbound and unfettered flux of matter over meaning. Accordingly, 'haptic perception privileges the material presence of the image' over its 'representational power',[39] in order 'to emphasize the tactile and contagious quality of cinema as something we viewers brush up against like another body'.[40] Drawn in close to the image, grazing across its surface and brushing up against it like another body, converting vision to touch, we are again invited through haptic visuality not only to see texture, but to feel it, to touch it, with our eyes. Moreover, in doing so we relinquish mastery's firm grip on spectator-screen relations and instead engage in a relationship of 'mutuality',[41] even 'a mutual dissolving of viewer and viewed, subject and object',[42] for unlike vision, touch is not 'unidirectional' and 'one cannot touch without being touched'.[43]

A third revolution to this *bodily* turn pushes this sense of mutuality, of reciprocity, and indeed of embodiment, deeper into our bodies, by suggesting that films not only draw us in close and invite us to brush up against them, akin to a skin-on-skin contact, but equally that they animate our musculature. Whilst Marks, then, foregrounds the skin-like qualities of film, Jennifer Barker ventures below a film's epidermis to postulate its 'muscular body'.[44] Taking John Ford's Westerns as an example, Barker notes how films

> make both intimate, inclusive gestures using close, circular compositions that gather us into a community or a family, and expansive gestures using monumental wide-angle vistas that are like someone throwing their arms open to take in the whole scene, making us feel small and yet exhilarated amidst the vastness of the American landscape.[45]

These gestures demand a very particular understanding of mimicry, with Barker positing that '[b]eyond thinking of spectators' identification with characters as being too complex to be called mimicry', we could alternatively consider mimicry [as] 'too complex to be only character centred', whereby 'viewers' bodily responses to films might be mimicry in another sense: not mimicry of characters, but of the film itself'.[46] 'Perhaps', she concludes, 'viewers respond to whole cinematic structures.'[47] In responding to whole cinematic structures, we thus transition from synaesthetic configurations to what Barker describes as a 'muscular engagement with the [film] wherein we straddle that threshold between "here and there," body and image'[48] — our 'here' being our bodies, wrapped up in the film's 'there', that is, its close, circular compositions or wide-angled embrace, and where once more we dissolve before the film, 'hitch[ing] ourselves to [its] body [...] liv[ing] vicariously through it',[49] rather than perched at arm's length across its frame.

Thanks to the *bodily* turn, we thus dismantle the strict, monologic contours of the window, the mirror and the picture frame in order to embark upon a direct dialogue with *Cléo*'s materiality — the black, textile triptych — to become 'visual "listeners"'[50] of its material surrounds who actually intersubjectively dialogue[51] with the film. And in its presence, following Jean-Luc Nancy's account of Japanese conceptual artist On Kawara's *Today* series,[52] we might hear the image announce:

> find me there where I am, and we will meet. You will recognize me by this, that I am only there for the encounter. And I will recognize you by the same. We will be there, you as well as I, only to find ourselves there. [...] We will find each other by each other.[53]

Nancy calls this invitation 'sight's date with vision',[54] and whilst the diurnal structure of Kawara's project and *Cléo*'s own temporal contours possess unexpected parallels, effectively rooting each in worldly (monochromatic) reality, Nancy's probing the nature of our dialogical encounter with the image echoes this article's primary intentions by positing the potential for a provocative corporeality whereby spectator and screen alike body forth, unbound and thus otherworldly.

Through a carpet tactilely

Cléo's clever opening sequence prepares us for this shift, that is, for our recasting the lesson in looking that the film relays in terms of a spectator's encounter with the filmic image instead of with Cléo's self-image. Patch-working together in vivid colour the warp and weft of the narrative with the ornament of the credits — with two different bodies, the time of the index and the time of the fiction, already encountering each other —, these moments of the film, owing to their many-hued palette, are, as mentioned above, frequently read as a space for fantasy. As the sequence advances it continues its playful allusions to the fleshy presences beyond the frame through Madame Irma's instruction to cut the deck. As Cléo does so, the filmic body follows suit and cuts from a tight framing of the protagonists' hands to a somewhat looser framing which incorporates the arms of each. In effect, the camera, like Cléo, responds to Madame Irma's directions and this 'Coupez, mademoiselle' could be said to address Varda as director, or Janine Verneau as editor, just as much as it does Cléo. Just, then, as the credits and narrative foreshadows are interwoven, the filmic body's response to the fortune teller's instructions does not so much mobilize a tension between the on- and off-screen space, but rather mobilizes a sense of each space partaking in a shared rhythm between image and spectator. A structural and diegetic coincidence reminiscent of Walter Benjamin's approximating the director with the surgeon,[55] a sense of a shared rhythm between image and spectator, works its way to the surface of the image thanks to this cut, effectively diffusing any tension between on- and off-screen space and formally implying that neither must fall silent while the other speaks.

The wider framing that this cut achieves reveals the surface upon which the tarot cards are spread to be the central medallion of a carpet that branches outwards towards thorny vines of flowers, which in turn neighbour still more decorative foliage patterning. Immanent to this carpet is an invitation, here specifically addressed to the spectator, not to get caught up in the festoons of its molar structure, but rather to relish in its '"molecular" materiality',[56] to decline a plunge into illusionistic depth, in favour of a graze across its tactile surface. Intriguingly here, the film itself attempts to belie its own attempts at casting off any discursive tropes through the tarot game itself which serves 'the "molar" politics of representation' in sketching out Cléo's fortune and the plot of the narrative, and as such risks carpeting over the molecular entirely.[57] Yet this textile invitation is in no way overwhelmed, or tamed,[58] by the molar and instead co-exists alongside it, because with each molar evocation the sequence enacts, spectatorial interest in the tactile is maintained, for the grain of the carpet's weave persists within the image as fabric margins, which themselves hem in the narrative impulses with which the tarot cards charge the sequence. With our eyes we thus brush up against the tiny stiches that make up the vast landscape of the carpet's seemingly boundless and florid desert, and whilst the brilliance of the prologue's colour blinds us to the richness of black, by extending a tactile invitation, *Cléo* here effectively inaugurates a spectator's co-incident, yet independent lesson in looking, by tying the latter to the textile.

FIG. 2.2. Tactile Margins

Such (productive) textile interplay is pursued further as Cléo shops for a new hat and it is here that we encounter the first panel of our black, textile triptych. Widely read as one of the most self-image-centric sequences of the entire film — through its 'literalization of the woman-as-image caught up as the pivot within the cinematic apparatus'[59] — it might appear a curious claim that it likewise makes space for a spectator, and indeed the city, amongst its contours. Yet while Cléo's various charades on the shop floor — intermittently the widow, the bride and the Southern belle — simultaneously foster the playful suggestion that our implication in and being with the image of another can be actualized as simply and cleanly as resting and removing a textile hemisphere upon and from one's head through the ornament of the hat, and hint at her construction from voyeuristic and narcissistic gazes, more subtly still, her role-play triggers the otherworldly qualities of black by tying it to the principles of imagination, fantasy and play, for as Cléo feigns the widow she declares how black really suits her.

Fig. 2.3. Black Widow

Immersed in this emporium, there is something wonderfully cosmic about the sequence's images, an impression which installs itself as soon as the camera takes up residence in the shop window and nestles itself amongst the items on show there, so obliging us to peer out from beneath the rims of the many textile orbs suspended above us. The curious shot/reverse-shot sequence which follows as Cléo and Angèle exchange glances with these floating discs attests to this notion for it suggests a mutual drawing together of two pseudo-celestial and earthly bodies, collapsing the distance between them and thereby anticipating the first panel of our black, textile triptych. Peeping out from the rims of hats, peering around their peripheries, throughout the sequence we are well aware that the hat shop is brimming with an urban lining and like a spectator, bystanders and onlookers can peek in at Cléo's antics through the shop windows. As Cléo scours the shop floor for her choice of headwear from the flying saucers stationed in the window, she passes a black sheet, draped across part of the glass store front and the first panel of our textile triptych, which momentarily blots out our view of her. The image she is replaced with continues the cosmic disposition of the hats stationed in the window, for pinned upon this twilight textile expanse is a series of white ellipses resembling palm-sized galaxies.

Almost imperceptibly, the intermingling of the microcosmic star systems and the reflection of the city caught up in the diaphanous glass surface of the window

Fig. 2.4. Panel One — Black Window

converts vision to touch, in a move which carries over the tactile vision inspired by the carpet's textile surface. Its cosmic disposition here disperses the image across its outermost layer, collapsing it onto one single plane. There is thus a further invitation to graze the image's surface, rather than to gaze at it as distinct forms dissolve and texture takes over this black expanse. However, it is not all *plain grazing*, that is, we do not simply brush up against it because the image does not resist figuration entirely and as our attention lingers on its surface we come to make out human forms which multiply the longer we look, hinting at the archival reality encroaching upon the fancy of Cléo's game of dress-up. As such, the image triggers a synaesthetic configuration, which borders on the edge of touch and of vision, placing us on the edges of each of these sensations too. Before this first panel of our black, textile triptych, a spectator is therefore able to graze across the image's surface, *seeing and feeling its texture*, independently of Cléo's own journey of self-discovery, and vision, and whereby she bodies forth as one sensory perception acts as a conduit for another, where her sense of sight is pervaded, co-opted by her sense of touch enabling it to see and feel what her hand can touch, implicating her entire bodily existence in her vision. Accordingly, then, the black(-and-white) reality reflected in the window becomes pregnant with otherworldly qualities, as our own graze across its surface seeks not to decipher its worldly, archival recording, but intersubjectively to dialogue with its contours, with its material, surficial excess unbound by history there where we meet.

A second makeshift performance space — Cléo's apartment — emboldens our embodied look upon the film's imagery and, decked out in the brilliance of white, the space resembles a blank canvas within which Cléo (again) indulges in a series of different looks, including an angel,[60] until she finally slips into what the existing critical canon view as her ultimate costume change: her anonymizing black dress. At home, gone is the clutter and archival lining of the shop floor, and without any critical intervention the space itself appears wholly otherworldly for, except for a very discreet reference to Edith Piaf, we are given no indicator of when, or indeed where, we are, curious for a locale which technically speaking breaks the film's topographical coherence. We might once more question how in this space there is room for a spectator beyond Cléo's self-image, and indeed for our interrogation of black since the sequence is seemingly devoid of pure white's polar opposite. However, here we encounter the two further panels of our black, textile triptych and far from being empty, that is, uncluttered, the suffocation bred into the sequence by Cléo's pervasive performativity ultimately erupts into a devastating musical and emotional crescendo as she sings 'Sans toi'. Generally considered the 'hinge'[61] or pivot of her transformative narrative, her poignant performance prefaces the fundamental hinge of our own textile odyssey.

First accompanied by Bob on the piano, as the camera moves towards her with an encircling, gentle sweeping motion, this diegetic music very soon, and again almost imperceptibly, becomes extra-diegetic as orchestral string music is invisibly woven into the musical body of the image. Cléo too, seemingly instinctively, becomes aware of this extra-diegetic dimension and turns her body towards this imagined concert hall and towards us, the actual spectators. The words she sings speak of a material, corporeal existence which Cléo herself feels is slipping away from her; that is, if her fears are well placed and as the camera coils around her, the rich albeit stagnant landscape in which she is enveloped when at home is entirely erased, and the image again collapses into one single plane. Standing before this black, textile backdrop, the second of the film, she cuts a desperate and desolate figure, and unlike the first display pinned to black fabric, Cléo here is a lonely, solitary planet and not situated among a constellation of neighbouring galaxies. Although its music and lyrics may not have been written by Cléo, they act as a catalyst to her consciousness, reacting with her psyche, and therefore rather than using this performance as a further disguise, after so many during this sequence alone, Cléo is instead undone by it. Its impact on a spectator, however, feels quite different, for despite its planar address, as her performance plays out the film provokes a muscular verticality in its encounter with the spectator. An experience of such muscularity might seem surprising given the sequence's visual and kinetic stasis for apart from the movement of her lips as Cléo sings, a single teardrop falling down her cheek is the only visible movement in the frame until the number is over, when the camera rapidly retreats from her figure to reveal her heightened despair. In spite of the static, though, Cléo's sung soliloquy dialogues with a spectator, spilling 'outside the room, visually and audibly' — *and muscularly* — 'bursting out of the space'[62] of her apartment and the frame by means of its audio puissance which in throwing itself wide open invites a spectator to respond to its invited embrace. While Cléo, then, is undone by her performance, it causes us to be done up with the film, as we body forth and hitch our bodies to its acoustic swell to become caught up both here and there. Whereas, then, the acoustic resonance of the radio broadcast heard as Cléo travels back home from the Rue de Rivoli rooted us firmly into the reality of 21 June 1961, here such resonance flowers into fantasy and play.

According to existing responses to the film, a sense of fantasy and play already radiates from our triptych's second panel, with Sandy Flitterman-Lewis considering it 'an apotheosis of the fetishized woman's image'[63] and Valerie Orpen 'an anti-

FIG. 2.5. Panel Two — Black Background

realistic (and hyper-real) orchestral and reverberating rendition of the song's last few stanzas'.[64] Whilst a play of textures, including colour, movement and music, is also keenly felt by other commentators, for example, Steven Ungar notes how, in isolating Cléo's head against the fabric background, Varda 'set[s] off the matt textures of skin and dressing gown against the black curtain and hard brilliance of drinking glasses atop the upright piano'.[65] Yet the existing canon's focus on Cléo's star turn here implies that these materials draw their power from Cléo's star power, from her self-image, meaning they retain the monologic character Cléo's self-image imposes upon the film. Our encounter with the third and final panel of out textile triptych very much jettisons this attachment for good.

Through the black, textile triptych finally

Overwhelmed by her performance, Cléo decides to escape the dry confines of her apartment and venture out into the city alone. A heated exchange with Bob ensues and captured in extreme close-up his head functions as a wipe across the outer plane of the screen. Cléo hurries into a corner and steps behind the black curtain draped there. Drawing the curtain in a counter movement to the wipe enacted by Bob's head, Cléo declares herself to be dressed in black and thus black garners its second mention of the film which through Cléo's costume change deepens its links to fantasy, to play.[66] With the third curtain we conclude the triptych of black textile surfaces we encounter throughout the film and importantly it is the only tablet of our triptych that is permitted to be the sole perceptible object of the frame, and we may, for a moment or two, suspect an analogue glitch through its evoking the actual material of the film stock. Yet far from the filmic body being broken here, it instead instigates a sense of breaking free, not least in Cléo's escape from her apartment and entourage, but equally through its offering a spectator one of the most emphatically independent and intersubjective moments of the whole film.

Our moves through this triptych illustrate this hypothesis, for if imagined hinged

FIG. 2.6. Panel Three — Black Hole

together, we move from a series of galaxies, to a lone planet and finally to a black hole. In essence, upon each encounter the surficial content of each panel thins out. The first iteration's synaesthetic configuration collapsing into Cléo's solitary figure, the acoustic muscularity of Cléo's sung soliloquy itself collapsing into the most singular image of the entire film. So singular that we could refute its very being there as image at all and playfully and formally implying that Cléo's star turn in the preceding tablet becomes a supernova and what remains is an abyss, a blank, a nothingness. But in our being there with the image, through our encounter with it, both in isolation and as part of the film's black, textile triptych, its existence cannot be denied because we meet and find each other at the threshold of the screen. Despite appearances, then, the final black, textile panel of our triptych does not present a void or a vacuum, but instead a moment for a fully embodied spectator to literally body forth before *Cléo*'s imagery, probing deeper than our skin and our musculature and into our own vitality. We are '[called on] to auscultate ourselves, to listen to our own living bodies and our own subjectivity',[67] as well as the body of the film, for it is only if we look, listen and feel carefully that we come to understand that quiet at all.

Thinking thus, black, or rather our encounter with the colour as a large fabric expanse, could be described as *Cléo*'s *couleur locale*, or its *carnation*, which Nancy describes as

> A singular intensity — itself protean, mobile, multiple — of a fleshy event, or of skin as an event of existence [...] the (peculiar) flutters, colours, rhythms, and subtleties, of a place, of an event of existence.[68]

By design the form of the triptych lends itself to the very principles which charge *carnation* because although technically one picture, each separate tablet affords us a different view of a similar theme, making it multiple and protean. Similarly each is the site of a singular intensity through its encounter with the spectator, its 'event of existence', because with each encounter of each fabric panel, we encounter a singular moment in the filmic body. Plunged into darkness, then, the third tablet of our textile triptych, and its earlier attenuated shadings, is not eclipsed by its black shroud, but rather charged with the unfettered, kinetic energy of *carnation*, and as such it does not foreclose an event horizon, but instead a notional horizon of event, that is, an embodied encounter with a spectator at the threshold of the screen. And although not necessarily boundless in its creative yield, it is certainly liberated from a determinate fixity of meaning, hence its singularity, thanks to its own peculiar flutters, colours, rhythms, and subtleties, unlike the peculiar flutters, colours, rhythms, and subtleties of death with which Cléo vision inflects the cityscape and our own.

Although Nancy stresses how *carnation* and *couleur locale* are not meant in the pictorial sense of either word, when describing how the material burst of a red ribbon in Rembrandt's 'Bethsabée au bain' 'makes the whole canvas vibrate and grabs our attention',[69] in his joint-authored text with Federico Ferrari, it is difficult not to extrapolate such reasoning. Especially if juxtaposed with his comments on Kawara's *Viet-Nam* triptych, from the *Today* series, and how the red magenta used is quite literally the paintings' *couleur locale* because it serves as 'the *datum* of a bloody spatter', that is, blood spilled on the landscape itself.[70] Somewhat indirectly, this *datum* of a bloody spatter returns us to the non-theory of actual embodied praxis, for neither is *lived* theoretically, but rather each is a record of a lived event enabled by and charged with the vitality of our lived bodies. As the film's *couleur locale* and its vehicle for embodied perception, black and its iteration in each pane of *Cléo*'s black, textile triptych, does not flutter in isolation, but, rather, requires our enabling bodies before it, whilst we in turn require it in order to learn to look with our entire bodies. In encountering the black, textile triptych in this way, we may, then, flicker its sombre hues with our own personal singularity, that is, with our own properly, productive subjective vision inflected with its own peculiar flutters, colours, rhythms and subtleties. *Cléo de 5 à 7* is not therefore exclusively an archival recording — that is, a lesson in looking at the city and its populus — or a lesson in looking lived vicariously through Cléo, but is instead a recording of the present spectatorial encounter with the film, its rhythm paced by the black, textile triptych. An encounter which breaks with conventional criticism of the film by aligning black with elements of fantasy and play, rather than these being exclusive to the film's colour prologue through their eschewal of watertight meaning.

Admittedly, however, *Cléo de 5 à 7* enacts a far more provocative gesture in its intimate intertwining of (a) colour and embodiment, which may well solve the enigma of its abyssal runtime, for despite advertising itself as 'Cléo from five to seven', the film only runs until a little after six thirty, expectantly concluding with Cléo's test results. With this absent yet present "extra" time, Roy Jay Nelson suggests that Varda 'seems to be encouraging us to shatter the mirror [since] from 6:30 (Cléo's time), when the screen goes black, until 7:00, the hour promised by the title, we are on our own, without a mirror, in search of our natural selves'.[71] Reminiscent of the aforementioned auscultation, at the film's close we are thus completely and utterly confronted with ourselves, by means of which, fundamentally, we might identify with Cléo's own position, for she too is confronted with herself. As the screen is consumed by black for a final time, then, here the at times flimsy juncture between art and reality is once more exposed, as the reality of the film (five to six-thirty) tips over into our own corporeality (six-thirty to seven and beyond), whereby the film does not trail off into nothingness, but into ourselves. *Cléo*'s missing thirty minutes, then, are not missing at all, but instead give us time to be in and with our bodies. Rather than simply relaying a mimetic representation of our reality, *Cléo* thus confers a truly productive vision upon the spectator through inviting us to body forth as well as to hold onto ourselves in front of the film by eschewing the dissolving the *bodily* turn promotes. In effect, then, *Cléo de 5 à 7* offers this very turn a revised approach to the spectatorial body. However, whilst enabling our bodies and ultimately giving itself over to them, somewhat eerily, *Cléo de 5 à 7*, and the mortal bounty its narrative places on the head of the figure of the female star, cannot avoid becoming fundamentally caught up with the 'real life' in which Cléo's perambulatory odyssey is embedded, that of 21 June 1961, through to the October 1963 death of Edith Piaf who, like black, garners audio and visual mention on three occasions throughout the film, to accentuate once more the tenuous line between art and 'reality'.

Notes to Chapter 2

1. Vivian Sobchack, *The Address of the Eye: A Phenomenology of Film Experience* (Princeton: Princeton University Press, 1992), 77–78.
2. Steven Ungar, *Cléo de 5 à 7* (Basingstoke: Palgrave Macmillan, 2008), 35 and 44–45.
3. Barbara Koenig Quart, *Women Directors: The Emergence of a New Cinema* (New York: Praeger, 1988), 142.
4. Sandy Flitterman-Lewis, *To Desire Differently: Feminism and the French Cinema* (New York: Columbia University Press, 1996), 38.
5. Ungar, 36.
6. François Penz, 'From Topographical Coherence to Creative Geography: Rohmer's "The Aviators Wife" and Rivette's "Pont Du Nord"', in *Cities in Transition: The Moving Image and the Modern Metropolis*, ed. by Emma Wilson and Andrew Webber (London: Wallflower Press, 2008), 123–40 (126).
7. Valerie Orpen, *Cléo de 5 à 7* (London and New York: I. B. Tauris, 2007), 17.
8. Orpen, 44.
9. Flitterman-Lewis, 270. My emphasis.
10. Ibid., 39.
11. Orpen, 7.
12. Ibid.
13. Ungar, 71.
14. Orpen, 75–76.
15. Roy Jay Nelson, 'Reflections in a Broken Mirror: Varda's Cléo de 5 à 7', *The French Review*, 56 (1983), 735–43 (740).
16. Ungar, 74.
17. Flitterman-Lewis, 274
18. *Ibid.*, 275
19. *Ibid.*, 277. My emphasis.
20. *Ibid.*, 77.
21. *Ibid.*, 268–69.
22. Nelson, 738.
23. Ungar, 66.
24. Sobchack, 17.

25. *Ibid.*, 285.
26. *Ibid.*, 172.
27. As we saw above with regards to Cléo's vision investing the city's surrounds with the presence of death.
28. Laura U. Marks, 'Thinking Multisensory Culture', *Paragraph*, 31 (2008), 123–37 (123).
29. *Ibid.*
30. Laura U. Marks, *The Skin of the Film: Intercultural Cinema, Embodiment, and the Senses* (Durham and London: Duke University Press, 2000), 150.
31. Sobchack, 214.
32. *Ibid.*
33. *Ibid.*, 271.
34. *Ibid.*
35. *Ibid.*, 78.
36. Marks (2000), 162.
37. *Ibid.*
38. *Ibid.*
39. *Ibid.*, 163.
40. *Ibid.*, xi-xii.
41. *Ibid.*, 184.
42. Laura U. Marks, 'Haptic Visuality: Touching with the Eyes', *Framework: The Finnish Art Review*, 2004, 78–82 (81).
43. Marks (2000), 149.
44. Jennifer M. Barker, *The Tactile Eye: Touch and the Cinematic Experience* (London: University of California Press, 2009), 79.
45. *Ibid.*, 79.
46. *Ibid.*, 74.
47. *Ibid.*
48. *Ibid.*, 72.
49. *Ibid.*, 75.
50. Sobchack, 272.
51. Ibid., 24.
52. The *Today* series is an ever-growing database of paintings that simply display the date of the image's creation upon a monochromatic background, the date's typescript determined by where Kawara is in the world on the day of the painting's creation.
53. Jean-Luc Nancy, 'The Technique of the Present', *Tympanum*, 2000 <http://www.usc.edu/dept/comp-lit/tympanum/4/nancy.html> [accessed 19 September 2015]
54. *Ibid.*
55. Walter Benjamin, 'The Work of Art in the Age of Mechanical Reproduction', in *Illuminations*, ed. by Hannah Arendt, trans. by Harry Zohn (New York: Schocken Books, 1985), 217–51 (233).
56. Anna Powell quoted in Martine Beugnet, *Cinema and Sensation: French Film and the Art of Transgression* (Edinburgh: Edinburgh University Press, 2007), 6.
57. *Ibid.*
58. Laura U. Marks, 'Thinking Like a Carpet: Embodied Perception and Individuation in Algorithmic Media' (Keynote at the The Cinema of Sensations, Cluj-Napoca, Romania, 2012)
59. Flitterman-Lewis, 278.
60. Jenny Chamarette, *Phenomenology and the Future of Film: Rethinking Subjectivity Beyond French Cinema* (Basingstoke: Palgrave Macmillan, 2012), 114.
61. Flitterman-Lewis, 277.
62. Janice Mouton, 'From Feminine Masquerade to Flâneuse: Agnès Varda's Cléo in the City', *Cinema Journal*, 40 (2001), 3–16 (6).
63. Flitterman-Lewis, 276.
64. Orpen, 37.
65. Ungar, 59.
66. The third mention follows later and is spoken, via an intertitle, by Godard's character in the silent film with reference to his 'lunettes maudites' which skew his worldview.

67. Lisa Coulthard, 'Haptic Aurality: Listening to the Films of Michael Haneke', *Film-Philosophy*, 16 (2012), 16–29, (28).
68. Jean-Luc Nancy, *Corpus* (Paris: Métailé, 2006), 17. My translation.
69. Jean-Luc Nancy and Federico Ferrari, *Nus Sommes: La peau des images* (Brussels: Yves Gevaert, 2006), 21. My translation.
70. Nancy (2000).
71. Nelson, 742.

CHAPTER 3

L'Une chante, l'autre pas: Music, Movement and the Utopian Community

Phil Powrie

L'Une chante, l'autre pas (1976) is one of Varda's least known films, a 'feminist musical' as Varda herself labeled it.[1] It focuses in part on the struggle for the legalization of abortion. A feminist musical group, Orchidée, takes the struggle into towns and villages throughout France. They perform nine songs in the course of the film. The words were written by Varda herself, and they sound like political tracts with their 'paroles militantes' [militant lyrics],[2] as Varda labels them. While male critics were generally favourable to the film, a number of contemporary women critics took the film to task. Françoise Audé in her influential *Ciné-modèles, cinémas d'elles* of 1981, called the music 'charmante plutot que mordante' [charming rather than biting], brushing the film off: 'Tout cela est sucré' [It's all a bit sugary].[3] Françoise Oukrate, writing in *Écran*, was even more critical, suggesting that the film's message was fatally compromised by playing to the gallery:

> Toutes ces féministes-là sont bien jolies, bien sympathiques: Pomme est à croquer. Suzanne, la douce, maternante à souhait. Tout le monde fond. Les 'Orchidées', épanouies, embaument. Dommage tout de même que l'on nous matraque un peu trop leurs chansons sans nous faire assister, tiens par exemple, à leur vie quotidienne pendant leurs tournées de chanteuses aux champs, leur vie de filles ensemble. Mais cela aurait risqué de donner dans le subversif. Voilà bien ma mauvaise nature qui ressort. Parce que contrairement au chœur laudatif de tous ces messieurs de la critique, je vends la mèche, moi femme, féministe, Personne n'est parfaite. En dépit de ses dires: 'j'ai fait un film de femme, je n'ai pas fait un film féministe', Agnès Varda est devenue malgré elle aux yeux de toute la critique virile 'notre féministe de choc'. Voilà donc un film féministe à la portée de tout le monde. C'est Walt Disney au MLF.
>
> [All those feminists are pretty and nice: Pomme is good enough to eat. Suzanne, gentle and incredibly motherly. You melt inside. The 'Orchids', fragrant, blossom. Shame though that we're bludgeoned by their songs, but we don't see, for example, their daily lives during their tours in the countryside, their life of women living together. But that might have been a tad too subversive. I guess it's my evil nature coming out. Because unlike all those gentlemen critics falling over themselves to praise the film, I'm going to let the cat out of

> the bag, me, a woman, a feminist. No-one's perfect. Despite what she's said — 'I've made a women's film, I haven't made a feminist film' — Agnès Varda has become whether she likes it or not in the eyes of male critics 'our star feminist'. So here we have a feminist for all and sundry. It's Walt Disney for the Women's Movement.][4]

It is fair to note that Varda herself includes this witheringly sarcastic criticism in *Varda par Agnès*.[5] Part of what I wish to do here is to counter this critique by showing how the film can now be seen as considerably more effective in its work than Oukrate's narrowly political position allows.

In some respects the film is dated. In *Varda par Agnès*, Varda comments that the band's tour of France seems 'datée, baba cool, militante et désuète à nos jeunes filles qui s'habillent Agnès B' [dated, hip, militant and old-fashioned for our young girls who dress in designer clothes].[6] She talks nostalgically of the period: 'Comment ne pas sourire avec tendresse en repensant aux longues jupes en coton indien, aux sabots, au pain complet, à l'utopie, aux hommes à cheveux longs, aux fleurs brodées sur les jeans, aux bijoux d'argent' [It's impossible not to smile tenderly when you think of long Indian cotton dresses, clogs, wholemeal bread, utopia, men with long hair, jeans embroidered with flowers, silver jewellery].[7] Not only is the film dated, but Varda herself has dismissed its importance within the larger body of her work, locating it within a very specific conjuncture: 'Sur le moment et avec le recul, *L'Une chante, l'autre pas* n'a jamais été pour moi une des étapes de mon travail de cinéaste. J'ai seulement fait le point [...] en proposant une fiction documentée sur la lutte des femmes entre 1969 et 1976' [Then and now, *L'Une chante, l'autre pas* was never for me a key stage in my work as a filmmaker. I just took stock [...] and proposed a documentary fiction on women's struggles between 1969 and 1976].[8] As if this were not damning enough, the film, with its nine songs, clearly belongs to that most invisible of genres in the French cinema, the musical, even though many of the critics of the period did not identify it as such.

However, this film is more significant than Varda or indeed her critics allow. This is partly because the musical has in recent years made a comeback in French cinema. I would therefore like to consider the film from the point of view of the interaction between music and image. In so doing, I will show how the music, both the songs and the incidental music, is key to the transformative potential of the film. This is not so much because of the proselytizing lyrics of the songs, but because of the way in which the music functions to create a community in movement. My analysis of the film will show how there is tension between stasis and movement, domesticity and nomadism, 'masculine' views of the world and 'feminine' views of the world. These are familiar binaries in Varda's films, suggesting that the film is much more obviously part of Varda's œuvre than the comments above might have indicated. And, secondly, my analysis of the music will show how these binaries, neatly encapsulated in a metaphorical sense by the title of the film, *L'Une chante, l'autre pas* [One Sings, the Other Doesn't], are undermined to create a mobile domestic community which shares many characteristics with Varda's other films.

As *L'Une chante, l'autre pas* is one of Varda's less well-known films, I shall give a brief synopsis. We are in 1962. The film articulates feminist politics of the period through the relationship of two women. Pomme, a schoolgirl, befriends Suzanne, the stay-at-home mother of two children, who is five years older than her. More resilient and resourceful than the quieter Suzanne, she pays for Suzanne's abortion by lying to her parents, and supports her morally when Suzanne's photographer-lover Jérôme commits suicide. Pomme wants to be a singer, and we see her taking part in a rock n roll recording session. More than a decade later, in 1976, Pomme has become a protest singer for the all-woman band Orchidée, while Suzanne works in a family planning clinic. The two women meet again at a demonstration for the legalization of abortion associated with the MLAC (Mouvement pour la Liberté de l'Avortement et de la Contraception [Movement for Free Abortion and Contraception]). Pomme marries Darius, an Iranian, whom she had met on a trip to Amsterdam where she had gone for an abortion. She and Darius move to Iran briefly; but they break up, because he expects her to be a stay-at-home wife. The film presents both as about Pomme and Suzanne's enduring friendship, despite a decade-long separation, during which they communicate by postcard, and their common struggle for women's rights.

That struggle is complementary, and reflects the film's title. Suzanne, the quieter of the two, is shown listening to women as they come to her for help in the family planning clinic. Pomme, on the other hand, is more outgoing; we see her expressing her views forcefully throughout the film, partly through the protest songs with their militant lyrics. Alison Smith neatly encapsulates this difference: 'What is interesting about Suzanne to the audience is what she *does* with her situation — what is important about Pomme is more often what she *is* or presents herself as being'.[9]

The nine songs place *L'Une chante, l'autre pas* within the musical genre. As mentioned above, this genre has made a comeback since the mid-1990s. During the thirty years stretching from the advent of the sound film to the end of the 1950s the musical was an important popular genre. René Clair experimented with the musical in the early 1930s, with films such as *Sous les toits de Paris* (1930). By the late 1930s the musical had become a highly visible and popular genre, with the Big Band films of Ray Ventura and the extremely popular film spectaculars of the three operetta tenors, Tino Rossi, Luis Mariano and George Guétary. The musical became the province of New Wave directors after the 1950s. While Godard experimented with the genre in *Une femme est une femme* (1961), Jacques Demy ensured that the musical remained a visible genre during the 1960s, with his two signature films *Les Parapluies de Cherbourg* (1964) and *Les Demoiselles de Rochefort* (1967), at the same time as the early rock n roll films of Johnny Hallyday emulated Elvis Presley's film successes. There were very few musicals made during the 1970s and 1980s. There has been a resurgence since the mid-1990s, however. These include what one might call the auteur musical as well as more popular musical films. In Alain Resnais's *On connaît la chanson* (1997), inspired by Dennis Potter's 1978 TV series *Pennies from Heaven*, the actors lip-synch 36 snippets of pre-recorded French pop songs. His later *Pas sur la bouche* (2003) is a reworking of a 1925 stage operetta, in which the actors sing the songs themselves as musical numbers. In François Ozon's *8 femmes* (2002), eight actresses each sing a different song. While Resnais and Ozon share a fascination with songs popular some thirty to forty years before their film musicals, the songs in the musicals of Christophe Honoré and Olivier Ducastel/ Jacques Martineau were composed for their films. Alex Beaupain was the composer for Honoré's *Les Chansons d'amour* (2007), whose narrative is based on his 2006 record *Garçon d'honneur*, and for his later *Les Bien-Aimés* (2011). Jacques Martineau wrote the lyrics, and Philippe Miller the music in Ducastel and Martineau's *Jeanne et le garçon formidable* (1998) and *Crustacés et coquillages* (2005). The songs may be contemporary, but these films are in several ways (which I do not have the space to go into here) clear homages to those of Jacques Demy.

In the 2000s, there have been mainstream films that are close to musicals, focused on the music-hall (*Faubourg 36*; Christophe Barratier, 2008), or a singer, such as bio-pics on Claude François (*Cloclo*; Florent Emilio Siri, 2012) and Edith Piaf (*La Môme*; Olivier Dahan, 2007), and *Quand j'étais chanteur* (Xavier Giannoli, 2006). The last two won Césars, suggesting a resurgence of the musical genre. And at the time of writing biopics on the singers Yves Montand and Dalida are in production.

It will be clear from this brief overview of the genre that it has been and currently is a major film genre, but one that did not see many films during the 1970s and 1980s. With the exception of some films by Demy (*Une chambre en ville*, 1982; *Parking*, 1985; *Trois places pour le 26*, 1988), there were only two other notable films in these decades, both by women directors. One of them is Chantal Akerman's *Golden Eighties* (1986), and the other, twelve years earlier, is *L'Une chante, l'autre pas*. In what follows, reprising work by Rebecca DeRoo, I will show how the film subverts the conventions of the musical in its formal strategies, and how it subverts the notion of a fixed identity in its narrative strategies.

L'Une chante, l'autre pas as subversion

Four fundamental points can be made about the musical as a genre, at least as it was established during the 1940s and 1950s in both Hollywood and France. The first is that its purpose is to establish a utopian community. Second, in the case of musicals that use singers as protagonists, known as the 'backstage musical', the narrative usually moves towards the establishment of a major musical event, and that event brings closure. Third, the musical's function is to establish strong identities, especially if the narrative is about the rise of a singer from obscurity to fame. Finally, running in parallel with the previous three points, is the heterosexual boy-girl narrative, whereby there is a parallel established between the musical event and marriage or its equivalent. The success of the singer who establishes a star identity parallels the success of the couple, and their integration within a broader community.[10]

As DeRoo points out, *L'Une chante, l'autre pas* undermines the conventions of the genre using what she considers to be Brechtian strategies.[11] First and foremost, musicals are generally not 'political' in the militant sense. The longest song of the film is 'Amsterdam-sur-eau' [Amsterdam on the Water]. Pomme and the acquaint-ances she has made at the abortion clinic decide to take a sightseeing tour on the Amsterdam canals. Pomme sings the following song as the group floats down the canal. Its lyrics focus on abortion and read more like a poetic political tract:

FIG. 3.1. 'Amsterdam-sur-eau' (courtesy Artificial Eye).

Glissant sous les ponts d'Amsterdam,
Sur un bateau-mouche hollandais,
Nous les éclopées de la baise,
Nous les mamselles, nous les madames,
Les maladroites et les niaises,
Les distraites et les abusées,
On a fait ne vous en déplaise
La croisière des nanavortées.

C'est pas romantique le vaporetto
Après la clinique,
Amsterdam-sur-eau,
Tulipes et vélos, je m'en souviendrai.

En voyant passer les vélos,
On a parlé de la pilule,
De nos amours au fil de l'eau,
De nos enfants, de nos ovules.
On a ri, on a dégoisé,
Sans avoir peur du ridicule,
Sur un bateau trop pavoisé,
Baladant des nanavortées.

Quarante ans ou seize, c'est le même lot,
Le même malaise.
Amsterdam-sur-eau,
Tulipes et vélos, je m'en souviendrai.

[Sliding under the bridges of Amsterdam,
On a Dutch sightseeing boat,

Go the women crippled from fucking,
The damsels and madams,
The clumsy and silly madams,
The absent-minded and the abused,
We're taking if you please,
A cruise for abortionees.

A boat's not romantic
After the clinic,
Amsterdam on the Water,
I'll remember the tulips and the bikes.

Watching the bikes go by,
We talked about the pill
About our loves over the years,
Our kids and our ovules.
We laughed, chattered away,
Unafraid of ridicule,
On a boat decked with too many flags,
Carrying abortionees.

In your forties or your teens, it's all the same,
It's the same unease. Amsterdam on the Water,
I'll remember the tulips and the bikes.]

DeRoo explores this sequence in some detail, showing how the occasionally playful lyrics, encapsulated in the neologism 'nanavortées' (nanas + avortées [chicks + aborted), and the stereotype of the sightseeing tour are in tension with the situation (the women have just had an abortion) and the visuals (shots of surgical equipment in the clinic, and exhausted patients). Moreover, the women's melancholic immobility as Pomme sings in the boat is at odds with the generally more lively song and dance routine of the musical; one thinks here of Anna Karina dancing in *Une femme est une femme*, or the complex and colourful dance routines of *Les Demoiselles de Rochefort*, performances in both of these films being modeled on the Hollywood musical.

Second, as DeRoo also points out, musicals focus on the establishment of strong heterosexual couples rather than female friendships. In this film the focus is the personal development of each of the two women, and the strength of their friendship over the years, signaled by their postcard correspondence. Darius questions how this friendship can survive without face-to-face contact. Pomme retorts by affirming the strength of the ties between the two women: 'Suzanne, c'est comme l'amour, mais sans salades [...] Suzanne et moi ça va tout seul' [Suzanne, it's like love, but without the complications [...] Suzanne and me, it's really easy].

DeRoo lists other familiar Brechtian strategies, such as the use of props that undermine theatrical illusion in the song 'La Femme-bulle' [Bubble Woman]. There is a similar use of props in a parody of silent films, which in many ways echoes the short silent film of *Cléo de 5 à 7* (1962). DeRoo draws out the implications of these Brechtian strategies:

> Varda's reluctance to provide a single resolution to feminist issues mirrors her refusal to employ a single narrative thread or to resolve the story neatly with a happy, uncomplicated ending. Varda's film reminds us of the aesthetic

Fig. 3.2. 'La Femme-bulle' (courtesy Artificial Eye).

> and political significance of speaking in the plural, confronting and continually undermining expectations in order to deny the idea of a complete resolution.[12]

The film is open-ended, without any obvious resolution or closure in the manner of a standard narrative. Life goes on. Suzanne was a single mother at the beginning of the film, but she is settled with Pierre at the end. Pomme, who was married to Darius, has split up with him, and is herself now a single mother. The epilogue's voice-over, by Varda herself, explains how the children are growing up, but that the challenges of being a woman remain. There is a sense of continuity, but not of closure, still less of fixity. It is this sense of openness, of lack of closure, as explored by DeRoo, which will serve as the background point for my analysis of the music track in the film, and its intersection with specific cinematographic devices, such as the extended tracking shot.[13]

Objects and subjects

First, extending DeRoo's point about lack of resolution, I want to show how the songs as a group function to destabilize any notion of a fixed female identity. The first twenty minutes of the film dwell on Suzanne and her partner Jérôme, who is a photographer. We see row upon row of women and children in the black-and-white portraits pinned to his walls. Suzanne explains that he cannot sell enough of them to make ends meet. He comes across as a head-in-the-clouds, stereotypically tortured artist; indeed, Ruth Hottell draws attention to a portrait of Baudelaire in the couple's flat, suggesting that Varda is critiquing the nineteenth-century romantic hero.[14] Jérôme says in the first few minutes of the film that he is trying to capture

FIG. 3.3. Jérôme's objectifying photographs (courtesy Artificial Eye).

FIG. 3.4. The portrait of Baudelaire (courtesy Artificial Eye).

Fig. 3.5. Rock n roll and 'man's business' (courtesy Artificial Eye).

the truth of the women he photographs. Pomme, however, comments robustly that all of the women in the photos are sad and presented as victims. He also tries to 'capture' Pomme, stripping her naked in both the literal and the figurative sense; but he is unsuccessful, complaining that he cannot get through to her 'truth'.

Jérôme literally frames the women, rendering them immobile, like an entomologist might frame butterflies, their differences and individualities rendered the same through framing, the black and white colour, and the poses he has asked his subjects to adopt. We could almost say that he 'monotonizes' his subjects. The film's project, then, is to construct a female-centred identity rather than one imposed by a man, as Smith explains: '[Jérôme] is not unmasking reality, but replacing one image (the pose, created by the woman) with another, which he has created. [...] The episode functions as a prologue for the gradual construction of a female-centred identity'.[15]

The contrast between masculine and feminine ways of representing the world is established early on in the film with music. Pomme, keen to pursue a career as a singer, is hired as part of the backing vocals for a recording session. We see the bare-chested lead singer wearing dark glasses and chewing gum, imbued with his self-image as a rock n roll star. The lyrics to the song are ironic; we hear 'c'est le rock n roll, c'est une affaire d'hommes' [it's rock n roll, it's a man's business] repeated twice. The song goes on to describe a self-contained boys-own world where fun is, as the lyrics put it, for boys to chew gum while clapping their hands.

What both Jérôme and the singer have in common is an attachment to a fixed image: that of his subjects whom Jérôme tries to fix as objects, and that of his fixed self-image for the rocker. The film will develop antitheses to these fixed objects. Jérôme's photos are echoed and counteracted in the film by the many colourful

FIG. 3.6. The postcards exchanged between the two women (courtesy Artificial Eye).

FIG. 3.7. Orchidée's performance locations (courtesy Artificial Eye).

Sections of film	*Time*	*Type of music/Titles of songs*
Titles and Prologue: 'une affaire d'homme' [men's business]	0	Quartet
	4	Choir
	20	Quartet
	22	Rock n roll
	26	Quartet
Touring with women	30	'Mon corps est à moi'
	31	'Je vous salue les Maries'
	36	'Ni cocotte'
	40	'Amsterdam-sur-eau'
	49	'Sera-ce un garçon?'
Iran: 'une affaire d'homme' [men's business]	58	Persian music
	1.02	Quartet
	1.04	Persian music
	1.06	Quartet
	1.08	Persian music
	1.14	Quartet (Pomme and Suzanne together again)
Touring with women and men	1.27	'Ni cocotte'
	1.32	Guitar/flute (François/Zorro picked up)
	1.33	'Quand on est presque mère'
	1.38	'Les mœurs domestiques' (instrumental)
	1.40	'Papa Engels'
	1.43	'Mon corps est à moi'
Touring with women	1.45	Flute (François leaves)
	1.45	Quartet and women's voices
	1.46	'La femme bulle'
Epilogue	1.51	'Bubble bubble gum rock'
	1.51	(instrumental)
	1.52	Quartet and women's voices
		Guitar (François returned)
Credits	1.54	'Quand on est presque mère'

Table 3.1. Music in the film and when it occurs (figures are minutes)

postcards that the two women exchange during their decade-long separation. This is very different from Jérôme's attempt to capture the so-called truth of his subjects, which only succeeds in turning them into objects. The function of the postcards is to locate a variety of moments in space and time, abolishing both in the act of communication, the postcards' splashes of colour contrasting vividly with Jérôme's black and white photos.[16]

In the case of the music, the rock n roll is superseded in the remainder of the film by a very different kind of music: folk. This is posited as the exact opposite of the rock n roll in a number of fairly obvious ways: the location of the songs constantly changes as the group tours, unlike the claustrophobic and cluttered recording studio; the group, indeed, is more often outside than inside, in farmyards and village squares, on small make-shift stages, with tiny audiences. And the focus of the songs is not the bubble-gum, shades and bare-chested posturing of the rock n rollers; it is the world of women and their search for identity in movement, indeed, identity in a movement.

The tension between subjects and objects in Varda's work is fundamental. In a previous article, I explored the way in which her approach to the object is connected to that of the surrealists: 'Her cinema is a cinema that crosses the boundaries between the object and the subject to create the space of the imaginary. Objects, like *le hazard objectif* [objective chance] of the surrealists, reveal traces of hidden subjectivities';[17] and I suggested that 'what matters is not where you are, nor where you are going, but movement, transformation, becoming, of the object and of the subject'.[18] As Varda's voice-over says of Pomme, who realizes that staying in Iran with her husband Darius will fix her identity as a stay-at-home wife, 'le danger c'était de s'arrêter' [the danger lay in stopping].

The commitment to movement and transformation has to negotiate a precarious equilibrium between rootedness, which threatens to become the seizure of immobility, and movement, which generates continuity. Too much of one or the other, and the balance becomes impossible. Too much of the subject in movement means that identity slips away; too much of the object, and identity becomes frozen and inauthentic. The trick is to keep both in play; as Macha Makeïeff says in *Les Glaneurs et la glaneuse: deux ans après* (2002): 'Les objets nous contiennent' [objects contain us].

We see that commitment and its tensions at key moments in Varda's films. At its simplest, it is the frequent contrast between human flesh and inanimate material: for example, the sculpture class in *Cléo de 5 à 7*; the naked man in a Paris street in *Les Dites caryatides* (1984), contrasting with the caryatids, as Isabelle McNeill points out in her chapter in this book; the wooden statue of the Buddha contrasted with live bodies in *Les Plages d'Agnès* (2008). It can also be a contrast between still and moving images, such as the installation in the Sète triptych, with videos playing on either side of a photograph.

The commitment to movement is also conveyed by camera movement. For example, the sculpture class in *Cléo de 5 à 7* does not simply contrast flesh and inanimate matter; it also contrasts the static nature of the sculptures and Cléo's fluid movement through the sculptures with tracking shots. Similarly, in *Sans toit ni loi* (1985) the extended tracking shots of Mona walking emphasize the restless search for identity, but identity in movement. Mona walks, those she meets subsequently try to pin her down as they stand still in front of the camera; but Mona carries on walking, errant and erratic, in more senses than one. More broadly, to return to *Cléo de 5 à 7*, the whole film is about movement across Paris in what could be conceived as a long travelling shot, just as in *L'Une chante, l'autre pas* Pomme travels around the country with the musicians.

In *Cléo de 5 à 7* and *Sans toit ni loi*, the identity of the women is never fixed, nor is there any obvious closure. We find out almost incidentally that Cléo has cancer, and the end of the film suggests a new beginning rather than the closure of death. While Mona dies, the point of the film is to demonstrate how she cannot be given a fixed identity; she is transient, unattainable. Similarly, in *L'Une chante, l'autre pas* Jérôme complains that Pomme resists him, when he photographs her: 'Vous vous défendez' [You are holding back], he says, to which she retorts: 'C'est seulement que je ne veux pas avoir l'air accablé que vous aimez' [it's just that I don't want to have the stricken look you like so much]. Pomme underlines this unattainability later in the same scene. He says that he wants to capture her in her naked truth, which she cheekily interprets literally, offering to pose nude. But this is no better for Jérôme, who still complains that she escapes him. Pomme comments on this unattainability, saying: 'Je sais pas quoi penser de moi. C'est comme si je n'étais pas une vraie fille' [I don't know what to think of myself. It's as though I wasn't a real girl]. It is a curious statement, in that it could be taken to mean that her unattainability for him means that she is not real for herself, in other words that only the gaze of a man can turn her into a subject, although clearly she would in that case be an objectified subject. But it is an ambiguous statement, as it could also indicate her inability, indeed her resistance to being objectified, as is suggested by the fact that at one point she places her hands over her face. The resistance to her 'naked truth' being captured is emphasized in a later scene during which we again see Pomme without clothes, the costume song 'Sera-ce un garçon?' [Is It a Boy?] which is about being an expectant mother. We see Pomme looking very pregnant, with her breasts bare and wearing an extravagant hat, looking enormously tall as she is perched on a colleague's shoulders, he being hidden beneath her long white dress. Pomme stops the rehearsal to complain that her vision of the song, which she has written, has been altered by having a second dancer looking pregnant. The man on whose shoulders she has been perched says 'nous on existe sans parler' [we exist without speaking], to which she retorts, recalling the scene with Jérôme: 'Moi, j'existe comme je peux' [I exist as best as I can]. Quite apart from the irony of the man hidden underneath her dress

FIG. 3.8. 'Sera-ce un garçon ?' (courtesy Artificial Eye).

saying that he does not speak, and thus underlining the role of the quiet male in the film, the scene emphasizes Pomme's agency: not only is she the author of the song, but her retort returns us to the struggle for female agency more generally.

And yet, despite the resistance to objectification, it could be argued that the end of the film seems to suggest domestic closure and immobility rather than the more open endings of *Cléo de 5 à 7* and *Sans toit ni loi*. I want to argue that the film's music works against closure, undermining binaries. It works with camera movement in the final sequence's long travelling shot to maintain community, while also maintaining the possibility of perpetual movement.

Music and movement

Music is key in its relationship with the movement of travelling in Varda's films, whether by the characters or the camera, or the combination of both, reminding us of her statement that cinema is music (see Hannah Mowat's chapter in this book). In *Cléo de 5 à 7*, a song separates the two halves of the film into inauthentic image and authentic image, as Cléo leaves her apartment and travels around various locations, often with extended tracking shots, as she walks or drives around Paris. And as Smith points out, 'Pomme is [...] a complement of Cléo in that both must address [...] the question [...] of how a woman whose vocation is to be looked at affects the situation of all women.'[19] I mentioned two types of music above, the men's' rock n roll and the women's folk. But there are in fact three other significant types of music, all of which play an important part in the film's musical structure, and its effects (see Table 3.1). They complicate what might otherwise have been seen as a simplistic binary between male and female music, between reification and self-realization, between object and subject; indeed, as Mowat suggests in her chapter in this book, 'music is not merely an accompaniment for Varda; it is what helps to stitch the visual constituents together during the viewing process'.

The first of these is string quartet music, which accompanies the opening credits and is linked to Jérôme and Suzanne. The second is Persian music, linked to Pomme and her Iranian husband Darius. And the final type is the flute and guitar music associated with the itinerant musician François (played by François Wertheimer, the composer of the quartet music, as well as three of the songs). As I hope to show, these different types of music form a complex and shifting matrix, whose function is to effect change.

The most complex of the different types of music is the string quartet, because its connotations shift during the course of the film, from the deeply negative to the considerably more positive. At the beginning of the film the quartet is most obviously linked to Jérôme and his melancholy; we hear it in the cemetery during his funeral. It returns alongside the Persian music in a long section without any songs. In this section of the film, the quartet signals Suzanne's solitude, the Persian music signaling Pomme's distant location. Shortly afterwards the quartet accompanies their happy reunion; although the music has shifted away from its previous negative connotations of solitude, its association with Jérôme is still in the background as Pomme recalls the events after his suicide with Suzanne. Nonetheless, the women's friendship has begun to shift the melancholic connotations of the quartet and its association with masculine solipsism and female loneliness. This shift away from the melancholic is completed by the end of the film when we hear it again. This time, however, it is accompanied by women's voices, suggesting strongly that the shift away from male melancholia towards a community of women has been realized.

The other music associated with a man is the quiet guitar and flute music of the itinerant father and son musicians who join the group. They join the group for a while, and we hear the flute accompanying the women. The father and son move on, but return in the epilogue to figure in an extended community.

The music therefore functions as a triangulated process in the film. Between the two poles of male individualistic and inauthentic rock n roll on the one hand and female folk collectivity on the other, we find a mobile set of music that enables the movement from the one to the other. The string quartet is mobile by virtue of its changing connotations, taking us from male melancholia, loneliness and death to a female-focused utopian community where men are presented as impermanent. The quiet folk music of the father and son musicians is mobile in a different way, in that we associate it with a nomadic lifestyle; it therefore functions as a signifier of the impermanence of men, their evacuation allowing for the construction of female community. Men disappear, as Pomme leaves Darius, and the father and son musicians move on, and this is emphasized by Varda's voice-over during the epilogue, transcribed below *in extenso*. It is accompanied throughout by François the guitarist (François II in the voice over of the epilogue), who hums quietly while playing his guitar.[20] The second half of the epilogue consists of one long panning shot which occasionally pauses, as detailed below, and which lasts 2 minutes 13 seconds. The camera movement is significant, and I shall comment on it below:

> Deux ans plus tard, c'était l'été, et pour la première fois Suzanne et Pomme se retrouvaient sans drame, sans naissance, sans panique. Pour une fois c'était les vacances avec des amis dans une grande maison louée. On riait, on mangeait, on se baladait, on faisait de la musique. Et puis on regardait les photos anciennes; on les avait emmenées exprès. On comparait les images, on parlait, on discutait. Pomme était très fière de sa petite Suzanne qui avait plein de tantes et quelques oncles à défaut de père. C'était ça la vraie famille. Et elle rêvait au jour où Darius viendrait aussi ici en vacances avec le petit Parviz Guillaume et sans doute une nouvelle épouse et un autre enfant. Elle était toujours aussi optimiste, Pomme. Marie avait changé. Elle avait à présent 17 ans et un amoureux, Théodore, qu'elle présentait comme Théothime, mon copain intime. [*beginning of left pan*] Joëlle et Micou n'avaient pas changé. François 1er, retrouvé depuis Bobigny, vivait maintenant avec Doudou. Il accompagnait les tournées de temps en temps. Zorro, le fils de François II, normalisé et tondu par l'école, vivait toujours avec son père fils-père. Ils ne se quittaient pas aux vacances scolaires. Marie, elle, elle était rentrée en terminale, et elle voulait toujours faire du chinois. Elle avait aussi un peu envie de devenir photographe, comme son père. Pomme se sentait bien. Elle aimait la douceur des crépuscules d'été au bord du lac. Mathieu avait changé. Il était parfois sauvage ou alors très confiant avec Pierre, qui était décidemment l'homme qui convenait à Suzanne, femme patiente et passionnée. [*pan stops*] Pierre lui confirmait qu'elle avait bien mené sa vie. Tout allait bien pour elle, pour eux. Et puis elle aimait voir et savoir que Pomme devenait enfin contente et cohérente [*start of right pan as Suzanne leans towards Pomme*] après avoir tant bagarré contre les autres et contre

> elle-même. Leur amitié allait très bien. [*pan stops on Pomme and Suzanne*] C'est sûr, elles étaient très différentes; l'une chantait, l'autre pas. Mais elles étaient aussi pareilles. Elles avaient lutté pour conquérir le bonheur d'être femme. [*pan right continues*] Peut-être leur lutte optimiste pouvait servir à d'autres, à Marie par exemple qui devenait une femme. Personne ne pensait que ce serait plus facile pour elle. Mais ce serait peut-être plus simple, plus clair. [*pan stops; shot lasts another 15s focused on Marie before the start of the credits sequence*]
>
> [Two years later it was the summer, and the first time Suzanne and Pomme were together again without a drama, without a birth, without panic. For once it was the holidays with friends in a big house they had rented. There was laughter, food, walks, music-making. And they looked at old photos which they had brought on purpose. They compared the pictures, they talked, they discussed. Pomme was proud of her little Suzanne who has loads of aunts and a few uncles instead of fathers. This was true family. And she dreamt of the day when Darius would come on vacation here as well with little Parviz Guillaume and no doubt a new wife and another child. She was ever the optimist, Pomme. Marie had changed. She was seventeen and had a lover, Théodore, whom she introduced as Théothime, my special boyfriend. [*beginning of left pan*] Joëlle et Micou hadn't changed. François the First, found again since Bobigny, now lived with Doudou. He went on tour with them occasionally. Zorro, François the Second's son, normalized and hair shorn by school, was still living with his unmarried father. They were inseparable during the school holidays. Marie had started sixth-form and wanted to study Chinese. She also wanted a bit to be a photographer, like her father. Pomme felt good. She liked the softness of the summer twilight by the lake. Mathieu had changed. He was sometimes wild or very trusting with Pierre, who was just the man for Suzanne, who was a patient and passionate woman. [*pan stops*] Pierre confirmed that she had led a good life. Everything was going well for her, for them. And then she was happy to see and to know that Pomme was at last happy too and consistent [*start of right pan as Suzanne leans towards Pomme*] after her long struggles with others and with herself. They had a good friendship. [*pan stops on Pomme and Suzanne*] True, they were very different; one sang, the other didn't. But they were also the same. They had fought for the happiness of being a woman. [*pan right continues*] Perhaps their optimistic fight could help others, Marie for example who was becoming a woman. Nobody thought it would be easy for her. But it would perhaps be simpler, clearer. [*pan stops; shot lasts another 15s focused on Marie before the start of the credits sequence*]]

There are several points to be made about this final sequence. First, it constructs a careful balance between nomadism and domesticity: the families have come together in a holiday location, so there is not the kind of domestic fixity one might expect.

Second, men are in a variety of ways on the fringes of the female-centred group: fathers are absent (Darius is in Iran, Suzanne has uncles rather than a father); new arrivals are literally diminutive ('Théodore, qu'elle présentait comme Théothime' [Théothime, my special boyfriend]);[21] young boys have changed ('Zorro [...] normalisé et tondu par l'école' [Zorro [...] normalized and hair shorn by school]; 'Mathieu avait changé' [Mathieu had changed]); two of the three other men have the same generic name and could literally just be any Frenchmen, distinguished only by a royal number (François 1er, François II). And as I suggested above, the

FIG. 3.9. The humming guitarist played by François Wertheimer (courtesy Artificial Eye).

humming guitarist played by Wertheimer suggests withdrawal and discretion, the etymology for the latter word indicating separation. The only exception is the almost ironically named Pierre, Suzanne's rock, who nonetheless exists only in relation to Suzanne ('Pierre lui confirmait qu'elle avait bien mené sa vie' [Pierre confirmed that she had led a good life]).

Third, in this reconfigured familial group comprising interlocking family ties and friendships, which Varda considers to be 'la vraie famille' [true family], it is the women who count: Suzanne and Pomme of course, and importantly Marie, who is Suzanne's daughter in the fiction, and Varda's real daughter. The pan starts on two members of Orchidée, stops on Suzanne and Pierre (although as I have already pointed out, Pierre is positioned relative to Suzanne), starts again as Suzanne leans towards Pomme, pauses on the two of them as Varda uses the title of the film to describe their roles, and starts again as the voice over talks about the legacy of the women's movement and what it may have brought to Marie, on whom the camera stops for a full fifteen seconds. In other words, it is women and their world that mobilize the camera in its ostentatious pan, and it is women who are the clear focus of the group. 'La vraie famille' [true family] is not just loose, but essentially matriarchal. The pan manages to retain a productive balance between the notion of a community and its continuity, at the same time as indicating that the community will never stay still, that its members will evolve, and that there is a transmission from one generation of women to another. The music in the sequence also contributes to the sense of equilibrium.

The pan is accompanied by François's guitar music, which is a synthesis of music by the lone male and the quiet folk of Orchidée. The film's score posits differences between male and female associated music, as indicated above; but by the end of

FIG. 3.10. Marie, Varda's real daughter (courtesy Artificial Eye).

the film, through the careful use of a variety of musical types, it incorporates the male-connoted music, at the same time as Pomme and Suzanne create an ideal extended community.

When Varda said in an interview for the *Cahiers du cinéma* that she had 'tout fait passer dans les chansons' [put everything into the songs] she was referring primarily to the political message.[22] As she explained, 'un discours on ne l'écoute pas' [no-one listens to speeches]. I hope to have shown that the music more generally 'fait tout passer' [makes everything pass], including false images and posturing self-images, to produce a sense of continually redefined and itinerant female identities. As Varda comments, 'music seems to be the only way to convey what isn't evident and/or feelings that lie beyond the characters' decisions: a momentary sense of grace, an internal difficulty, the feeling of being inexplicably stuck, little failures, unexpectedly sweet times'.[23]

Bibliography

ALTMAN, RICK, *The American Film Musical* (London: British Film Institute, 1989)
AUDÉ, FRANÇOISE, *Ciné-modèles, cinémas d'elles* (Lausanne: L'Age d'Homme, 1981)
DEROO, REBECCA, 'Confronting Contradictions: Genre, Subversion and Feminist Politics in Agnès Varda's *L'Une chantre, l'autre pas*', *Modern & Contemporary France*, 17:3 (2009), 249–65
FEUER, JANE, *The Hollywood Musical* (Bloomington: Indiana University Press, 1982)
HOTTELL, RUTH, 'The Role of Female Spectators in Agnès Varda's *Le Bonheur* and *L'Une chantre, l'autre pas*', *Cinema Journal*, 38:2 (1999), 52–71
OUKRATE, FRANÇOISE, '*L'Une chante, l'autre pas*', *Ecran*, 57 (1977), 65–66

POWRIE, PHIL, 'Heterotopic Spaces and Nomadic Gazes in Varda: From *Cléo de 5 à 7* to *Les Glaneurs et La Glaneuse*', *L'Esprit créateur*, sp. no. 'Watch This Space: Women's Conceptualisations of Space in Contemporary French Film and Visual Art', 51:1 (2011), 68–82

SMITH, ALISON, *Agnès Varda* (Manchester: Manchester University Press, 1998)

VARDA, AGNÈS, *Varda par Agnès* (Paris: Cahiers du cinéma, 1994)

VARDA, AGNÈS, *Agnès Varda: Interviews*, ed. and translated by T. Jefferson Kline (Jackson: University of Mississippi Press, 2014)

Filmography

Bien-Aimés, Les (Christophe Honoré, 2011)
Chansons d'amour, Les (Christophe Honoré, 2007)
Cléo de 5 à 7 (Agnès Varda, 1962)
Cloclo (Florent Emilio Siri, 2012)
Crustacés et coquillages (Olivier Ducastel/Jacques Martineau, 2005).
Demoiselles de Rochefort, Les (Jacques Demy, 1967)
Dites caryatides, Les (Agnès Varda, 1984)
Faubourg 36 (Christophe Barratier, 2008)
Glaneurs et la glaneuse: deux ans après, Les (Agnès Varda, 2002)
Golden Eighties (Chantal Akerman, 1986)
Jeanne et le garçon formidable (Olivier Ducastel/Jacques Martineau, 1998)
Môme, La (Olivier Dahan, 2007)
Parapluies de Cherbourg, Les (Jacques Demy, 1964)
Parking (Jacques Demy, 1985)
Plages d'Agnès, Les (Agnès Varda, 2008)
Quand j'étais chanteur (Xavier Giannoli, 2006)
Sans toit ni loi (Agnès Varda, 1985)
Sous les toits de Paris (René Clair, 1930)
Trois places pour le 26 (Jacques Demy, 1988)
Une chambre en ville (Jacques Demy, 1982)
Une chante, l'autre pas, L' (Agnès Varda, 1976)
Une femme est une femme (Jean-Luc Godard, 1961)

Notes to Chapter 3

1. 'Agnès Varda Talks about the Cinema', in *Agnès Varda: Interviews*, ed. and trans. by T. Jefferson Kline (Jackson: University of Mississippi Press, 2014), pp. 64–77 (p. 77).
2. Agnès Varda, *Varda par Agnès* (Paris: Cahiers du cinéma, 1994), 110–11. All translations are mine.
3. Françoise Audé, *Ciné-modèles, cinémas d'elles* (Lausanne: L'Age d'Homme, 1981), 145.
4. Françoise Oukrate, '*L'Une chante, l'autre pas*', *Écran*, 57 (1977), 65–66 (p. 65).
5. Varda, *Varda par Agnès*, 256.
6. *Ibid.*, 110.
7. *Ibid.*, 111.
8. *Ibid.*, 110.
9. Alison Smith, *Agnès Varda* (Manchester: Manchester University Press, 1998), 109; Smith's emphasis.
10. See Jane Feuer, *The Hollywood Musical* (Bloomington: Indiana University Press, 1982) and Rick Altman, *The American Film Musical* (London: British Film Institute, 1989) for the standard views of the Hollywood musical.
11. Rebecca DeRoo, 'Confronting Contradictions: Genre, Subversion and Feminist Politics in

Agnès Varda's *L'Une chantre, l'autre pas*', *Modern & Contemporary France*, 17:3 (2009), 249–65.

12. *Ibid.*, 259.
13. See Phil Powrie, 'Heterotopic Spaces and Nomadic Gazes in Varda: From *Cléo de 5 à 7* to *Les Glaneurs et La Glaneuse*', *L'Esprit créateur*, sp. no. 'Watch This Space: Women's Conceptualisations of Space in Contemporary French Film and Visual Art', 51:1 (2011), 68–82 for a previous exploration of the tracking shot in Varda's films.
14. Ruth Hottell, 'The Role of Female Spectators in Agnès Varda's *Le Bonheur* and *L'Une chantre, l'autre pas*', *Cinema Journal*, 38:2 (1999), 52–71 (p. 61).
15. Smith, *Agnès Varda*, 110.
16. Such colour contrasts are not unusual in Varda's work as for example in the contrast between the opening credit sequence of *Cléo de 5 à 7* and the remainder of the film; see Francesca Hardy's comments on this sequence in this book.
17. Powrie, 'Heterotopic Spaces', 68.
18. *Ibid.*
19. Smith, *Agnès Varda*, 109.
20. François Wertheimer, who plays François II, has collaborated with Varda on a number of films. McNeill points out in her chapter in this book that in his music for *Les Dites Cariatides* he works to undermine gender stereotypes. The figure he plays in *L'Une chante, l'autre pas* similarly deconstructs the powerful male, as we shall see; in both films his singing becomes humming, signaling a kind of withdrawal of the male voice.
21. The suffix '-thime' can be construed as a diminutive.
22. '*L'Une Chante, l'Autre Pas*: Inteview [sic] with *Agnès Varda*', in *Agnès Varda: Interviews*, pp. 78–88 (p. 84).
23. *Ibid.*, 85.

CHAPTER 4

Lara Croft dans un champ de patates: A Ludomusicological Approach to Agnès Varda

Hannah Mowat

The prospect of placing Agnès Varda in an academic context is a daunting one. Her response to aspiring theoreticians is robust and unambivalent. She has long complained of '[c]ette réputation d'intellectuelle qu'on me colle sur le dos... c'est lourd... et faux' [this reputation for being an intellectual that people make me shoulder... it weighs me down... and it's phoney] (Narboni, Toubiana and Villain 1977: 21) and, more worryingly for this author, announces that '[j]e souffre un peu de voir que mes films sont pris comme des sujets à thèse' [I suffer a little from seeing my films used as subjects for theses] (Bibi 2012: para. 5 of 6)...[1] Her moving images, she insists, are designed to be *fun*. Her filmmaking process '[c]'est un jeu, c'est une *jam*, c'est un tissage, une partie de ping-pong' [is a game, a jam session, a woven design, a round of ping pong] (Varda 1994: 16). But why should fun be antithetical to the academic enterprise? This chapter seeks to bring together the two through the emerging discipline of ludomusicology: a field in which soundscape is inseparable from the act of gameplay.[2] I take my lead from Roger Moseley's ample and indispensable definition of the term:

> In my view, ludomusicology involves the study of both the musically playful and the playfully musical. Bringing music and play into contact in this way offers access to the undocumented means by which composers, designers, programmers, performers, players, and audiences interact with music, games, and one another. It promises to account for competitive behavior, the acceptance and evasion of protocols and constraints, the pleasures of rhythmic bodies in motion, and the dizzy delight taken in exhibitions of virtuosity. Ludomusicology is thus more concerned with performativity [...] than it is with the text-based preoccupations of representation, meaning, and interpretation. In other words ludomusicology recognizes that music and digital games are not merely to be read, seen, or heard, but played. Music, from this perspective, constitutes a set of cognitive, technological, and social affordances for behaving in certain ways, for playing in and with the world through the medium of sound and its representations. For their part, digital games offer rules — which is to say possibilities bound by constraints — for entering into relationships with the world that are simultaneously material and imaginary, real and virtual. (Moseley 2013: 283)

Performativity and playfulness within spheres real and virtual seem delightfully promising starting points for a discussion of Varda's work. Perhaps rather more unexpectedly, so, too, does video gaming. The title of this chapter is taken from an interview with Varda's son, Mathieu Demy (INA 2001). Asked what fictional heroine she would choose to be, he unhesitatingly dubs her 'Lara Croft in a potato field'. But what on earth do a leather-clad gaming icon and a lilac-clad 87-year-old have in common? Rather more than one might imagine, it transpires. Given that Varda's filmic endeavour is, and has always been, 'de donner une coloration ludique aux choses les plus sérieuses' [to give the most serious of things a ludic hue] (de Bruyn 2012: para. 8 of 19), in view of her stated belief that 'le cinéma c'est de la musique' [cinema is music] (cited in Decock 1996: 162), and, as I shall demonstrate in the following, taking into account her ongoing fascination with virtual gameplay, it is my intention to marry these aspects of her work under the auspices of ludomusicology, in order to examine how Varda's on-screen minds and bodies respond to the playful machinations and choreographic potential of their accompanying soundtracks.

While acknowledging Varda's considerable portfolio of photographs and installation pieces, my focus will be on her filmmaking. I shall look, in reverse chronological order, at three of her moving-image works that combine the ludic with the sonic to address 'the musically playful and the playfully musical' (Moseley 2013: 283): a section from the first episode of Varda's 2011 television series, *Agnès de ci de là Varda*; her 1987 feature, *Kung-fu Master*; and her 1966 sci-fi outing, *Les Créatures*. Specifically, I shall examine how they make use of gameplay soundscapes to support and extend their respective narratives, whereby music offers a way of 'playing in and with the world' (*ibid.*). To clarify, I am applying the term 'gameplay soundscapes' quite literally to instances in which Varda's protagonists participate in a screen-based computer game with accompanying soundtrack. In each case, I shall consider the impact of these gameplay soundscapes on the bodies on screen to argue that they permit the latter to move in a virtual, and sonic, domain parallel to that of the everyday, and in so doing exceed those bodies' real physical and psychological confines to enter into rule-based (or rule-breaking) 'relationships with the world that are simultaneously material and imaginary, real and virtual' (*ibid.*). Choreographed gameplay, I argue, does not restrict Varda's bodies; it extends both their limits and their outreach — sometimes even beyond the human.

Varda/Lara: Agnès as Avatar

Varda relishes a good game. Her weakness for wordplay is well-known: the DVD extras christened 'boni' — '[c']est plus latin et surtout plus joli!' [it's closer to Latin and bonnier to boot!] — and the discs themselves that she refers to as 'galettes' [biscuits/pancakes] because she finds the word 'plus réjouissant' [more gratifying] (de Bruyn 2012: para. 6 of 19). When she takes a lead part in the on-screen fun and games, meanwhile, it is often as avatar and in disguise. This is identity as roleplay. Citing *Les Plages d'Agnès* (2008) in interview, Varda underscores the self-conscious artificiality of her on-screen persona, while also revelling in the authenticity of the humour that runs through the film: '"Je joue une petite vieille, rondouillarde et bavarde, qui raconte sa vie." Ça fait rire, et en plus c'est vrai' ['I'm playing a little old lady, plump and chatty, who's telling her life story.' It makes people laugh, and what's more, it's true] (Domenach and Rouyer 2008: 18). Recently, too, she has allowed herself to be depicted as a cartoon figure, the work of Christophe Vallaux.[3] Her eminently self-deprecating sense of fun has been amply documented. As Martin Knelman notes, 'what other 80-year-old woman would film herself wearing a potato costume?' (2008: para. 6 of 14) as Varda did to greet visitors to her *Patatutopia* installation at the 2003 Venice Biennale.

Demy's description of his mother as an earthier incarnation of the tomb-raiding, quasi-superhuman video-game heroine, Lara Croft, is thus no random analogy. It neatly captures both Varda's (spud-centric) attention to the real[4] — the rhizomatic and rooted — and her broader fascination with virtual fun and games.

Editing and *Cinécriture*: Piecing Puzzles...

Varda's more general love of the ludic is intrinsic to her filmmaking, and emerges in her frequent equation of jigsaw puzzles with the editing process. In her (written) autobiographical work, *Varda par Agnès*, she compares the construction of filmic narratives to the piecing together of a puzzle, both of which require her to 'reconstituer une image faite de fragments qui s'emboîtent' [reconstitute an image made up of fragments that slot together] (Varda 1994: 159). For all her affable self-mockery, there is a more sober side to her gameplay: there are *rules* to be acknowledged, 'la règle du jeu', as she tells Jane Birkin in *Jane B. par Agnès V.* (1987), doubtless intentionally evoking Jean Renoir's 1939 film of the same name and its caustic critique of societal norms. And these rules, it seems, are sometimes there to be broken. Hence, while Varda admits to being an avid jigsaw fan, she notes, too, that she has, over the years, become less concerned with completing the picture than with the ongoing process of puzzling itself. In dialogue with Birkin in *Jane B. par Agnès V.*, she compares this process to that of film editing. 'C'est comme quand on fait un puzzle', she says. 'On pose des petits morceaux par-ci, par-là, et puis ça se dessine doucement et il y a encore un trou au milieu, un vide...' [It's like doing a puzzle. You lay down a few pieces here and there, and then the picture slowly starts to form and there's still a hole in the middle, a void...] (cited in Brioude 2006: 101).

An aesthetics of incompletion that is simultaneously an ethics of inclusion starts to take shape. Ludic to the last, her 2006 installation, *L'Île et Elle*, at the Fondation Cartier, was organized around the same principle of montage and play. 'Mon bric-à-brac personnel, j'ai réussi à le représenter comme un puzzle à reconstituer' [I've managed to represent my personal bric-à-brac as a jigsaw to be pieced together again], she concluded, proudly (Nave 2009: 23). Puzzles, in their enduring incompleteness, become infinitely reconfigurable — and personalizable. Visitors to the exhibition were to find themselves invited to interact with its constituent elements in order to construct a version of Varda's life story that would inevitably also contain some of their own. Even her most recent exhibition, *Triptyques atypiques* (8 February-5 April,

FIG. 4.1: *Cinq bacheliers*: calculated voids[5]

2014), ongoing at the Galerie Nathalie Obadia in Paris as this chapter was being written, included a brand-new, asymmetrical piece, *Cinq bacheliers* (2013), that is also literally a (167-piece) jigsaw (Fig. 4.1).

Three pieces have yet to be placed, leaving as many voids for the onlooker to fill with personal projections. The mathematical discrepancy between the title and image, meanwhile, offers a further conundrum as we struggle to equate the figure five with the eight figures before us. Even as we juggle permutations and seek out body doubles, Varda's lopsided triptych teases us with the simultaneous prospect and impossibility of rule-based, arithmetic resolution: 167, like the three of the triptych and the five of the title, is a prime number and as such, indivisible.

... Finding Rhythms

While Varda's fondness for games is oft-cited,[6] her attention to her soundscapes is not. Yet music is not merely an accompaniment for Varda; it is what helps to stitch the visual constituents together during the viewing process. She never intends for music to remain unnoticed, choosing to use it 'que là où on peut l'entendre' [only where it will be heard] (Varda 1994: 208). Speaking of the score commissioned for *Sans toit ni loi* (1985), she insists that she was seeking 'de la musique pour un film, pas de la musique de film' [music for a film, not film music] (*ibid.*: 209). Ultimately, music is yet another jigsaw to be rearranged, and Varda enthusiastically recycles refrains from one film in another, transposing, for example, elements of Pierre Barbaud's score for *Les Créatures* (of which more in due course) to her 1984 short, *7 p., cuis., s. de b., ... à saisir.* As she tells Emmanuel Levy, the same pieces can be revitalized in new contexts, so that 'excerpts of music separated from the scenes they originally accompanied take on another meaning. It is another [f]acet of the puzzle' (Levy n.d.: para. 24 of 34). The musicologist, Claudia Gorbman, has lamented the relative lack of critical scrutiny that these soundtracks have received to date, arguing that music is 'a structuring element in Varda's filmmaking', central to Varda's proprietary concept of *cinécriture* [cine-writing] (2008: 27). She appeals to researchers to pay it the attention it is due. I wish to respond to this call and enfold the musical into the broader discussions of Varda's work.

Let me first situate music more clearly in relation to Varda's vocabulary. *Cinécriture* is a highly inclusive term, encompassing as it does each and every facet of film 'style' (Varda 1994: 14): all of the phases, techniques, resources and materials required to form a film, from premise to post-production. And within this holistic, artisanal filmmaking process — Varda's cottage-industry of creation — music plays a vital role, as Gorbman has pointed out (2008: 27) and Varda confirmed (Knegt 2001: para. 26 of 32). Varda is a '*mélomane*, a music lover', Gorbman notes (2008: 27) — but I am reminded, too, of the broader definition of the term that the young soldier, Antoine (Antoine Bourseiller), brings to *Cléo de 5 à 7* (1962) when he describes the eponymous Cléo (Corinne Marchand) as 'mélomane. Pas celle qui aime la musique; celle qui aime le mélo' [a melomaniac. Not the kind who loves music; the kind who loves melodrama]. Wordplay links music to (sensationally self-conscious, deliberately performative) narrative — but arguably also, by association, to 'méli-mélo': a multiform mix of disparate things that echoes Varda's associative approach to montage.

Varda, then, is a *méli-mélomane*, and music, like her constituent jigsaw-images and narratives, forms a crucial part of an eclectic and highly subjective editing process. However, it is a process that nonetheless serves to bring a certain order to the aleatory. Hence, it is above all *rhythm* that Varda seeks (Marvier 2000: 47); a (once again, mathematically based) means of pacing her images from within. As she puts it, '[l]a musique intérieure quand on filme, c'est le tempo' [when you're making a film, your internal music is all about tempo] (Narboni, Toubiana and Villain 1977: 25). Editing and choreography, both underpinned by the same concern for rhyme and rhythm, are indivisible in the broader process of *cinécriture*; the 'metronome' that has gone hand-in-hand with the 'violin' since Varda published her foreword to the screenplay to *Cléo de 5 à 7* equating the former with '[l]e temps mécanique' [mechanical time] and the latter with 'la durée subjective' [subjective duration] (1962: 9). Hence, in the following, my focus on music will be on its potential to *choreograph* the body within a ludic context. Where Gorbman focuses on the relationship between diegetic and non-diegetic sound, my interest is in the influence of the sonic field on the body in the domains, real and virtual, of gameplay. My approach is not musicological; it is ludomusicological.

Sidestepping Senescence: *Agnès de ci de là Varda*

The first episode of the TV travelogue, *Agnès de ci de là Varda*, includes a section set in the late Chris Marker's studio. Apart from their close friendship, based in no small part on a shared fondness for felines, Varda and Marker are both members of what has become known as the Left Bank Group: artists and filmmakers working alongside the French New Wave without ever quite being called into — or indeed wanting to join — its inner sanctum. We barely glimpse their hands before the camera is swiftly steered towards Marker's computer screen, introducing Varda to his virtual museum complex on the Second Life internet platform,[7] where he delights in persuading her online incarnation to dance alongside an avatar of his cherished cat, Guillaume-en-Égypte (Fig. 4.2).[8]

FIG. 4.2. Marker and Varda dance the Gee (simplified score)[9]

Drawn to the way in which Varda and Marker — she already well into her eighties, he a venerable nonagenarian — embrace the ludic possibilities inherent in this parallel world, I also want to consider *why* this virtual choreographing of the body proves so compelling to Varda. There is evidently much humour to be derived from the visual incongruity, but we should not forget — as Gorbman reminds us — that Varda's underlying intent is so often 'seriously playful' (2010: para. 13 of 18). Willing as she is to acknowledge the outer traces of old age, as the unremitting close-ups of her hands and hair in *Les Glaneurs et la glaneuse* or of Jacques Demy's frail and faltering body in *Jacquot de Nantes* (1991) testify, Varda nonetheless recoils from the prospect of mental decrepitude and its defining feature, 'radotage', the act of rambling on incoherently. The fact that a body will die is infinitely more acceptable to her than the possibility that it may outlive its mind. In her vehement assertions that she does not ramble, a deep-seated fear of senility emerges. She defends her repetitions in interview as the inevitable outcome of the process of feverishly marketing her films (Heti 2009: para. 6 of 82; Varda 1994: 183), but cannot entirely mask her revulsion at the implications inherent in the term. '[C]ette horreur qu'est le radotage' [that dreadful thing known as rambling on] evokes her mother, Mamie, stricken in old age by dementia, and Varda reacts against it violently, viscerally, and with hyperbolic horror: 'Répétage et radotage sont les deux mamelles flétries des vieilles qui ne se décident pas à mourir' [repetitions and ramblings are the two sagging breasts of old women who can't make up their minds to die] (Varda 1994: 212). Capable as she is of marking the inexorable passage of time, rendering the dying eerily beautiful, the thought of losing her mind greatly unsettles her. Awareness, we might surmise, is key. It is one thing to repeat deliberately; quite another to do so without realizing it. Though happy to label herself as a person whose recollections can only be triggered by association (*Les Plages d'Agnès*, while superficially autobiographical, is, we learn, a film subject 'aux hasards de la mémoire' [to the random will of memory] [Tranchant 2008: para. 6 of 12]), the prospect of losing *complete* control of recall absolutely horrifies her, and is inextricably linked to the lowering threat of cerebral senescence.

Varda thus cherishes quick-wittedness, and has derived much pleasure from drawing attention to her 24-hour work ethic and almost preternatural ability to multitask, often at lightning speed. Despite her transition to what might be termed 'national treasure' status in recent years ('J'ai la sensation d'être aimée. Plus aimée qu'admirée, d'ailleurs' [I feel I'm loved. Loved more than admired, I might add], she comments, wryly [Libiot 2012: para. 10 of 17]), collaborators and critics have on occasion balked at her uncompromising attitude (the 'Abécédaire' included in *Varda par Agnès* features a characteristically curt entry under 'P' for 'patience': 'Je n'en ai pas' [I don't have any] [1994: 27]). Her formidable speed and vivacity are evoked repeatedly, if not always with appreciation then certainly with awe. Charles Ford, in a barbed appraisal of her work, has recourse to the codes of character assassination beloved of human resource departments when he paints her as possessing 'une forte personnalité' [a strong personality] (Ford 1972: 110). Anatole Dauman, the Argos Films producer with whom she enjoyed what can charitably be described as an uneven professional relationship, nonetheless recalls her 'énergie infatigable' [tireless energy] (Gerber 1989: 57). Chris Darke, writing for *Sight & Sound*, is almost literally bowled over by this 'frighteningly energetic septuagenarian' (2008: 22), while Sandra Benedetti struggles to keep up with an interviewee so 'terriblement volatile' [terribly volatile] that she darts from room to room mid-conversation (2011: para. 6 of 6). Varda freely admits that her sheer velocity can be trying: 'Je suis un peu "speedy" comme ils disent pour tout ce qui est travail. Je fatigue les gens qui travaillent avec moi. Par une extrême rapidité dans ce que je fais et ma demande' [I'm what they call a bit 'speedy' when it comes to work. I exhaust the people I work with. Because I'm so fast at what I do, and so demanding] (Decock and Varda 1988: 384) — although she does subsequently stress that her hyperactivity is entirely organic in origin, crediting her favourite rosemary *tisane*: 'That's my speed. Hot water and herb' (Heti 2009: para. 71 of 82).

Inevitably, though, Varda has been forced to admit that her body is slowing down. She now acknowledges her frequently aching legs (Marvier 2000: 47), and incorporates imagery of her physical frailties into her moving images: the liver spots and white hair of *Les Glaneurs et la glaneuse* (Mireille Rosello notes Varda's refusal to beautify these traces of age, seeing in them 'the already defeated fight against time' that defies the recuperative urge at the heart of the film [2001: 34]), but also a brief glimpse of herself navigating a museum in a wheelchair in *Agnès de ci de là Varda*. Fascinatingly, however, she counters this increasing immobility by underscoring the galvanizing impact it has on her film work: restricted physical movement generates more moving images. Her aching extremities leave her more time to run hot baths and daydream, which in turn plays a crucial role in breathing vitality into vague ideas, triggering '[u]n mouvement de film, un bout de dialogue, un mouvement qui s'arrête sur un objet...' [a film-movement, a snippet of dialogue, a movement that comes to rest on an object...] (Marvier 2000: 46). The wheelchair, too, lends a new mobility to her images as she confides in a 2010 radio interview with Laure Adler, noting how it enables her to circumvent the rules to capture 'strictly forbidden travelling shots' in airport security zones (cited in Barnet 2011: 109).

Waning physical force, harnessed in the interests of the moving image, allows Varda to 'break the rules' while outstripping — or outwitting — her age. Through their Second Life selves, co-opting the virtual to establish a 'double vie' [double life] and creating avatars that can be programmed to dance in time to sonic cues, Varda and Marker are able to tap into superhuman powers, executing virtual acrobatics that their ageing bodies, if not their enduringly sharp minds, can no longer perform. When Varda takes a tumble in Marker's vertiginous virtual museum, there are no broken bones; instead, she summons up another soundscape, courtesy of the multi-talented Guillaume. She requests a piano rendition of Domenico Scarlatti's Cat Fugue. 'Ça me remontera' [that'll lift me up again], she says, and so it does, both figuratively and literally. Once more, virtual music restores the integrity of the physical body, infusing it with a 'second life' that has much in common with a 'second youth', allowing Varda to be subversive without any of the horrors that accompany a 'second childhood'. This is liberation through ludomusicology: 'the acceptance and evasion of protocols and constraints, the pleasures of rhythmic bodies in motion, and the dizzy delight taken in exhibitions of virtuosity', as Moseley puts it (2013: 283). In many ways, the gameplay soundscapes of Second Life in *Agnès de ci de là Varda* open up a 'double life' in reverse that Varda has, in diversifying into gallery-based installation work, continued to expand. In the press release accompanying *Triptyques atypiques*, she is cited as describing herself as 'une vieille cinéaste devenue jeune artiste visuelle' [an old filmmaker who has become a young visual artist] (Varda, Obadia et al. 2014: para. 1 of 8). Even as she grows older, her work rejuvenates her and (virtual) art reverses (actual) age. As Varda once said, '[j]e pense [...] que le passage vers le troisième âge est comme une adolescence'. [I think [...] that the transition to the third age is like an adolescence] (Delvaux 1991: 54).

Keeping Adolescence under Control: *Kung-fu Master*

And what of films in which adolescence itself takes centre-stage? I turn to *Kung-fu Master*. On first viewing, at least, it appears to have little in common with the genial Second Life sequence featured in *Agnès de ci de là Varda*. Yet the relationship between virtual soundscapes and the body in play is once again pivotal. Varda describes the film in a section of *Varda par Agnès* that riffs on the homonymic relations between 'jeu' and 'je': [l]e jeu, encore le jeu: au casino j'entre comme joueuse dans le jeu du film. Mathieu, lui, joue Julien qui joue au jeu vidéo et l'appareil de ce jeu joue dans le film, etc., etc.' [gameplay, gameplay again: in the casino [scene], I enter the film-game as a gambler. Meanwhile, Mathieu plays Julien who plays a video game, and the arcade-game apparatus plays [a part] in the film, and so on and so forth] (Varda 1994: 189). This is a film that repeatedly establishes a link between gameplay and the self, and an *aural* link at that.

Based on a draft script by Jane Birkin, *Kung-fu Master*'s subject matter has been described by *Sight & Sound*'s Jill Forbes as 'tailor-made, one imagines, to frighten British distributors' (1989: 124). The 40-year-old Mary-Jane, played by Birkin, finds herself ineluctably drawn to one of her daughter's classmates, 14-year-old Julien (Mathieu Demy). What follows is a tale of grooming and seduction that somehow manages to maintain a strange degree of innocence, partly because all signs of physical consummation, bar one kiss, are kept firmly out of sight — banishing the obscene off-screen — but partly also because of Birkin's sheer boyishness. As Georgiana M. M. Colvile has remarked, we are left with the impression that Mary-Jane is caught up in a yearning for her *own* adolescence, by which token 'elle aimerait autant *être* Julien que l'*avoir*' [she would like to *be* Julien as much as she'd like to *have* him] (2009: 154) — a view that Birkin appears to confirm by describing the boy as 'une projection romanesque de moi au même âge' [a fictional projection of myself at that age] (cited in Varda 1994: 186).

Yet Varda does not turn a blind eye to the less salubrious side of the story and its undercurrent of predation. After all, attempts to resuscitate lost youth do not appeal to her: in *Les Plages d'Agnès*, Varda watches her efforts to re-enact an old photograph fail, and notes drily that '[e]ssayer de se revoir enfant, c'est courir à contre-sens' [trying to see yourself as a child again is like swimming against the tide]. Rather than support Mary-Jane's retrograde desire to relive her teens, then, what Varda does, in *Kung-fu Master*, is to create an alternative, virtual — and, in many respects, adult — space for *Julien*; one over which he has control, and in which he can play out, and win, the narrative of conquest. This space is the eponymous 1980s video arcade game, Kung-fu Master, at which Julien excels, and with which he — and above all, his gestures — are inextricably linked.

FIG. 4.3. Mary-Jane's refrain, with sonic seascape in the background (not transcribed)

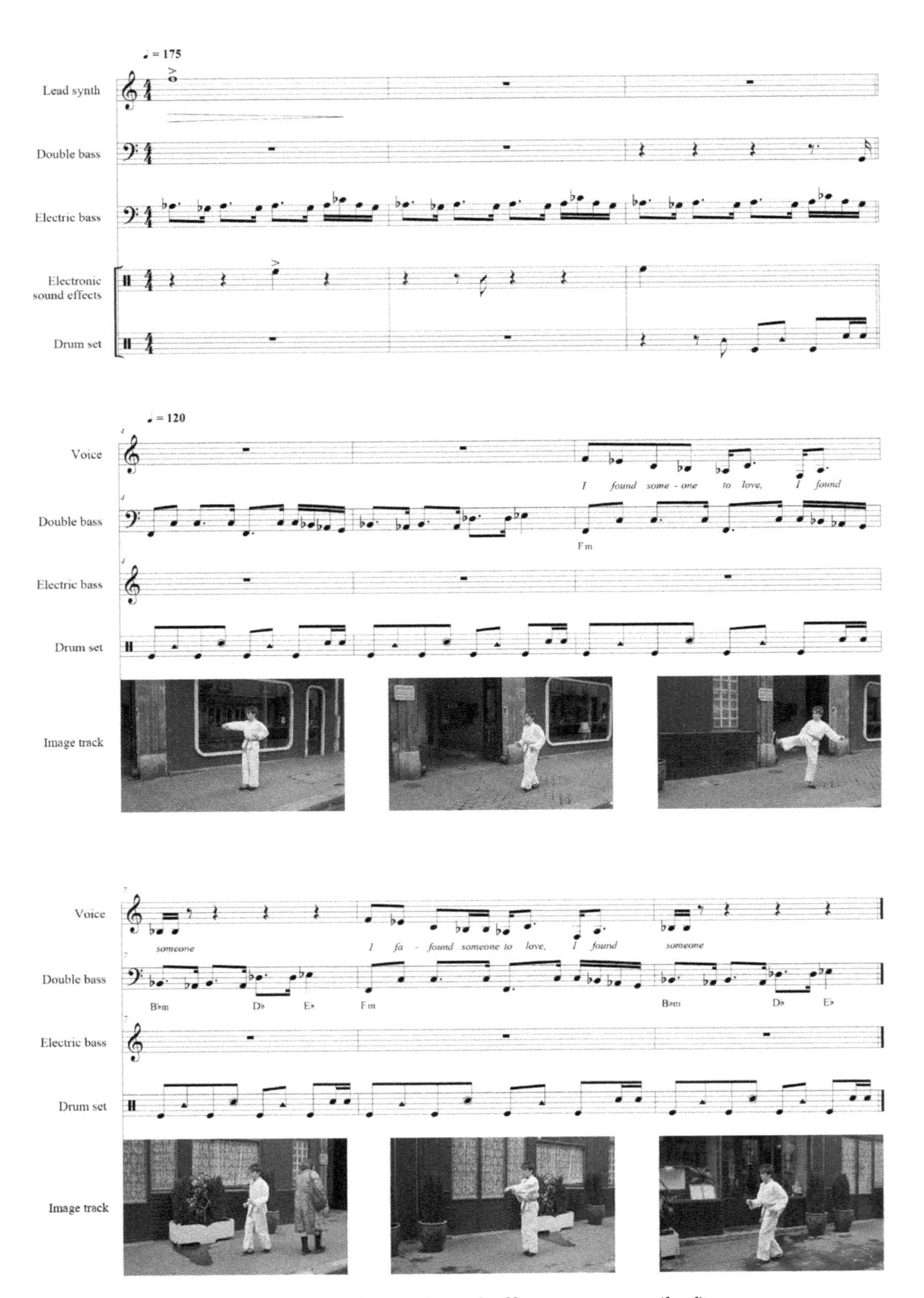

FIG. 4.4. Enter Julien (sound effects not transcribed)

Even as the film opens, the music accompanying the credits shifts from a dreamy refrain, itself rhythmically underscored by rolling waves, henceforth associated with the ethereally out-of-touch Mary-Jane (Fig. 4.3), to the quick-fire soundtrack that dominates Julien's after-school hours, quite literally informing his every move (Fig. 4.4). The track is a mash-up, starting with the 8-bit theme that accompanies the Kung-fu Master arcade game, which then segues into the first bars of the almost equally frenetic pop hit, 'Someone to Love', by the French band, Les Rita Mitsouko.[10]

As Julien chops and kicks his way across the screen, the tinny thuds and shrieks of battling video-bodies punctuate the sequence. These asynchronous noises simultaneously provide a bridge linking gameplay soundscape and contemporary pop song, and a stand-alone sound-effects track. Whereas the waves follow the flow of the Bruzdowicz 'Mary-Jane' theme, Julien's acrobatics are out-of-synch, independent of the rhythms of his after-school soundscape. Even though he is depicted as a video-game character, his movements, compared to those of the older woman, have a greater degree of autonomy with regard to the music associated with them.

Within Julien's gameplay soundscape, therefore, the disposition of the various tracks defines a (superhuman) universe that is uniquely his. Furthermore, this is a universe to which, crucially, Mary-Jane has no access. During their first encounter alone in a café, she avidly watches Julien at the controls of the arcade game. She comes up behind him, moving ever closer. The boy's focus, however, remains the screen: the game world that incorporates Julien but excludes her (Fig. 4.5). 'Il était complètement dans son jeu: habile, passionné' [He was totally immersed in his game: skilful, all fired-up], she observes, wistfully, in voiceover.

Tellingly, too, the video-game soundscape is only present when Julien is in the frame. Julien, however, does manage, albeit briefly, to co-opt Mary-Jane's sonic environment. In the film's penultimate sequence, after the couple has been forcibly and permanently separated by scandalized relatives, we witness Julien, alone in the arcade, completing the game, the theme tune overwritten by the airy refrain that opened the film and is clearly associated with the older woman. Lest we deduce that the recurrence of the refrain denotes a further encroachment on the part of Mary-Jane, it is interrupted and overwritten by the diegetics of gameplay: the sonic echoes of kung-fu manoeuvres that bear witness, as noted above, to Julien's

FIG. 4.5. Mary-Jane fixates on Julien fixed to his screen

physical autonomy. In musical terms, Julien's virtual victory, it seems, allows him to gain control of the real, adult world of the woman who seduced him. At the same time, it permits him to reclaim that which is rightfully his; a conclusion we might draw from the title Bruzdowicz chooses for her Mary-Jane refrain: 'Adolescences' (see Bruzdowicz, Chamborédon et al. 1991: tracks 4 and 5). By establishing an alternative narrative in which he is the master, not the slave, gameplay and its sonic accompaniment offer Julien a measure of control beyond his years while confirming his claim to adolescence. The victory may be fleeting and mitigated by the ironic return, unwitnessed by Julien, of the arcade-game screen complete with original theme tune, announcing further tribulations in store (Fig. 4.6), but it is there nonetheless and finds no equivalent in the domain that Mary-Jane inhabits, from which the arcade-game soundtrack is enduringly absent. And there is a double finality to this: as Julien exits the arcade, sliding insouciantly down the central balustrade, a sign at the bottom of the stairs tells us that 'TOUTE SORTIE est considérée comme définitive' — strictly no re-entry allowed after leaving these premises.

Fig. 4.6. Ominous indicators, ignored

Julien, empowered by the parallel universe of the arcade game and its soundscape, has extended his physical victory briefly into the adult sphere while underscoring his claim to the teenage domain; Mary-Jane, on the other hand, never achieves the alternative existence she craves. There can be no move backwards to usurp youth, Varda suggests, whereas the young will inevitably progress into adulthood. Again, the complex relations between the on-screen bodies, their concomitant soundscapes and the principle of gameplay resonate with the remit of ludomusicology defined by Moseley. In *Kung-fu Master*, we are afforded an insight into various forms of performativity, whereby music provides 'a set of cognitive, technological, and social affordances for behaving in certain ways, for playing in and with the world through the medium of sound and its representations' (2013: 283) — and, in Varda's case, subtly redrafts the powers and perimeters of the bodies within that world.

Battling the Mid-life Crisis: *Les Créatures*

Thus far, I have looked at Varda's treatment of the extremes of age; now, I turn to its mid-point, taking as my focus Varda's sci-fi feature, *Les Créatures*. On first consideration, a ludomusicological approach might seem rather misplaced. With a release date of 1966, only the most rudimentary of computer games were in development, none of them with accompanying soundtracks. Yet the film's structure uncannily foreshadows the form that the genre was to take from the 1970s onwards. Frequently lauded as the forerunner of key movements — the New Wave, which she pre-empted by some five years with *La Pointe-courte* (1955) 'comme une hirondelle annonce le printemps' [as a swallow heralds the Spring] (Varda 1994: 6); and the debates around the 'male gaze' of the 1970s, which she broached in *Cléo de 5 à 7* more than ten years ahead of time (see, e.g., Flitterman-Lewis 1990: 40; Rollet 2009: 51) — Varda here again seems to forecast the advent of strategic, and computer-controlled, gameplay with its own accompanying sonic field.

Les Créatures might accurately be characterized as a film of in-betweenness and indecision. It is one of the few features for which Varda deemed it necessary to 'amollir' [tone down] her artistic vision, in part because the far more 'vicieux' [depraved] scenario she had in mind so deeply unsettled her husband, Jacques Demy (Varda 1994: 86), to whom the film is dedicated. By compromising, however, the film itself was compromised. Judged purely by its performance at the box-office, it counts among Varda's most spectacular flops. And yet, its very uncertainty, its embedded failures, are also central to its narrative, raising the possibility that this purported turkey is actually a relative success precisely *because* of its deliberate focus on the unaccomplished and incomplete. Varda, the arch-manipulator of bric-à-brac and leftovers, certainly suggests as much when she describes it using her favoured jigsaw analogy, noting that, once again, 'the idea of a puzzle structures the project' (Levy n.d.: para. 27 of 34). I shall look here at the ways in which Varda brings the playful and the programmatic together once again, this time within that epitome of the uncertain in-between: the mid-life crisis. At the same time, I shall explore how this relates to the film's motif of failure. What happens when music is 'out of tune', and games cannot be won?

Edgar (Michel Piccoli) is a hack suffering from writer's block after a car accident that leaves him scarred and his wife, Mylène (Catherine Deneuve), mute. They have moved to the island of Noirmoutier to recuperate. He is of a certain age, wedged uncomfortably between an irreversible past and a precarious future, and experiencing a full-blown mid-life crisis. Finding himself unable to churn out the potboilers that are his bread and butter, Edgar resorts to casting his neighbours in the role of protagonists for a sci-fi thriller he is struggling to complete. What fascinates me is the form that this struggle takes: on the one hand musical, on the other ludic, and in each case underpinned by the programmatic.

I turn to the film's orchestral score: a serial-music work by Pierre Barbaud, a pioneer in the field of algorithmic composition. Present only during Edgar's outdoor perambulations and imagined interactions with the surly islanders, this 'concerto déconcertant' [disconcerting concerto] is almost entirely computer-generated (Varda 1994: 208). A short documentary excerpt entitled 'Pierre Barbaud, compositeur et "ingénieur en émotions musicales"' [Pierre Barbaud, composer and 'musical emotions engineer'], included on the DVD of *Les Créatures*, sheds light on the cutting-edge technology used. The composer prepares a series of punchcards, randomly perforated, which are taken to a neon-lit 'salle du gamma' [gamma room] packed with monstrous computers (Fig. 4.7).

Fig. 4.7. Cards are punched for processing

Fig. 4.8. From punchcard to printout

Fig. 4.9. Numbers become notes

The cards are fed into these fearsome 'organes de calcul' [arithmetic organs], and the results printed off (Fig. 4.8). The cryptic eight-figure numbers thus generated — each representing a note, including its pitch, length, position, intensity and corresponding instrument — are then manually decoded and transcribed as traditional musical notation (Fig. 4.9).

The resulting score is both aleatory and algorithmic — and not always easy on the ear. Yet amidst the randomly generated, a space is left for the *deliberately* dissonant. One instrument escapes the 'arithmetic organs', and that is the highly chromatic solo violin part, handwritten by Barbaud to represent Edgar as he battles to master his mid-life crisis and regain control of his writing (see 'Violin I' in Fig. 4.10). His struggle with the in-between is thus transposed into music as the violin works to break free from the programmatic orchestral score that surrounds it.

FIG. 4.10. Serial (music) struggles: Edgar's violin versus the algorithmic orchestra[11]

FIG. 4.11. Virtual chess in *Les Créatures*

This struggle is simultaneously depicted through programmatic gameplay. Picking as his arch-villain an unassuming and solitary engineer, M. Ducasse, Edgar reimagines him as a monster; a warped genius with paedophile tendencies. The showdown is set in a secret lair in Ducasse's home and takes the form of an elaborate game of virtual chess. It features a board peopled with holograms of local inhabitants. Moves, and fates, are determined by rolls of the dice. A screen in the background visualizes each strategic attack and defence, accompanied in each case by the dissonant soundtrack. A metal claw hangs from the ceiling, poised to pounce should Edgar falter. Ducasse explains the rules:

> DUCASSE Vous avez trois chances surnaturelles et aussi votre confiance naturelle en l'humanité. Moi, j'ai toutes les chances de malfaisance que le hasard m'offrira. Voilà. L'ordre des cartes vous dira qui jouer. Les dés nous diront de combien de cases avancer.
>
> EDGAR N'oubliez pas que je suis venu pour gagner. Comment jugerons-nous des gains et des pertes?
>
> DUCASSE N'oubliez pas que c'est un jeu de l'échec. Si vous réussissez à maintenir un seul couple qui résiste à mes maléfices pendant tout le temps du jeu, vous aurez gagné et je disparaîtrai. Et si vous perdez, c'est *votre* couple qui sera détruit.
>
> [DUCASSE You have three superhuman jokers, as well as your natural belief in humanity. As for me, I have all the opportunities for wrongdoing that chance will afford me. And there you have it. The order of the cards will tell you who to play. The dice will tell us how many squares to move.
>
> EDGAR Don't forget that I came here to win. How will we decide what's been won and lost?
>
> DUCASSE Don't forget that this is a game of chess. If you manage to prevent just one relationship from succumbing to my wicked ways for the duration of the game, you will have won and I'll disappear. And if you lose, *your* marriage will be destroyed.]

Ducasse turns to the screen. A moving image appears, panning across a nearby beach. The camera pauses and zooms in on a mirror-image of Edgar, identically clothed and posed in contemplation (Fig. 4.11). As the music starts and the solo violin recommences its fight for survival, it seems that Edgar has made the transition from real to virtual terrain, re-configured as avatar.

Appearances, however, can be deceptive. It is easy to forget, in a film in which the division between (science-)fiction and the real is never clear-cut, that the evil Ducasse, too, is a figment of Edgar's (stymied) imagination. Few relations, it transpires, escape fictionalization in *Les Créatures*. Yet again, Varda's love of wordplay intervenes to scramble on- and off-screen genealogies. While 'Ducasse' recalls both a break-in ('le casse') and the broken (the scrapyard of 'la casse'), mirroring the character's criminal tendencies even as it presages his eventual disposability, the name finds its literary predecessor in Isidore Lucien Ducasse, author (under the pseudonym of the Comte de Lautréamont) of *Les Chants de Maldoror*, which Edgar is seen reading and which Varda cites as an early influence for the film (Varda 1994: 86). Lucien, meanwhile, is the first name of the actor playing the role of the maladjusted Ducasse: Lucien Bodard — who, in the real world beyond the confines of *Les Créatures*, is known primarily as an author and journalist. Conversely, the on-screen writer is associated with an off-screen actor, again by dint of his name: Edgar's surname is Piccoli — shared with the actor who plays him, Michel. This whirlwind of pen names, homages, borrowings and potential kinships hardly serves to multiply meaning, however; we are once again in the ludic realm of what the musicologist Moseley terms 'the dizzy delight taken in exhibitions of virtuosity' (2013: 283). Edgar's universe overflows with literary derivatives and linguistic affiliations, all of which place his purported adversary beyond the real.

If anything, Edgar's battle — for his career and his marriage — is pitched against *himself*. Retrospectively, his question as to how wins and losses will be attributed makes no sense: there are no victors in a conflict of one. In this light, Ducasse's reminder that 'this is a game of chess' assumes a new significance. A 'jeu de l'échec', in French, contains a double connotation; a game not only of chess, but also of *failure*. We are back in Varda's much-favoured world of wordcraft.[12] The constant visual reminders of the strategic game playing beyond the fringes of the everyday to be found in the film's props and décor — a novel named after a (self-sacrificing) chess gambit;[13] an intrusive abundance of chequered cloths and covers — are also a recurring reminder of the ever-present possibility of self-defeat. The musical battle played out in the soundtrack sets the 'real' of the solo violin against the 'virtual' (and thus *unreal*) forces of programmatic instrumentation. The central game of video-chess between Edgar and Ducasse, meanwhile, underscores the futility of such conflicts, positing the travails of mid-life not as a war to be won, but as a heavily fictionalised, one-sided and Quixotic enterprise in which, ultimately, the only victim is the self.

As early as 1966, Varda's fascination with the prosthetic qualities of programmatic gameplay and soundscapes was in place, offering her protagonist an alternative, if futile, means of circumventing the physical and mental limitations of his mid-life crisis. In ludomusicological terms, the soundscape that pits the algorithmic against the individual paves the way for 'competitive behavior, the acceptance and evasion of protocols and constraints', while the on-screen gameplay offers pseudo-rules and regulations designed to justify Edgar's initiation of 'relationships with the world that are simultaneously material and imaginary, real and virtual' (Moseley 2013: 283). Paralysed by writer's block, it seems Edgar's only resort is to create a parallel universe to which he can escape to play out his failures through computer-generated music and virtual avatars manipulable through rule-based gameplay. Perhaps what we have here is one of the earliest examples of computer gaming as procrastination.

Conclusion

This chapter has chosen a ludomusicological approach to Agnès Varda to explore 'the musically playful and the playfully musical' in her film work. Drawing on Moseley's definition of ludomusicology, it examines how she combines gameplay and soundscape in order to play 'in and with the world through the medium of sound and its representations', making and breaking rules to marry 'material and imaginary, real and virtual' (2013: 283). In so doing, it has sought to highlight how — and why — she explores these gameplay soundscapes not so much as an alternative but as a complement and an extension to the physical domain.

The Second Life sequence in *Agnès de ci de là Varda* offers its ageing protagonists a chance to translate their mental agility into physical mobility — a second adolescence defined by heightened sentience rather than impending senescence. The eponymous arcade game of *Kung-fu Master*, meanwhile, endows a teenage boy who could all too easily be configured as a victim with a measure of control — granting him a parallel environment which not only allows him to emerge victorious, but also to exclude the adult forces that otherwise hold sway over him. And *Les Créatures*, pre-dating commercial video games equipped with a soundtrack by more than a decade, serves up a computer-generated gaming platform in which strategic, avatar-led gameplay and a forerunner of computer-chip music allow its procrastinating protagonist to inhabit a virtual space in which he can stage a battle to distract him from the crushing stasis of a mid-life crisis. A ludomusicological approach to Varda is thus a fruitful one. Music and gameplay in the virtual sphere, Varda suggests, are puzzles whose possibilities far exceed the sum of their parts, offering a form of embodied control — or diversion — that, while ludic in nature, simultaneously breaches the confines of age and circumstance.

With a lightness of touch bordering on the joyful, Varda nonetheless raises weighty issues: the ravages of age; the vulnerability of youth; the difficulty of finding meaning in the midst of life. Harmony is attained by striking a balance between the serious and the ludic. As Varda observes, her work has always thrived on the approximation of extremes, and the liberty 'de dire quelque chose puis le contraire, et de me sentir moins piégée parce que je ne choisis pas une seule version des choses' [to say something and then the opposite, and to feel less trapped because I'm not opting for just one version of things] (Varda 1994: 67). As so often with Varda, this is not, however, to be confused with compromise. She is not seeking 'just one version of things', but a *just* version; her objective is thus not to balance at all costs: it is to achieve the *right* balance. What she strives for is the complementarity she finds in the palettes of the Impressionist painters, which was to inspire the tones (literal and figurative, visual and musical) of her 1965 feature, *Le Bonheur*, aiming for 'ce qui n'est pas tout à fait vrai dans la réalité, mais ce qui est tout de même une idée juste, une sensation juste' [something which isn't quite the case in real life, but which is nonetheless the right idea, the right feeling] (Fieschi and Ollier 1965: 50).[14] At base, it is on the editing table — amidst the puzzle-piecing and rhythm-making — that this delicate (and, indeed, ethical) equilibrium is established. Musing on the time it took her to complete *Les Plages d'Agnès*, Varda confides that the primary aim of an editor is to find 'le juste équilibre [...] entre le récit rieur, la pudeur et l'émotion' [the right balance [...] between a jocular narrative, a sense of modesty and emotion] (Domenach and Rouyer 2008: 21). Filmmaking, Varda tells us, is not a battle, but a balancing act between gameplay and gravitas. It is 'un projet de réconciliation' [a project of reconciliation] (Varda 2001: 28).

Acknowledgements

First, my heartfelt gratitude goes to Katia Makdissi-Warren for finding the time in her Vardaesque schedule to transcribe the excerpts from the soundtracks used in this chapter. Second, it strikes me that academic articles on cinema do not always acknowledge the sheer pleasure that moving images provide. I would like, then, to thank Agnès Varda. She may be one of my 'sujets à thèse', but only because I have had so much, and such serious, fun watching her films.

Bibliography

BARNET, MARIE-CLAIRE, '*Elles-Ils* Islands': cartography of lives and deaths by Agnès Varda', *L'Esprit Créateur*, 51:1 (2011), 97–111

BASTIDE, BERNARD, '"Mythologies vous me faites rêver!" ou mythes cachés, mythes dévoilés dans l'oeuvre d'Agnès Varda', *Études cinématographiques*, 56 (1991), 71–83

BENEDETTI, SANDRA, 'Agnès Varda: "Tant qu'il y a des pulsions de cinéma, ça m'intéresse"', *L'Express* (19 December, 2011) <www.lexpress.fr/culture/tele/Agnès-varda-tant-qu-il-y-a-des-pulsions-de-cinema-ca-m-interesse_1061715.html> [accessed 20 September 2015]

BRIOUDE, MIREILLE, 'Phèdre au labyrinthe: pour une cinétique du Je', in *Création au féminin, Volume 2: Arts visuels*, ed. by Marianne Camus (Dijon: Éditions universitaires de Dijon, 2006), pp. 97–105

COLVILE, GEORGIANA M. M., 'Autoportraits d'une autre: *Jane B. par Agnès V.* et *Kung-Fu Master*', in *Agnès Varda: le cinéma et au-delà*, ed. by Antony Fiant, Roxane Hamery and Éric Thouvenel (Rennes: Presses universitaires de Rennes, 2009), pp. 145–55

DARKE, CHRIS, 'First Person Singular', *Film Comment*, 44:1 (January/February, 2008), 22–23

DE BRUYN, OLIVIER, 'Agnès Varda: "Dans ce coffret, il y a mes trois vies créatrices en une"', *evene.fr* (29 November, 2012) <www.evene.fr/cinema/actualite/coffret-toute-varda-interview-Agnès-varda-1736766.php> [accessed 20 September 2015]

DECOCK, JEAN, 'Review: *Les Cent et une nuits d'Agnès Varda* by Bernard Bastide', *The French Review*, 70:1 (October, 1996), 161–62

DECOCK, JEAN and AGNÈS VARDA, 'Entretien avec Varda sur *Sans toit ni loi*', *The French Review*, 61.3 (February, 1988), 377–85

DELVAUX, CLAUDINE, 'Agnès Varda, *Jacquot de Nantes*: évocation d'une enfance heureuse', *24 images*, 55 (1991), 52–55

DOMENACH, ELISE and PHILIPPE ROUYER, 'Entretien avec Agnès Varda: Passer sous le Pont des Arts à la voile', *Positif*, 574 (December 2008), 17–22

FIESCHI, JEAN-ANDRÉ and CLAUDE OLLIER, 'La grâce laïque: entretien avec Agnès Varda', *Cahiers du cinéma*, 165 (April, 1965), 42–51

FLITTERMAN-LEWIS, SANDY, *To Desire Differently: Feminism and the French Cinema* (Urbana and Chicago, IL: University of Illinois Press, 1990)

FORBES, JILL, 'Agnès Varda: The Gaze of the Medusa?', *Sight & Sound* (Spring, 1989), 122–24

FORD, CHARLES, *Femmes cinéastes ou le triomphe de la volonté* (Paris: Denoël-Gonthier, 1972)

GERBER, JACQUES (ed.), *Anatole Dauman, Argos Films: Souvenir-écran* (Paris: Centre Georges Pompidou, 1989)

GORBMAN, CLAUDIA, 'Places and Play in Agnès Varda's *Cinécriture*', *pbs.org* (posted on 23 June, 2010) <www.pbs.org/pov/beachesofagnes/gorbman.php> [accessed 15 October 2015]

——, 'Varda's Music', *Music and the Moving Image*, 1:3 (Fall, 2008), 27–34

HETI, SHEILA, 'Agnès Varda [Filmmaker]', *The Believer* (blog) (October, 2009) <www.believermag.com/issues/200910/?read=interview_varda> [accessed 20 September 2015]

KNEGT, PETER, 'Decade: Agnès Varda on "The Gleaners and I" ', *IndieWire* (5 December, 2009, interview first published 2001) <www.indiewire.com/article/decade_Agnès_varda_on_the_gleaners_and_i> [accessed 20 December 2015]

KNELMAN, MARTIN, 'Interview with Agnès Varda', *The Star* (10 September, 2008) <www.thestar.com/entertainment/tiff/article/496378--interview-with-Agnès-varda> [accessed 20 September 2015]

LEVY, EMMANUEL, 'Agnès Varda at 80: Interview with the New Wave Director' (n.d.) <www.emanuellevy.com/interview/Agnès-varda-at-80-interview-with-the-new-wave-director-6/> [accessed 20 September 2015]

LIBIOT, ERIC, 'Agnès Varda, son univers décrypté à la lettre', *L'Express* (28 November, 2012) <www.lexpress.fr/culture/cinema/Agnès-varda-son-univers-decrypte-a-la-lettre_1192585.html> [accessed 20 September 2015]

MARVIER, MARIE, 'La leçon de cinécriture (interview)', *Synopsis*, 7 (May/June, 2000), 46–47

MOSELEY, ROGER, 'Playing Games with Music (and Vice Versa): Ludomusicological Perspectives on *Guitar Hero* and *Rock Band*', in *Taking It to the Bridge: Music as Performance*, ed. by Nicholas Cook and Richard Pettengill (Ann Arbor, MI: University of Michigan Press, 2013), pp. 279–318

NARBONI, JEAN, SERGE TOUBIANA and DOMINIQUE VILLAIN, 'Entretien avec Agnès Varda', *Cahiers du cinéma*, 276 (May, 1977), 21–26

NAVE, BERNARD, 'Rencontre avec Agnès Varda', *Jeune cinéma*, 322–23 (Spring, 2009), 17–25

PICANT, JÉRÔME, '*Sans toit ni loi* ou la boucle imparfaite', *Études cinématographiques*, 56 (1991), 141–54

ROLLET, BRIGITTE, 'Autres regards, autres histoires? Agnès Varda et les théories féministes', in *Agnès Varda: le cinéma et au-delà*, ed. by Antony Fiant, Roxane Hamery and Éric Thouvenel (Rennes: Presses universitaires de Rennes, 2009), pp. 49–59

ROSELLO, MIREILLE, 'Agnès Varda's *Les Glaneurs et la glaneuse*: Portrait of the Artist as an Old Lady', *Studies in French Cinema*, 1:1 (April, 2001), pp. 29–36

SERCEAU, DAVID, 'Les synthèses d'Agnès Varda (*Sans toit ni loi*)', in *Agnès Varda: le cinéma et au-delà*, ed. by Antony Fiant, Roxane Hamery and Éric Thouvenel (Rennes: Presses universitaires de Rennes, 2009), pp. 121–32

TRANCHANT, MARIE-NOËLLE, 'Agnès Varda: "Les souvenirs sont comme des bulles qui remontent" ', *Le Figaro* (17 December, 2008) <www.lefigaro.fr/cinema/2008/12/17/03002–20081217ARTFIG00368-Agnès-varda-les-souvenirs-sont-comme-des-bulles-qui-remontent-.php> [accessed 20 September 2015]

VARDA, AGNÈS (guest designer), *Zoetrope: All-Story*, 17:3 (Fall 2013)
——, *L'Île et Elle* (Éditions Acte Sud, 2006)
——, 'Au détour du miroir' (interview), *Lisières*, 13 (February 2001), 5–28
——, *Varda par Agnès* (Paris: Éditions Cahiers du cinéma and Ciné-Tamaris, 1994)
——, *Cléo de 5 à 7* (Paris: Gallimard, 1962)
VARDA, AGNÈS, NATHALIE OBADIA ET AL., *Press Release (French): Triptyques Atypiques*, (January, 2014) <www.galerie-obadia.com/show.php?show_id=2665&showpress=1&language=2&p=1&g=3> [accessed 15 October 2015]
VARDA, AGNÈS ET AL., *Les Plages d'Agnès: Texte illustré* (Paris: Les Éditions de l'Oeil, 2010)

Discography

BRUZDOWICZ, JOANNA (comp.), Emmanuel Chamborédon (ed.) et al., *Musique pour les films d'Agnès Varda* (Milan CD CH 347, 1991) [on CD]

Filmography

Agnès de ci de là Varda (2011), dir. by Agnès Varda, 'Tout(e) Varda' box set (ARTE Éditions, 2012) [on DVD]
Les Plages d'Agnès (2008), dir. by Agnès Varda, 'Tout(e) Varda' box set (ARTE Éditions, 2012) [on DVD]
Deux ans après (2002), dir. by Agnès Varda, included on the same disc as *Les Glaneurs et la glaneuse*, 'Tout(e) Varda' box set (ARTE Éditions, 2012) [on DVD]
Les Glaneurs et la glaneuse (2000), dir. by Agnès Varda, 'Tout(e) Varda' box set (ARTE Éditions, 2012) [on DVD]
Jacquot de Nantes (1991), dir. by Agnès Varda, 'Tout(e) Varda' box set (ARTE Éditions, 2012) [on DVD]
Jane B. par Agnès V. (1987), dir. by Agnès Varda, 'Tout(e) Varda' box set (ARTE Éditions, 2012) [on DVD]
Kung-fu Master (1987), dir. by Agnès Varda, 'Tout(e) Varda' box set (ARTE Éditions, 2012) [on DVD]
Sans toit ni loi (1985), dir. by Agnès Varda, 'Tout(e) Varda' box set (ARTE Éditions, 2012) [on DVD]
7 p., cuis., s. de b., ... à saisir (1984), dir. by Agnès Varda, included on DVD 1 of 'Varda tous courts', under the heading 'L'Essai', 'Tout(e) Varda' box set (ARTE Éditions, 2012) [on DVD]
Les Créatures (1966), dir. by Agnès Varda, 'Tout(e) Varda' box set (ARTE Éditions, 2012) [on DVD]
Le Bonheur (1965), dir. by Agnès Varda, 'Tout(e) Varda' box set (ARTE Éditions, 2012) [on DVD]
Cléo de 5 à 7 (1962), dir. by Agnès Varda, 'Tout(e) Varda' box set (ARTE Éditions, 2012) [on DVD]
La Pointe-courte (1954), dir. by Agnès Varda, 'Tout(e) Varda' box set (ARTE Éditions, 2012) [on DVD]

Videography

Institut national de l'audiovisuel (INA), *Portrait d'Agnès Varda par son fils Mathieu Demy* (Paris: INA, 2001), video interview <www.ina.fr/video/I00014298> [accessed 16 December 2015]

Notes to Chapter 4

1. All translations from the French are my own, unless otherwise stated.
2. This chapter was developed from a paper given at the Ludomusicology Research Group's conference, Ludo2013, held at the University of Liverpool from 12–13 April, 2013; see <http://www.ludomusicology.org/past-events/easter-conference/> [accessed 20 September 2015).
3. See, e.g., Varda 2006: 9–10, 48, 51 and 60–61; Varda et al. 2010: cover; and Varda 2013: 26–28.
4. Varda has an affection bordering on obsession for the humble potato, particularly of the heart-shaped variety. These feature prominently in *Les Glaneurs et la glaneuse* (2000) and its sequel, *Deux ans après* (2002), and take centre-stage, in their thousands, in the *Patatutopia* installation, but can be traced back to a single specimen, captured in a photograph dated 1953 (Varda et al. 2010: 40).
5. The photograph is my own.
6. E.g. Serceau 2009: 131, Picant 1991: 151–52, and Flitterman-Lewis 1990: 313 (*Sans toit ni loi*); Bastide 1991: 81, and Flitterman-Lewis 1990: 352 (*Jane B. par Agnès V.*); Levy n.d.: paras 24 and 27 of 34, and Nave 2009: 26 (*Les Plages d'Agnès*).
7. See maps.secondlife.com/secondlife/Ouvroir/191/70/40.
8. All screenshots were captured directly from the DVDs of Varda's work listed in the filmography.
9. The Gee is a pre-Gangnam Style South Korean dance craze spearheaded by the all-female band, Girls' Generation. The steps are synchronized to a rapid, regular and ultra-synthetic K-pop beat (see, e.g., www.youtube.com/watch?v=U7mPqycQotQ) hilariously at odds with the sedate and gently jazzy tune selected to accompany Marker and Varda's moves.
10. The song was released on the band's 1986 album, *The No Comprendo*.
11. Simplified excerpt from the opening credits, commencing shortly before the four-minute mark.
12. In 2006, Varda repurposed the feature in an installation piece for *L'Île et Elle*, entitled 'La Cabane de l'échec' [the cabin of failure], whose walls were crafted from strips of surplus film stock from *Les Créatures* (see Varda et al. 2010: 98–99; Varda 2006: 38–41). For a discussion of this and other of Varda's 'shacks', see the chapter by Gill Perry on 'Les Cabanes d'Agnès' included in this volume.
13. *Le Gambit des étoiles*, a 1958 sci-fi novel by Gérard Klein.
14. See also Catherine Dousteyssier-Khoze's contribution to this volume, '*Mise en abyme*, irony and visual cliché in Agnès Varda's *Le Bonheur* (1964)'.

CHAPTER 5

Re-viewing Varda's *Le Bonheur* (1964): Accident? Suicide? Or the Natural Order? That is the Question

Mark Lee

Having taught Agnès Varda's *Le Bonheur* in the context of an undergraduate French film class many times, I can safely say that, despite its seductive cinematography, music and cast, it ranks as one of the most controversial, initially confounding, even irritating works for my cohort of students, comprised in the majority of 19- to 22-year-old Canadians. The rather negative range of viewer reactions to *Le Bonheur* is, according to Sandy Flitterman-Lewis, quite peculiar to this film which she characterizes as 'a form of Brechtian outlining of a social situation that highlights certain elements while leaving the spectator in the productive position of forming his or her own conclusions'.[1] Indeed, a review of scholarship confirms that these reactions are in fact widespread and longstanding. Rebecca J. DeRoo, summarizing reception of the film from the mid-1960s until its more recent 2007 DVD release in the Criterion collection, concludes that 'it remains Varda's most misunderstood film, disparaged for its seemingly antifeminist themes and opacity'.[2] Likewise, Ruth Hottell speaks of a deliberate downplaying of grand human emotions in *Le Bonheur* 'to the point of outraging critics/spectators who missed the irony, the invitation to question'.[3] Some of the opacity, disparagement and outrage I have encountered derives partly from spectators' inability to arrive at a consensus about what exactly happens to one of the film's female leads — who dies during the course of the plot — and the ostensible downplay of mourning following her death; a question my students were particularly attuned to since we study this film alongside Kieslowski's *Trois couleurs: Bleu*, and Ozon's *Sous le sable* where the 'travail de deuil' [grieving process] is foregrounded. As we shall see, even the actresses who played the principal roles fail to agree on the sort of death the film portrays. I wish to flesh out some of the hypotheses surrounding the cause of death of the character Thérèse in *Le Bonheur* and to explore how highlighting a structure of substitution and replacement when re-viewing the film informs these hypotheses and perhaps Varda's own place in cinematic history.

First, an attempt at a basic plot summary of *Le Bonheur*. François and Thérèse are an apparently happily married couple in their twenties with two small children. François meets another woman, Émilie. They start an affair and François is even happier. During a picnic he tells his wife about the other woman and asks whether she can accept that the affair continue. Thérèse is disconcerted but seems to acquiesce. François is over the moon; they make love and fall asleep. Upon awakening, François sees that Thérèse is missing. With his two children in tow he searches the park and discovers that Thérèse has drowned and been pulled from the water. A few months later, after a burial and a summer vacation, Émilie assumes Thérèse's place in François' family. There are a series of faceless shots of Émilie's hands carrying out the same domestic tasks Thérèse performed earlier in the film. It seems that the women — who even look passably alike — are interchangeable.

Given that the character Thérèse does not overtly announce any intention of dying and that following her drowning there is no discussion of how or why it took place, the circumstances surrounding Thérèse's death indeed remain 'opaque', unresolved in the film and continue to be so even for spectators today. Faced with the absence of explicit explanation in the film, students have come up with various causes for her death — some more sophisticated than others. Let's run through a number of them before analyzing more closely the most commonly offered explanation, and then return to see where certain structures in the film direct us.

Without prompting, many student spectators attempt to find a moral cause and lesson in Thérèse's demise. While a few take the view that the film represents a society where infidelity is socially tolerated and consider her death an odd yet merely dramatic event in the plot, many more feel the urge to see her death through a moral prism of crime and punishment. In this version François is an unrepentant adulterer who has taken too much enjoyment in sinning and is therefore sanctioned for his transgression with the death of his cherished wife and mother of his children. However, the fact that once his short period of grieving is over François seems equally happy to restart his life minus Thérèse but with Émilie appears to invalidate the idea that he has suffered a severe punishment, and perhaps nullifies the very notion of fault in the film too.

The more psychologically sophisticated spectator might say that, in spite of François's claim to his wife that he has no intention of leaving her to start a new life with Émilie, Thérèse's demise performs nevertheless a sort of unacknowledged wish-fulfillment: both that Thérèse should suddenly disappear or die and that he should suffer for having secretly wished she disappear. Once again, however, François does not display signs of regret and no one else in the family appears on-screen to contest his new love or accuse him of callousness. The lack of remorse or consequence is what most disturbs not only my cohort of students but many other spectators. Hottell again reports the strong emotions provoked by *Le Bonheur* among commercial critics in the 1960s: 'It seemed like a sacrilege to many that Agnès Varda had excluded any kind of self-inflicted punishment that one would rightfully expect from penitent survivors.'[4]

Because it obliges students to take some distance from a knee-jerk reaction to find and assign fault, I encourage them to envisage Thérèse's death from an economic point of view or more precisely to examine it according to the economy of happiness exposed by François in the film. François already proclaims to be happy with Thérèse in his marriage. When with his mistress, Emilie, he analyzes the nature of his happiness, he claims he is not a different man since meeting her, but rather, 'Au contraire, je suis moi, encore plus' [On the contrary, I'm me, only more so], and that 'Le Bonheur ça s'additionne' [Happiness, it can be added on to].[5] Somewhat similarly, when François tries to explain the effect of his affair to his wife he describes it as a sort of bounty of nature: 'Ce sont des fleurs en plus, des pommes en plus. Ça s'ajoute, tu comprends?' [It's flowers, but more of them, apples, but more of them. It all gets added on, don't you understand?]. Thérèse's sudden, seemingly inconsequential death following this avowal is, as we have seen, disconcerting for most spectators, to say the least. While as Hottell remarks, '[t]he film's refusal to judge François and his egocentric philosophy of "du Bonheur en plus" in a direct manner causes a violent reaction in the spectator',[6] from an economic point of view Thérèse's demise suggests there is an upper limit to happiness (for the man), a limit beyond which something must give. In this plot it is Thérèse's life that gives. Her death is an economic fatality of excess.

Although it is not something students have remarked, continuing from this economy of excess it is tempting to see the logic of a Derridean 'supplémentarité' [supplementarity] at play here.[7] Emilie the mistress is a 'supplement' to François's already apparently full life. That is to say she is on the one hand, in this economy of domestic happiness, an *addition*, something extra added on to the ostensible already completeness of an established order. However, by a logic perhaps quite independent of individual will, the happiness added in by the affair with Émilie and represented by her character is on the other hand also a rival to and a potential replacement — or *suppléant* — for that supposedly already perfect, complete happiness. The internal conflict of Thérèse as supplement — both as addition and substitute — would call into question the stability, the supposedly perfect, original happiness. The result remains that Thérèse is a fatality of this economy.

For the majority of spectators, however, explaining Thérèse's death comes down to two broad possibilities: was it an accident? Or was it suicide? When giving a plot résumé some critics come out strongly on one side of the issue while others hedge their answer or remain neutral.[8] Since in the film itself no explanation is uttered, spectators feel the need to fill up the silence surrounding the death. Indeed, not only spectators but the actresses themselves carry the burden and feel the uncertainty of the film's silence. In a short 2006 piece, *Les Deux femmes du 'Bonheur'* — which appears as a supplement to the 2007 Criteron DVD edition of the film — Rosalie Varda-Demy interviews some forty years later the two women who played Thérèse and Émilie — Claire Drouot and Marie-France Boyer — about their experience of shooting the film and their thoughts on its plot. The two women in love with the same man who never had a speaking scene together in *Le Bonheur* finally get the opportunity to meet and talk on camera. It isn't long before the question of how the character Thérèse dies comes up for comment. The ensuing dialogue illustrates how to this day, even for the actresses involved, the cause of death is not clear-cut:

Boyer On sait qu'il s'est passé un drame. On le sait tout de suite.
Drouot Elle a été... faible.
Boyer Je pense qu'elle s'est suicidée, qu'elle est tombée dans l'eau, exprès, non?

Drouot Moi, à sa place je n'aurais pas fait comme ça. D'abord il y avait les enfants. Je ne serais pas partie me noyer. Jamais. [*shot inserted from Le Bonheur of Thérèse drowning*]
Boyer Moi je pense qu'elle est tombée dans l'eau.
Drouot Moi, je ne crois pas, non.
Boyer Tu ne crois pas, toi?
Drouot Non.

[*Boyer* We know something tragic has happened. We know it right away.
Drouot She was... weak.
Boyer I think she committed suicide, that she fell into the water, on purpose. Don't you?
Drouot If I were her, I wouldn't have acted that way. Firstly, there were the children. I wouldn't have gone off and drowned myself. Never. [*shot inserted from Le Bonheur of Thérèse drowning*]
Boyer I think she fell into the water.
Drouot Oh, I don't think so, no.
Boyer You don't think so?
Drouot No.]

We note that Drouot is firmer than Boyer in her conviction that Thérèse drowned herself. While Drouot doesn't agree with the suicidal act, for her that is nevertheless what took place. However, Boyer — the actress who plays Émilie — is more on the fence, saying first it is a suicide only to pull back from that affirmation to suggest it was *not* a willful act: 'elle est tombée dans l'eau'. After this difference of opinion, a marked and slightly uncomfortable silence is allowed to linger on camera between the two women and the interviewer. That silence, I would argue, reproduces the pregnant silence in the film. I will now investigate what the internal structure of repetition in the film might say to fill that silence and to instruct us about the nature of Thérèse's death.

As already stated, *Le Bonheur* is in part organized around a structure of repetition and substitution where one character, Thérèse, cedes or has her place taken over by another, Emilie, in a most concrete and visual manner. Varda gives us shots near the end of the film where Émilie closely reduplicates many of the day-to-day activities we had seen Thérèse perform earlier — cleaning up, changing flowers in a vase, putting the children to bed, going for a family walk in the countryside — where Émilie, in the role of mother, occupies the precise space Thérèse had taken during a similar outing at the beginning. The flagrant nature of this repetition with a substitution should alert viewers to its potential redeployment elsewhere and otherwise in the film. I ask students to look for other examples in their re-viewing of the film and to articulate what they might mean. Indeed, a closer examination does reveal the odd reproduction of what is arguably the film's key plot scene. Thus it is that, when François first admits his affair to his wife during what will turn out to be their last picnic together, the attentive viewer will recognize that he or she has *already* witnessed something uncannily similar earlier in the film. Here is the lead-in to François's avowal, performed lounging in the grass, once the children are asleep.

Thérèse Qu'est-ce qui te rend si content ? Raconte.
François C'est du bonheur, en plus. C'est difficile à expliquer. [*pause*] J'ai peur que tu ne comprennes pas. [*pause*] Je voudrais partager avec toi sans te faire de la peine.
Thérèse De la peine ?
François Tu as raison. Je suis maladroit.
Thérèse François, parle-moi.
François Non, laisse.
Thérèse Si, je t'assure. Je peux comprendre. Je ne suis pas si bête que ça.

[*Thérèse* What's making you so happy? Tell me.
François It's happiness, more of it. It's hard to explain. [*pause*] I'm afraid you wouldn't understand. [*pause*] I'd like to share it with you without hurting you.
Thérèse Hurt me?
François You're right. I'm tactless.
Thérèse François, speak to me.
François No, let's leave it.
Thérèse Yes, I assure you. I can understand. I'm not all that stupid.]

Students are brought to recognize that we have here an odd sort of *déjà vu*. While it is true that François has previously had a somewhat similar conversation with Émilie about happiness and his affair at her apartment, that is not the repetition evoked here. The trigger that we have already witnessed a same but different version of this scene is not initially obvious in *what* the characters say to each other — although it will be important — but in *how* they are filmed: a man and a woman in a countryside setting, the man initially in a reclining position with his back against a tree approached by a woman, both of them framed in a low, medium shot as they speak. Yes, *Le Bonheur* opens with a similar scene when the family is enjoying a Father's Day picnic in the countryside. But at the end of that Sunday outing, they stop by Uncle Joseph's home where unexpectedly another scene interrupts it. As the family arrives we get a shot of Joseph watering the garden, then another of his wife, Madeleine, in the house watching a film on television. A shot/reverse shot sequence establishes Madeleine as a viewer of this film-within-the-film, creating the interpretative condensation for a *mise-en-abyme*[9] where we are encouraged to view her viewing. In this television movie — an excerpt from Jean Renoir's 1959 *Le Déjeuner sur l'herbe* — we find another man and another woman in a very similar sort of composition as François and Thérèse during the later avowal scene. The numerous frames within the frame of the shot — a window, what appears to be a framed wedding picture sitting on the television set, the set itself — all serve to concentrate our attention on what is being performed without comment on the small screen. And, retrospectively it incites the viewer to ask, by an operation of repetition and substitution, whether the TV couple's exchange elucidates the future and final discussion between François and Thérèse and thus help us shed light on the opacity surrounding her death.

Before the arrival of her nephew and family we observe Madeleine watching the following sequence from *Le Déjeuner sur l'herbe*. On the small screen we have actor, Paul Meurisse, playing a supine professor Étienne Alexis, leaning back against a tree in a countryside setting, just as François will later do on his future picnic, and approached by a woman — actress Catherine Rouvel, playing country-girl, Nénette. Aunt Madeleine and we the spectators clearly hear the following dialogue:

> *Nénette* Monsieur, vous ne voulez pas me dire quelque chose ?
> *Professeur Alexis* [*sourire*] Te dire quoi ?
> *Nénette* N'importe quoi, pourvu que vous parliez. Vous parlez si bien.
> *Professeur Alexis* Où en étions-nous ?
> *Nénette* Hier vous avez commencé à parler de la révolution des espèces.
> *Professeur Alexis* L'évolution. [*sourire*] Quelle est l'origine de la vie organique? 'That is the question', comme disait Hamlet.
>
> [*Nénette* Sir, could you please tell me something?
> *Professeur Alexis* [*smile*] Say what to you?
> *Nénette* Anything at all, just as long as you speak. You speak so well.
> *Professeur Alexis* Where were we then?
> *Nénette* Yesterday you started to speak about the revolution of the species.
> *Professeur Alexis* Evolution. [*smile*] What is the origin of organic life? 'That is the question', as Hamlet would say.]

One need not know many details about the plot lines of *Le Déjeuner sur l'herbe* to grasp the nature of the relationship between this couple: a distracted, cerebral scientist (Meurisse) and an exaggeratedly naïve country woman (Rouvel). Might their briefly glimpsed relationship be a same but different version of the one between Thérèse and François? In the preceding sequence from *Le Bonheur* and elsewhere in the film, Thérèse shows herself to be deferential to an implicitly more knowledgeable, dominant François, with repeated references to Father's Day when husbands are to be honoured by their subservient wives. In the avowal scene this dynamic is especially evident when François says, 'J'ai peur que tu ne comprennes pas' and when Thérèse, telling him to speak forthrightly and defending herself replies, 'Si, je t'assure. Je peux comprendre. Je ne suis pas bête'. A clear parallel is being established both visually and in dialogue between the two couples.

Nénette's misapprehension of '**r**évolution des espèces' for '**é**volution des espèces' says all this and perhaps much more. Indeed, 'that is the question', precisely. Professeur Alexis briefly speaks in English. He cites something in a foreign tongue which simultaneously does and does not communicate what Varda (one could argue) seeks to say — but not too obviously — to her (French) viewer, through the insertion of a filmic *mise-en-abyme*. This elliptic, apparently off-hand reference in this conversation to Darwin's *Evolution of the Species* and to Shakespeare's *Hamlet* should, by substitution and replacement, guide our understanding of Varda's later iteration of this shot with Thérèse and François. Let's pause to gloss this before moving to the second and final inscription of this film into our film.

The guiding and vulgarized principal of Darwin's theory of evolution is the notion of a natural order based on survival of the fittest, where weaker members of a species — or weaker species all together — are replaced by stronger ones. How might this relate to *Le Bonheur* where Émilie replaces Thérèse? Might Émilie be a stronger, fitter, a 'new and improved' version of Thérèse? Perhaps. Thérèse is a mother and part-time seamstress. She and François married young; she is described as being more passive whereas Émilie a 'postière' [postal worker] with an independent income is described as being more active. Young, single, more outgoing and not inhibited by some traditional moral constraints, she is the slightly more modern, 'fitter' 1964 woman. Remember actress Drouot's comments about Thérèse: 'Elle a été... faible'. The Darwinian reference via Renoir suggests that Varda's characters are not making individual choices but following some larger natural order. In addition to the opening sequence in *Le Bonheur* of sunflowers filmed as if they were observing each other (perhaps following the natural arc of sunlight), Varda elsewhere in the film intersperses images of animals, notably from the Vincennes zoo, encouraging the notion that some broader instinct or species-driven non-cognitive instinct is at play. It corroborates the perception that François shows little remorse, that he seems virtually devoid of feelings of fault or guilt following Thérèse's death. When read through this intertextual reference, Thérèse is not only an economic fatality but the weaker victim of a Darwinian, species-wide and universal imperative.

The brief *Hamlet* reference — 'That is the question' — in our film-within-the-film, however, adds into the mix the hypothesis of suicide and, upon reflexion students are able to tie it directly into the plot lines of *Le Bonheur.* While Hamlet contemplates in his famous soliloquy the question of whether he should end it all, it is of course a female character, Ophelia, who driven to madness by a man, covered in flowers, is found drowned in a river, suspected of having committed suicide. When read through this intertextual reference, the Shakespearian reference becomes almost programmatic for how Thérèse's life will end. It raises the question in *Le Bonheur,* as in *Hamlet,* of whether Thérèse/Ophelia commits suicide or simply dies accidentally under the weight of her sodden clothes.

A few minutes after the first insert of the televised *Le Déjeuner sur l'herbe* into *Le Bonheur,* we get a final snippet of dialogue from the film. The television audio almost completely disappears into the background of the commotion created by the arrival of François, Thérèse and their two children, and the English-language subtitles do not translate what is being said on the small screen. This time François is set up visually in relation to the Professor Alexis character by having him framed lounging in a chair next to the television while Alexis appears on the small screen. Listening closely, we are able to discern what Renoir's scientist says about the concept of happiness and indirectly — by substitution — what Alexis tells the viewer about the cause of Thérèse's later death in *Le Bonheur.* There is a barely audible mention of 'la disparition des espèces' [disappearance of species], and then quite sententiously as the camera alternates between François, the television screen and his young daughter on the other side of the set, we hear Alexis state: 'Le bonheur, c'est peut-être la soumission à l'ordre naturel' [Happiness is perhaps submission to the natural order]. Given the double context into which this sentence falls, it appears to be a key pronouncement in Varda's film. In its light Thérèse's death looks less and less likely a mere accident. By substitution and replacement we are led to ask whether 'le bonheur, c'est peut-être la soumission à l'ordre naturel' is the very message Thérèse also hears in François's explanation of his extra-marital happiness, when this scene is re-enacted later in the film. Is Thérèse's happiness — not only on a personal but on a species or society-wide level — predicated on submitting to a Darwinian natural order? Her happiness, Francois's happiness, society's happiness would be found in fulfilling that submission, in giving way to the fitter Émilie, to the instinct of a dominant François.

Students note that at another point in the film, when Thérèse tells François she has refused a new sewing job from a disagreeable client, François is visibly happy with her decision. He says to Thérèse that, without even having to ask, 'tu fais toujours ce que je veux que tu fasses' [you always do what I ask of you]. Remembered later, these words are ominous for Thérèse. They belie a not too subtle form of coercion that apparently satisfies, makes happy, both parties, and perhaps the section of 1964 French society Varda implicitly here critiques.

The question asked of the actresses Drouot and Boyer in *Les Deux femmes du 'Bonheur'* is now slightly modified. Can we still ask if Thérèse *chooses* to die, casting her death more as a suicide, or does she submit to death in order to fulfil the happiness of an other/ of others, more along the lines of what Drouot seemed to suggest? For students and for all viewers the waters between individual choice and an external (marital, societal or 'species') pressure are muddied indeed. If we understand that she submits to a natural order, then her death, we might argue, if not a form of sanctioned murder, is at least a form of coerced suicide.

In conclusion, perhaps Catherine Rouvel's naïve character from *Le Déjeuner sur l'herbe* was unwittingly right. What is needed is a 'révolution' and not an 'évolution'. And Agnès Varda is part of it. We viewers are free to see a feminist or proto-feminist message in the very structure of substitution and replacement Varda employs in *Le Bonheur*, where Varda, who comes after and 'replaces' Renoir, substitutes his vision with her more subtly critical and subversive one: a step in that revolution.

Bibliography

Derrida, Jacques, *De la grammatologie* (Paris: Minuit, 1968).

DeRoo, Rebecca J, 'Unhappily Ever After: Visual Irony and Feminist Strategy in Agnès Varda's *Le Bonheur*', *Studies in French Cinema*, 8:2 (2008), 189–209.

Flitterman-Lewis, Sandy, *To Desire Differently: Feminism and the French Cinema* (New York: Columbia University Press, 1990, 1996 Expanded Edition).

Hottell, Ruth, 'Including Ourselves: The Role of Female Spectators in Agnès Varda's *Le Bonheur* and *L'Une chante, l'autre pas*', *Cinema Journal*, 38:2 (1999), 52–71.

Filmography

Bonheur, Le (Agnès Varda, 1964)
Deux femmes du Bonheur, Les (Agnès Varda, 2006)
Déjeuner sur l'herbe, Le (Jean Renoir, 1959)
Sous le sable (François Ozon, 200)
Trois couleurs: Bleu (Krzysztof Kieslowski, 1993)

Notes to Chapter 5

1. Sandy Flitterman-Lewis, *To Desire Differently: Feminism and the French Cinema*, rev. and expanded edn (New York: Columbia University Press, 1996), 234.
2. Rebecca J. DeRoo, 'Unhappily Ever After: Visual Irony and Feminist Strategy in Agnès Varda's *Le Bonheur*', *Studies in French Cinema*, 8:2 (2008), 189–209 (p. 189).

3. Ruth Hottell, 'Including Ourselves: The Role of Female Spectators in Agnès Varda's *Le Bonheur* and *L'Une chante, l'autre pas*', *Cinema Journal*, 38:2 (1999), 52–71 (p. 64).
4. *Ibid.*, 63. Hottell is citing and translating in this passage Yvette Bíró, 'Les Cariatides du temps ou le traitement du temps dans l'œuvre d'Agnès Varda', in *Agnès Varda*, ed. by Michel Estève (Paris: Minard, 1991), p. 49.
5. All translations are mine.
6. *Ibid.*, 65.
7. I refer here to the notion of 'supplément' developed in '... Ce dangereux supplément...' in Jacques Derrida, *De la grammatologie* (Paris: Minuit, 1967), pp. 203–34.
8. DeRoo states matter-of-factly in her plot résumé that Thérèse 'commits suicide later that same day'; see DeRoo, 'Unhappily ever', 189. Hottell attenuates that judgment by describing 'the (supposed) suicide of the first wife' or by reporting that on a surface level Thérèse 'seems to remove herself voluntarily'; see Hottell, 'Including Ourselves', 62. Flitterman-Lewis's résumé stays initially neutral, stating 'his wife is found drowned'; see Flitterman-Lewis, *To Desire*, 232.
9. See Catherine Dousteyssier-Khoze's wider examination of *mise en abyme* and her complementary reading of the function of Renoir's film in *Le Bonheur*.

CHAPTER 6

Mise en abyme, Irony and Visual Cliché in Agnès Varda's *Le Bonheur* (1964)

Catherine Dousteyssier-Khoze

Agnès Varda resorts to various types of images in *Le Bonheur*: photographs; posters; stamps; film intertext. This chapter explores how these images function within the film, what the relationships are between them, and how they participate in the complex politics and aesthetics of the film. In particular I shall focus on the strategy of *mise en abyme* as defined by Dällenbach in his monograph *Le Récit spéculaire: essai sur la mise en abyme*[1] (translated as *The Mirror in the Text*[2]): 'a *mise en abyme* is any aspect enclosed within a work that shows a similarity with the work that contains it'.[3] According to Dällenbach, 'its essential property is that it brings out the meaning and form of the work'[4]. In *Le Bonheur*, one can argue that *mise en abyme* raises awareness as to the different images used; it shows how they are costructed and what their effects are. Through the various instances of *mise en abyme*, we are encouraged to engage with the possibility (or probability) of visual irony; to identify the representation of happiness as cliché; and, ultimately, to reject it or distance ourselves from it.

Le Bonheur's context and reception: Varda's mixed signals

Released in 1964, *Le Bonheur* occupies a special niche, both in Varda's output and in Nouvelle Vague cinema. Of course, the Nouvelle Vague directors are undeniably keen on *mise en abyme*, and *Le Bonheur* is no exception in this respect. The films of Godard and Chabrol, to name but a few, are filled with mirrors and reflections of all kinds (see for instance *À bout de souffle* [1959] and *À double tour* [1959]), and so is Varda's *Cléo de 5 à 7* (1961): indeed, the eponymous character is constantly trapped in an elaborate game of mirrors which draws the viewer's attention to the complexities of viewpoint and perception.[5] In fact, the Nouvelle Vague is, arguably, to Cinema what the *fin-de-siècle* novel is to literature, namely that, through its reflexive, self-conscious quality and its fascination with *mise en abyme*,[6] it paves the way for (post) modernity.

But *Le Bonheur* mostly stands out because of the unique way in which *mise en abyme* engages with cliché and visual irony. We can certainly agree with Rebecca DeRoo that 'Varda employed a sophisticated strategy of visual irony in *Le Bonheur* that disputes the film's narrative and conservative notions of domestic harmony' (even though DeRoo's exclusively feminist focus fails to account fully for Varda's complex politics and aesthetics of irony).[7] As we shall see, the main purpose of visual irony, as facilitated by *mise en abyme*, is to increase the viewer's awareness as to the constructed nature of the images they are seeing and to deconstruct clichés (about happiness, male-female relationships, family life, consumer society). In terms of reception, this strategy backfired to a large extent. Audiences did not 'get' *Le Bonheur.*[8] As DeRoo put it, 'although *Le Bonheur* won the Silver Bear at the 1965 Berlin Film Festival and the 1965 Louis Delluc Prize, it remains Varda's most misunderstood film, disparaged for its seemingly antifeminist themes and opacity.'[9] One could draw useful parallels with one of Claude Chabrol's films of the period: indeed, four years earlier, *Les Bonnes Femmes* (1960) was the victim of a somewhat similar misunderstanding/misreading. In it, Chabrol portrayed the (dull) lives of four female shop assistants in post-war Paris, one of whom ends up murdered at the end by a mysterious boyfriend. Because of the absence of a narrative voice, the representation of the tedium and banality of everyday life, as well as the lack of depth of the female characters, were interpreted by critics and audience alike as a sign of arrogance and cruelty on the director's part. Such are the potential pitfalls of second-degree narrative (and/or irony and humour). It requires active participation, decoding, on the viewer's part, and leaves space for some ideological overcoding or distortion to occur.

Chabrol vehemently denied the accusations of misogyny and arrogance in his treatment of the *bonnes femmes* of the title, arguing instead that his clichéd and shallow female characters were supposed to convey and denounce alienation.[10] Varda, for her part, was sending very mixed signals about *Le Bonheur* in that, for a long time, she refused to acknowledge both the presence of irony and to support a feminist reading of the film. Hence the label of 'opacity' of meaning which often accompanies the film.

Le Bonheur is a demanding film for its audience, not because of a degree of experimental formalism and anti-narrativeness which characterize some of Godard's films, but because its simple, understandable plot sounds uncanny. What Guy Austin said about *Les Bonnes Femmes* — '[it] is perhaps above all a film which explores spectatorship. [...] It is aware of itself as a spectacle and frequently challenges the audience's expectations and desires'[11] — is also true of *Le Bonheur.* Varda's film is a glossy (and perverse) fairy-tale in which Prince Charming dares to swap princesses (after his failed attempt to keep both of them), with no visible consequences: what will the viewer make of it? Both films require from the audience the identification of critical distance beyond the perceived neutrality. As Joël Magny put it when commenting on *Les Bonnes Femmes* (his assessment works just as well for *Le Bonheur*):

> Les personnages n'ont aucune profondeur [...]. Le sens du film ne saurait venir d'eux et ne peut s'appréhender que dans ses structures proprement cinématographiques. L'abstraction de sa conception et de sa construction mène au plus concret: l'image et le cinéma lui-même.[12]
>
> [The characters have no depth whatsoever [...]. The meaning of the film is not to be derived from them and can only be reached through its inherent filmic structures. The fact that its conception and construction are so abstract points towards the most concrete: the image and cinema itself.]

The analysis will therefore focus on the ways in which Varda's own 'miroir piégeant'[13] works — how the image is constructed and how it points, right from the beginning, towards cliché and an ironic reading of *Le Bonheur*.

The sunflower as icon of irony

From the very beginning of the film, there is a playful interrogation on the nature of the image, of the spectacle we are about to engage with. Indeed, the opening credits, which show the dance of the sunflowers, can be perceived as a *mise en abyme* of the whole film. Via the playful montage and the role of the music, the sunflowers are almost anthropomorphized and, conversely, the characters from *Le Bonheur* can easily be assimilated to colourful flowers, without psychological depth, who will gracefully move about or dance in the world of the film. The sunflower (or more generally, the flower) motif is recurrent throughout the film, in the guise of various objects (yellow colander or lampshade) or real flowers, and therefore encourages a symbolic reading: the sunflower is always turned towards the sun; by nature it is looking for the sun (or happiness), and this is what defines François's behaviour in the film. (Thérèse herself, who wears a sunflower-printed dress at the beginning of the film, is a sunflower woman whose only sun is François.) The sunflower comes to epitomize happiness itself, as the title *Le Bonheur*, appearing in yellow letters above the flower, tends to suggest. But more interestingly perhaps, this fragmented sequence, made of multiple brief shots or snapshots of the sunflowers from different angles, attracts the viewer's attention on its very form, on the framing process and we are therefore encouraged to ask ourselves how this sequence relates to the rest of the film. In particular, there is one intriguing, obsessively recurrent close-up on a single sunflower (which also serves, significantly, as the opening shot of the film). In this close-up, it is the camera, i.e. the eye, the image-maker, which seems

Fig. 6.1. *Le Bonheur*, opening credits

to play the role of the sun. Therefore, more than on the sunflower, it is on the sunflower-as-image that Varda focuses, on the process or making of the sunflower. The sunflower becomes, arguably, an icon of irony and provocation. And this, of course, has a fundamental impact on our perception or interpretation of what follows, namely the representation of the family in the countryside. Rather than a family, if we are to take the hint from the opening credits, we are dealing with *the image of a happy family*, i.e. with a construct, a mere cliché.

The filmic intertext

The use of filmic intertext is another key type of *mise en abyme* in *Le Bonheur.* As film within the film, it is one of the most efficient ways of making the viewer question the status of what they are seeing. This is perhaps a more surprising or unusual practice for Varda. Indeed, critics keep discussing the relationship between her films and other arts such as photography, painting and music (see for instance Alison Smith's volume on Varda and the art-image[14] and the section entitled 'Varda et les arts' in *Agnès Varda: le cinéma et au-delà*),[15] but they are paying much less attention to the ways in which her films engage with other films. As Bernard Bastide put it, 'la culture iconique de Varda est et restera essentiellement plastique, plus que cinématographique'.[16] This is justified by Varda's own cultural background in which painting, drama and poetry occupied pride of place, not cinema. Unlike her Nouvelle Vague contemporaries, she was not a film buff and had never written any film criticism when she started her career. As she herself admitted, 'je peux compter sur les doigts les films que j'avais vus avant vingt-cinq ans'[17] and she clearly states that neither *Le Bonheur* by Marcel L'Herbier (1935) nor by Medvedkin (1934) have influenced her film.[18] However, in *Le Bonheur,* she resorts, in typical Nouvelle Vague fashion, to the use of filmic intertext in the guise of an extract from Jean Renoir's *Le Déjeuner sur l'herbe* (1959). So, what is the diegetic function of the Renoir quotation?

Varda introduces the film in a subtle and realistic way during François and Thérèse's visit to the uncle and his family, on the way back from their picnic in the countryside. The TV is switched on, and seems at first to function as mere background noise. But insidiously it comes to the fore, and through a framing shot of the TV set (frame within frame) it becomes impossible for the viewer to ignore it any longer. The two main characters from Renoir's *Le déjeuner sur l'herbe*, Professor Etienne Alexis et Nénette (played respectively by Paul Meurisse and Catherine Rouvel) are lying under a tree and the professor, reflecting on a turn of events which made him forget all about his research on artificial insemination and favour instead the joys of nature and sexual intercourse with Nénette, is saying: 'Le bonheur, c'est peut-être la soumission à l'ordre naturel.' Because of the magic word 'bonheur', it is of course difficult not to see this sentence as a key or a clue (or a red herring?), playfully planted here by Varda. As an intertext, it encourages the viewer to look for parallels or differences, for some relevant/meaningful connection between the diegetic worlds of Renoir's and Varda's films. Or, to refer to Riffaterre's approach to intertextuality, the reader (or viewer in our case) identifies the 'foreign body' of the intertext, 'whose assimilation will signal or trigger the replacement of meaning by significance'.[19] However, 'significance' turns out to be quite cryptic: what can be seen in *Le déjeuner sur l'herbe* as Renoir's philosophizing, his own hymn to nature and recipe for happiness, raises many questions when one tries to connect it to *Le Bonheur* and its characters. Indeed, François and Thérèse have already submitted to the natural order, as defined in Renoir's film, insofar as they have reproduced naturally (they are parents to two picture-perfect children) and they clearly have not lost touch with the joys of nature/sex: they are just back from their own picnic or 'déjeuner sur l'herbe' in the countryside. In other words, they have already found 'le bonheur' according to Renoir. And yet, as the rest of the film shows, submission to this type of natural order is not quite enough for one of them as François will seek to 'add up' an ingredient to this recipe for happiness. Ironically, what François longs for is a more extreme submission to or version of the 'natural' order: i.e. a world in which males are fully entitled to satisfy a few females and, possibly, have a few families (or apple-trees), all in perfect freedom and harmony. His metaphors, significantly, belong to the natural world:

> Toi et moi et les petits, on est comme un champ planté de pommiers, un champ carré, bien net, et puis j'aperçois un pommier qui a poussé en dehors du champ, en dehors du carré, et qui fleurit en même temps que nous. Ce sont des fleurs en plus, des pommes en plus, ça s'ajoute.
>
> [You and me and the children, we are like a field full of apple trees — a very neat, square field. And then, I see an apple tree which grows outside the field, outside the square, and it is in blossom, just like us. More flowers, more apples; it all gets added on.]

What the Renoir intertext emphasizes, in my view, is how François's child-like, naive, seemingly unconscious perversity lies in presenting as 'natural' and innocent a version of happiness that is likely to be shocking to the average viewer (especially the female viewer). And, no doubt, one of the reasons the film is so chilling is that, once his more controversial and greedy version of happiness[20] has failed, François can smoothly and effortlessly come back to a Renoirian definition, with a different woman. After all, as a (sun)flower woman, it is only 'normal' and natural that Thérèse should fade away and be replaced by another flower (see the recurrence of the vase-of-flowers motif in the film).

The filmic *mise-en-abyme* serves to emphasize the perversity of François's consumerist approach to happiness and thereby reinforces the politics of irony at work in *Le Bonheur*: i.e. the indirect questioning of a world in which the family and women are nothing but products.

Posters and adverts: the world as soap bubble

The montage underlines the ease with which we switch from poster to diegetic reality and vice versa in *Le Bonheur*. For instance, just after one of François's visits to the post office, a close-up on a street advert for soap 'Un savon d'homme!' is immediately followed by a shot showing François shaving in front of a mirror, which makes it look as though his entire life is a poster or advertisement. And, indeed, François's world is as flat and glossy as an image: he is a poster boy cast in *Le Bonheur* as a happy husband/father/representative of the working-class. A rapid sequence of snapshot-like shots gives us insights into Thérèse and François's everyday life (Thérèse ironing, baking, sewing; the children looking cute; the close-up on the vase of flowers; François locking the door...) and tends to confirm that their world boils down to a series of simple, easily recognizable (and therefore perfectly reproducible) actions/images. The fact that this poster-like world is reproducible is confirmed at the end of the film with a very similar and perfectly symmetrical sequence of everyday chores: the only significant, or rather not so significant difference — a mere detail as it turns out — is that one woman (Émilie) has replaced another (Thérèse).

François and Thérèse's idyllic version of the family is certainly very similar to a poster, a colourful advertisement, or the representations of family life as featured in some women's magazines of the 1960s: on the subject, see DeRoo's convincing analysis, which shows that, in *Le Bonheur,* Varda provides a critique (or a parody, one could argue) of such women's magazines as *Elle* or *Marie-Claire.*[21] Without any fear of sounding anachronistic, one could also indulge in some freewheeling intertextuality à la Barthes[22] by referring to the famous ad for Nestlé's morning drink Ricoré, aired in France in the 80s and 90s. In it, we have the perfect family (wealthy middle-class family in this case) having breakfast in a sunny garden. Everyone, children and adults alike, is smiling and happy; the ad is very colourful and the tune catchy and joyful. The box of Ricoré is bright yellow and so are the breakfast bowls (which, one might note in passing, might remind of sunflowers, both in terms of shape and colour — this is even more noticeable in the 1990s version of the ad). If taken at face value, *Le Bonheur* is very reminiscent of the Ricoré ad. And, in a way, this anachronistic reference helps us understand better what Varda was after and what *Le Bonheur* is really about. As she said herself: 'Dans un monde où les médias nous envoient des images préfabriquées du bonheur, il est intéressant d'en démonter les clichés'[23] [Because we live in a world in which the media keep throwing prefabricated images of happiness at us, it is interesting to try to dismantle such clichés]. *Le Bonheur* is a proleptic antidote to the Ricoré ad. Thérèse/François and their children belong to a smooth, colourful, picture-perfect and, of course, very cliché-ridden world. Interestingly, they lead a poster-like life in a world that is itself full of posters, hence the *mise en abyme* effect. In *Le Bonheur,* posters seem to function as mirrors or reflections, as clues that the characters' lives are too smooth, too *papier glacé.* As already mentioned in the example of the shaving scene, it is as if the characters had escaped from the posters and images which are to be found everywhere in the diegetic world. There is a constant dialogue in the film between posters and life, hence the blurring of the borders between the two. 'Reality' looks like an image: the colours and brightness of the diegetic world are very similar to those of the posters that are seen everywhere in the city and they are reinforced by them.

In another Barthesian 'pleasure of the image'-type intertextual trip, one could also look back in time for another type of cliché. The world of *Le Bonheur* is as colourful, light and happy as a Chéret poster.[24] The bright primary colours of the posters to be found in *Le Bonheur* can of course remind us of pop art but the predominance of yellow is also very much in the style of the *fin-de-siècle* poster designer. Thérèse in particular — light, evanescent, luminous — could be a perfect Chéret poster girl.[25]

The presence of posters everywhere in the film encourages a reading of the diegetic world as cliché and construct. François and Thérèse's world is a bright bubble about to burst and the various posters and images serve as clues of that, for instance when they expose François as a liar: when asked by his wife whether he prefers Brigitte Bardot or Jeanne Moreau, he replies that he likes her, Thérèse, best but the following shot shows posters of both actresses in his workshop. The montage here pinpoints a small 'crack' or betrayal and, of course, this scene has a proleptic value in that it foreshadows the bigger betrayal to come. Moreover, Émilie looks strikingly similar to some of the images/posters pinned on a door in his workshop (Sylvie). She is an image that he falls in love with and cannot resist; François behaves like a consumer, he has to have her. His outlook on the world is as simple and shiny as a poster. Despite the reference to nature to justify his relationship with Émilie (see the metaphor of the apple orchard), he treats women / family as a commodity, a product. The link between family and product is further reinforced when Émilie jokingly says '40 centimes; c'est pas cher pour une famille'.

More images/clichés: stamps and photographs

Varda keeps insisting, in a rather systematic way, on the connections and similarities between image and 'reality'. See, for instance, the link shot between the birds at the zoo and the bird on the stamp, and conversely, in the same sequence, the shot between the Chagall stamp that Émilie is looking at and François looking at her. Reality becomes an image (birds) and in turn the image/the stamp/the painting become reality (Chagall's newlyweds, 'Les Mariés de la Tour Eiffel' [1938–1939] function here as a proleptic *mise en abyme* of the couple François and Émilie will soon make). Varda undeniably encourages the viewer to reflect on the status of the image and its relationship to 'reality'; there is a constant and fluid exchange between the two and, as a consequence, it becomes difficult to disentangle them. In *Le Bonheur*, reality (i.e. the diegetic world) is constantly de-realized through its contact with/contamination by an image or another, and, indeed, the entire film seems to have soaked up the bright colours of the images.

There would also be much to say about the use of photos and snapshots in the film, especially wedding photos and snapshots as POV shots (projection of Émilie's mind?) or the photo of François as a widower by the seaside. The photograph inevitably raises questions about the status of the image and, in Varda's *œuvre* as a whole, it has a particular role: 'The still photo, when it appears in Varda's films, appears, inevitably, as an object, and quite frequently as a collection of objects.'[26] One might wonder, more specifically, how the photo relates to other images in *Le Bonheur*. Photos are frequently associated with a sense of loss and nostalgia in Varda's films[27] but this effect is somehow subverted in *Le Bonheur* owing to the proximity of so many other images. A sort of cross-contamination occurs, which emphasizes that images just circulate; they can easily be replaced and reproduced (that is certainly the case with the coded wedding photo). Just like the postcard in other films by Varda[28], the photo is mostly understood here as an object for mass consumption. The personal and the nostalgic that photographs can be imbued with do not catch on for long in *Le Bonheur.* Photographs are just part of a vast collection of images or, more precisely, clichés.

Whether they be film images, posters, stamps, photos, the very *accumulation* or mass presence of images is bound to arouse suspicion as to the nature of the diegetic world. In Dällenbach's words, these embedded images 'bring out the meaning and form of the work'.[29] Varda seems to be telling us, what if that world was nothing but a mirage, a colourful visual construct? Indeed, all visual clues point to the fact that the world in which François, Thérèse and Émilie circulate is fake or at least no more real than the images with which they interact so freely. Via this innovative use of visual *mise en abyme*, *Le Bonheur* can be read as Varda's hidden feminist and anti-consumerist manifesto.

'L'ère du soupçon' or 'the unbearable slipperiness of irony'[30] in *Le Bonheur*

Critics widely commented on the absence of a narrative voice, on the perceived neutrality of the film, or on the fact that there was no judgment passed on François's behaviour, for instance, and Varda was often criticized for it. She denied any feminist dimension to *Le Bonheur* and 'when asked whether the title of her film was ironic, [she] baldly refuted the claim'.[31] In a way, this uneasiness on Varda's part goes hand in hand with the dialectics of fascination/repulsion for the power of the image, which lies at the heart of the film. As mentioned earlier, the film was often misunderstood by audiences and critics alike. This all seems to refer to the fact that, as pointed out by Hutcheon (and many other theorists of irony such as Muecke or, more recently, Schoentjes),[32] irony is indeed a 'risky business' which can be 'unbearably slippery' at times[33] – all the more so when the suspected 'ironist' eschews responsibility and seems to leave the viewer free to decide for themselves what is going on in the film. As DeRoo put it, 'To the very end [...] the film's working-class women appear happy and do not acknowledge the irony of their situations: it is for the viewer to recognize the distinction.[34]

Does it make *Le Bonheur* a candidate for 'non-intentional' irony,[35] i.e. for irony as a reading/viewing grid, as a 'strategy of interpretation'[36] (and indeed, one might argue, as one of the most satisfactory of such strategies)? Is irony merely in the 'eye of the beholder' in *Le Bonheur*? Hutcheon argued in *Irony's Edge: the theory and politics of irony* that the most convincing and comprehensive theoretical model for irony would need to encompass three distinct strands within irony theory, that is,

> what is usually called the intentionalist position (ironist only); the reverse position that all irony is a function of reading (interpreter only); and the position that there is a shared responsibility (for both) in the use and attribution of irony.[37]

In *Le Bonheur,* the very undecidability as to agency and where the ironic 'intentions' lie, if any, leads to a blurring of the film's ethics. Is there a critical or satirical dimension to it? And if so, what are its targets? *Le Bonheur* is the ultimate visual 'tarte à la crème'; it is fully booby-trapped and it seems that irony is still the best way out (of the cliché). When faced with the recurrent use of visual *mise en abyme*, it is indeed in the viewer's best interest to start questioning the status of the images they are seeing insofar as this increased awareness helps to deconstruct and reject the cliché of the happy family.

From a generic point of view, *Le Bonheur* — which plays with the musical genre (key role of Mozart's music; parody of the sugariness that can be associated with the genre) and, very briefly, with the melodrama — also functions well as a parody of the fairy tale: Thérèse does not make food, she makes 'honey' (in François' words); the multiple shots in which François takes Thérèse in his arms after she was pulled out of the river belong to the iconography of Prince Charming and Sleeping Beauty. The film starts where the fairy tale usually ends with a 'And they lived happily ever after' (which could have been an alternative title for the film) and, by quickly disposing of the seeds of melodrama, it manages to retain or regain some sort of 'happily ever after' at the end. The film's circular structure emphasizes the similarities between the family walk in the opening credits and at the end. Apart from the change of season, the colour of the sweaters, and a different wife/mother, nothing much has changed. The transition is as smooth as when François was swapping dancing partners at the *bal musette*. This is 'repetition with a difference', i.e. parody according to Hutcheon's definition: parody is 'repetition with critical difference that allows ironic signalling of difference at the heart of similarity'.[38] Indeed, there is more than enough scope for irony or rejection to surface. As Alison Smith put it: 'The process is violent in proportion to the amount which the spectator has invested in the cliché.'[39] Thérèse's death is but a blip in the colourful and irrepressible, all-powerful, cruel but beautiful, world of the cliché. And one can go much further than DeRoo's approach to *Le Bonheur* as 'feminist critique'. What the film critiques above all else is the siren-like, seductive power of visual clichés (including, but not limited to, that of the perfect wife and mother). Through a series of visual *mises en abyme*, Varda shows happiness as pure visual cliché, and as a perfectly reproducible product. As a thorough and subversive examination of the power of the image / of images, *Le Bonheur* remains to this day one of Varda's — and, indeed, French Cinema's — most provocative statements.

Bibliography

Agnès Varda: le cinéma et au-delà, ed. by Antony Fiant, Roxane Hamery and Éric Thouvenel (Rennes : PU de Rennes, 2009)

Austin, Guy, *Claude Chabrol* (Manchester: Manchester University Press, 1999)

Barthes, Roland, *Le Plaisir du texte/The Pleasure of the Text* (Paris : Seuil, 1973)

La Belle Époque de Jules Chéret. De l'affiche au décor, ed. by Réjane Bargiel and Ségolène Le Men (Paris, BnF 'Les Arts décoratifs', 2010)

Dällenbach, Lucien, *Le Récit spéculaire: essai sur la mise en abyme* (Paris: Seuil, 1977) / *The Mirror in the Text*, trans. by Jeremy Whiteley and Emma Hughes (Chicago: The University of Chicago Press, 1989)

DeRoo, Rebecca J., 'Unhappily ever after: visual irony and feminist strategy in Agnès Varda's *Le Bonheur*', *Studies in French Cinema*, 8:3 (2008), 189–209

Gide, André, *Journal 1889–1939* (Paris: Gallimard, 'Bibliothèque de la Pléiade', 1948)

Hutcheon, Linda, *Irony's edge: the theory and politics of irony* (London; New York: Routledge, 1994)
——*A Theory of Parody: The Teachings of Twentieth-Century Art Forms* (New York and London: Methuen, 1985)
Magny, Joël, *Claude Chabrol* (Paris: Cahiers du Cinéma, Collection 'Auteurs', 1987)
Muecke, Douglas Colin, *The Compass of Irony* (London: Methuen, 1969)
Murat, Pierre, 'Agnès Varda par Agnès Varda', *Télérama*, no. 1873 (4 December 1985)
Nelson, Roy Jay, 'Reflections in a Broken Mirror: Varda's *Cléo de 5 à 7*', *The French Review*, 56 (5 April 1983), 735–43
Riffaterre, Michael, 'Sémanalyse de l'intertexte', *Texte*, 2 (1983)
Schoentjes, Pierre, *Silhouettes de l'ironie* (Geneva: Droz, 2007)
Smith, Alison, *Agnès Varda* (Manchester: Manchester University Press, 1999)
Varda, Agnès, *Le Bonheur* [1964], DVD, Artificial Eye, 2011

Notes to Chapter 6

1. Lucien Dällenbach, *Le Récit spéculaire: essai sur la mise en abyme* (Paris: Seuil, 1977), p. 16.
2. *The Mirror in the Text*, trans. by Jeremy Whiteley and Emma Hughes (Chicago: The University of Chicago Press, 1989).
3. *The Mirror in the Text*, p. 8. ['Toute enclave entretenant une relation de similitude avec l'œuvre qui la contient', *Le Récit spéculaire*, p. 18.]
4. *The Mirror in the Text*, p. 8.
5. See Roy Jay Nelson, 'Reflections in a Broken Mirror: Varda's *Cléo de 5 à 7*', *The French Review*, 56 (5 April 1983), 735–43.
6. Let us not forget that the term was coined by Gide in the 1890s. See André Gide, *Journal 1889–1939* (Paris: Gallimard, 'Bibliothèque de la Pléiade', 1948), p. 41. Even though Gide refers to much earlier practices — from Velásquez to Shakespeare — it is no surprise that the device should be named and theorized in the 1890s, at a time when the 'novelist's novel' was particularly prevalent.
7. Rebecca J. DeRoo, 'Unhappily ever after: visual irony and feminist strategy in Agnès Varda's *Le Bonheur', Studies in French Cinema* 8:3 (2008), 189–209 (p. 189).
8. See Lee, p. [pagination/cross-reference]
9. DeRoo, *ibid.*
10. The mise-en-scène seems to point to that, for instance in the zoo scene where the women are seen through the bars of a cage, thereby reminding the viewer that the shop in which they work (and by extension the society in which they live) also function(s) as a cage/prison. Whatever these uneducated working-class women do, they do not stand a chance. Chabrol went as far as to say that his was 'un film profondément marxiste'. See Guy Austin, *Claude Chabrol* (Manchester: Manchester University Press, 1999), p. 28.
11. Guy Austin, *Claude Chabrol* (Manchester: Manchester University Press, 1999), p. 28.
12. Joël Magny, *Claude Chabrol* (Paris: Cahiers du Cinéma, Collection 'Auteurs', 1987), p. 175.
13. Magny, p. 174. Magny applies the phrase to Chabrol's *Les Bonnes Femmes.*
14. Alison Smith, *Agnès Varda* (Manchester: Manchester University Press, 1999), pp. 32–48.
15. *Agnès Varda: le cinéma et au-delà*, ed. by Antony Fiant, Roxane Hamery and Éric Thouvenel (Rennes: PU de Rennes, 2009).
16. 'Agnès Varda, une auteure au féminin singulier', in *Agnès Varda: le cinéma et au-delà*, p. 21.
17. Pierre Murat, 'Agnès Varda par Agnès Varda', *Télérama* no. 1873, 4 December 1985.
18. Varda interview; DVD bonus material [*Le Bonheur*, Artificial Eye, 2011]
19. Michael Riffaterre, 'Sémanalyse de l'intertexte', *Texte*, 2 (1983), p. 173. Le lecteur repère la 'trace de l'intertexte', trace 'intratextuelle', car elle 'se trouve insérée, ou enkystée, dans le texte — corps étranger dont l'assimilation signalera le remplacement du sens par la signifiance' (p. 173). [The reader identifies an intertextual trace, which is intratextual insofar as it is inserted in or rather embedded within the text — like a foreign body that, once assimilated, will allow the replacement of *meaning* by *significance*'.]

20. See Mark Lee's point on François's 'economy of happiness' ('Le bonheur, ça s'additionne'), p. 89 above.
21. DeRoo, p. 196.
22. *Le Plaisir du texte* (Paris: Seuil, 1973): 'Je savoure le règne des formules, le renversement des origines, la désinvolture qui fait venir le texte antérieur du texte ultérieur [...] pp. 58–59. ['I savor the sway of formulas, the reversal of origins, the ease which brings the anterior text out of the subsequent one'. *The Pleasure of the Text*, translated by Richard Miller (New York: Hill and Wang), p. 36.]
23. DVD interview, bonus material.
24. When asked, during the November 2012 Varda conference organized by Marie-Claire Barnet, whether she was familiar with the work of fin-de-siècle artist Jules Chéret and whether his posters were a source of inspiration for the representation of Thérèse, Varda answered both questions in the negative. The parallel, however, still has the merit of emphasizing the poster-like quality of Thérèse.
25. See, for instance, the Saxoléine poster girl, in *La Belle Époque de Jules Chéret. De l'affiche au décor*, ed. by Réjane Bargiel and Ségolène Le Men (Paris, BnF 'Les Arts décoratifs', 2010).
26. Smith, *Agnès Varda*, p. 48.
27. Smith, p. 50.
28. See Smith's analysis of Varda's *L'Une chante, l'autre pas*, in Smith, pp. 50–51.
29. *The Mirror in the Text*, p. 8.
30. Linda Hutcheon, *Irony's edge: the theory and politics of irony* (London and New York: Routledge, 1994), p. 116.
31. DeRoo, p. 207.
32. Douglas Colin Muecke, *The Compass of Irony* (London: Methuen, 1969); Pierre Schoentjes, *Silhouettes de l'ironie* (Geneva: Droz, 2007).
33. Linda Hutcheon, *Irony's edge*, pp. 9, 116.
34. DeRoo, p. 207.
35. Hutcheon, p. 118.
36. Hutcheon, p. 117.
37. Hutcheon, p. 119.
38. Linda Hutcheon, *A Theory of Parody: The Teachings of Twentieth-Century Art Forms* (New York and London: Methuen, 1985), p. 26.
39. Smith, p. 43.

CHAPTER 7

Ways of Seeing in Agnès Varda's *Les Dites Cariatides* (1984)

Isabelle McNeill

In 1936, Robert Musil observed the curious tendency of monuments to be unseen:

> There is nothing in the world as invisible as monuments. There is no doubt they are erected in order to be seen, indeed to arouse attention, but at the same time they are somehow impregnated against attention: it runs down them like water on oilcloth, without stopping for an instant (Musil 1986: 320).

The caryatids that adorn the façades of certain Parisian buildings do not seem to be monuments. They have not, on the whole, been designed with a specific commemorative purpose in mind. Yet these sculptural columns depicting the feminine form were nonetheless, in Musil's terms, erected in order to be seen and to arouse attention. Despite this, how many of us notice them as we walk past? Intended as an ostentatious display, they have become part of the furniture, something our gaze simply glances off without coming to rest. It is as though time has endowed them with a second skin and, just as skin resists water, their surfaces seem to resist attention. There is a sense in which caryatids might be understood as monuments. The word monument comes from the Latin *monere*, meaning 'to remind', and its current usage has travelled through the Old French fourteenth-century word *moniment*, meaning simply, 'anything that preserves a memory of something' (OED). Like all art, like all architecture, the caryatids do in fact preserve a memory of something: as Agnès Varda puts it in the commentary of her short documentary about them, they are, 'une certaine idée de la femme en architecture' [a certain idea of woman in architecture].[1] They embody certain ideas about femininity and buildings, conserving traces of past tastes and attitudes in the midst of the contemporary city.

Agnès Varda's film, *Les Dites Cariatides* [The So-Called Caryatids] (1984), a commission from TV channel TF1, penetrates the epidermal layer of familiarity that screens the caryatids from our view. Writing about the film in her book *Varda par Agnès*, the filmmaker explains that although she was aware of about ten caryatids in Paris, through the making of the film she discovered around fifty (Varda 1994: 266). A two-minute sequel made in 2005 (*Les Dites Cariatides bis*) shows that the subject has continued to interest her and features, as titles in English tell us, 'some caryatids of Paris that Agnès forgot in 1984'. That she frames these films as a personal discovery in the city alerts us to the idea that they are engaged with the act of looking. She writes of the 1984 film: 'Nous qui avons pour métier de regarder, de faire voir ou d'informer, nous ne regardons jamais assez' [Those of us whose trade it is to look, to shape the vision of others or to inform, can never do enough looking] (1994: 266). Varda is concerned not just with seeing but with a certain *way of seeing* that goes beyond the surface and informs the vision of both filmmaker and spectator.

I propose to examine the ways in which the 1984 film *Les Dites Cariatides* both offers ways of seeing to the spectator and, in so doing, reveals ways of seeing that are crystallized in the architectural forms of the caryatids. It might seem odd, with a body of work as vast as Varda's, to dedicate an entire essay to the discussion of a film that lasts less than twelve minutes. Yet not only is *Les Dites Cariatides* rich with references that spin out beyond the short span of its viewing time, it also ties in with broader questions that traverse Varda's work. It is part of an ongoing filmic exploration of Paris, a city that has for a long time been the site of Varda's home and production company, Ciné-Tamaris, in the rue Daguerre. On the DVD collection of short films, *Varda Tous Courts*, *Les Dites Cariatides* is presented among the 'Parisian' shorts, while the film and its tiny sequel can be found together on the 'Édition Collector' of two of Varda's most well-known films 'about' Paris, *Cléo de 5 à 7* (1961) and *Daguerréotypes* (1975). Varda's cinematic Paris is heterogeneous, but some common threads are apparent. One is the relation between the city and the female subject. This is sometimes explored through the protagonist of the film, as in *Cléo de 5 à 7*, at other times in the figure of the filmmaker herself: the 'femme enceinte' [pregnant woman] whose filmic diary forms the images of *L'Opéra-Mouffe* (1958), or the young mother who, in *Daguerréotypes*, made a film about the shopkeepers in the rue Daguerre, partly because it kept her close to her home and small baby (Varda 1994: 143), something she underscores later in the autobiographical film, *Les Plages d'Agnès* (2008). Paris has also provided a location (among others) for exploring social issues: from the relation of the urban poor to food and consumption in *L'Opéra-Mouffe* and *Les Glaneurs et la glaneuse* (2000) to the fascinating yet problematically conservative stasis of the local community in *Daguerréotypes*.

As we shall see, the twin ideas of women and society are important aspects of *Les Dites Cariatides*. However, these themes are bound into a preoccupation that weaves through Varda's œuvre: the cinematic rendition of time. Time is so insistently explored in Varda's works that Yvette Bíró and Catherine Portuges have declared that, 'time itself is the main protagonist of Varda's films' (1997: 1). *Les Dites Cariatides* excavates the temporal strata of urban architecture, reanimating the relation between past and present. I have discussed elsewhere the way Varda's works tend to mobilize the virtual pasts of objects, in order to 'fold private experience into a broader cultural space in which we can all share' (McNeill 2009: 284). This arises from an understanding of the filmic (in its broadest sense) as a powerful means of animating objects, revealing them to be points of intersection between individual and shared memories (McNeill 2010: 56). Thus the stooping motion of gleaning in Jean-François Millet's painting *Les Glaneurs* (1857, Musée d'Orsay, Paris, France) is animated through repeated mobile images of gleaning in *Les Glaneurs et la glaneuse*, releasing the political significance of a gesture that incorporates poverty and resourcefulness, waste and recuperation. In *Les Dites Cariatides*, Varda evokes cultural memory, through music,[2] allusion and quotation, and in so doing defamiliarizes and demystifies the caryatids, freeing them from their mute stillness. In this way the film excavates the temporal strata of urban architecture, reanimating the relation between past and present.

This is a process that recalls the materialist historiography of Walter Benjamin, who 'sought a way to actualize historical material that would uproot and *shock* what has been constructed as "the present"' (Pensky 2004: 181). Watching Varda's film, one might comprehend the caryatids as another instance of the commodity fetishism that Benjamin analysed in what he termed the 'phantasmagoria' of nineteenth-century Paris (1999a:14). An audiovisual fascination with skin as stone, and with the clothing or undressing of the human body as urban ornament, characterizes *Les Dites Cariatides.* This interest in what happens to the body when put into the service of architecture echoes Benjamin's view of fashion as that which 'couples the living body to the inorganic world' in a 'fetishism that succumbs to the sex appeal of the inorganic' (1999a: 19). We can detect this interest elsewhere in Varda's oeuvre, thinking of the wax works and plaster heads, juxtaposed with images of a naked baby and an elderly woman in *7 p., cuis., s. de b.* (1984), or the uncanny move between a close-up on intertwined mannequin limbs and a close-up on real bodies engaged in lovemaking in *Documenteur* (1980–81). With the caryatids, however, this juxtaposition seems more obviously akin to Benjamin's work in exposing the strange displacement from people to things that nineteenth-century French culture enacted so strikingly as capitalism flourished. The façade of the Opéra Garnier and the bourgeois façade in general have been explicitly linked to Benjamin's analyses of the commodity economy by Anne Higonnet et al in an article published the same year that *Les Dites Cariatides* was made, which is to say in the midst of the materialistic 1980s (Higonnet et al 1984: 399). As Margaret Cohen puts it, for Benjamin, 'the lost past flashes to view because it resonates with the crises and challenges that present themselves with great urgency in the historian's present' (2004: 201). When Varda alludes in the commentary to Marx's *Capital* as part of the context of the 1860s, when many of the caryatids were erected, she explicitly acknowledges the connection between this architectural mode, the rise of capitalism and its critique. Later, in *Les Dites Cariatides bis*, Varda powerfully captures the caryatids' embodiment of the commodification of the female form with the inclusion of images of caryatids on the rue Réaumur, framing publicity posters showing women in erotically charged poses (Fig. 7.1). Looking at the architecture of the past returns our gaze to the present.

Margaret Cohen flags up Benjamin's 'blind spot to gender' (2004: 220, n. 8). This is one reason — as will be clear later in my discussion — that it is helpful to turn also to the work of John Berger, whose Benjamin-inspired approach to art history was acutely aware that both the gaze and its object are always underpinned by relations of gender and power. *Ways of Seeing* is the title of his seminal television series from the early 1970s and the published book that followed it (Berger 1972). Berger and his collaborators, Mike Dibb, Sven Blomberg, Chris Fox and Richard

FIG. 7.1. Caryatid and publicity poster,
Les Dites Cariatides bis (2005)

Hollis, examined in words and images the ideologies embedded in Western art and, following Benjamin, argued that this aspect of art was often concealed in traditional art criticism. For Berger, 'if we "saw" the art of the past, we would situate ourselves in history. When we are prevented from seeing it, we are being deprived of the history that belongs to us' (11). Here Berger uses inverted commas around the verb 'to see' in order to emphasize that there are different ways of seeing. He does not mean to suggest that there is only one way of reading a work of art. On the contrary, he continually reminds us that looking is relational and contingent: 'Although every image embodies a way of seeing, our perception or appreciation of an image depends also upon our own way of seeing' (10). It is precisely this intricate combination of situation in history and personal vision that I find so compelling in *Les Dites Cariatides*. To analyse in depth Varda's short exploration of the caryatids is, I suggest, to witness her understanding of film's unique power to activate a dynamic relation between personal and collective, past and present.

Varda's first task is to make us see the caryatids anew. The most obvious way she does this is through the use of camera movement. Throughout the film, slow, steady shots travel up the caryatids, from feet to faces. Varda often uses a vertical tracking shot rather than tilting the camera upwards on its axis, allowing us to view the caryatids from angles that would be impossible when walking along the street. She allows us to contemplate their forms of fabric and flesh, as well as their city-worn textures, closely and cinematographically. Although freeing our view from its grounded axis, this recurrent upward movement evokes a lifting upwards of the gaze. Occasionally a tilt is used as though to underscore this human possibility of looking up in the city. In a shot that hints at Pierre-Auguste Renoir's rainy Parisian street scene *Parapluies* (1885–86, National Gallery, London, UK), pedestrians huddling under umbrellas walk past an initially immobile camera, the slanting rain flickering across the image. As Varda's commentary draws attention to the appearance of caryatids in Parisian architecture in the 1860s, the camera tilts upwards to reveal a full-length pair, just above the heads of those walking below. As well as exemplifying the upwards movement in the film, this shot demonstrates how the movement of the camera is combined with the movement of the city itself to animate Varda's still subjects. In this sequence, and frequently throughout the film, Varda moves the camera rather than using a cut, emphasizing the multi-dimensionality of urban space. So when moving between close-ups on caryatids who form a pair, Varda tends to use a whip pan from one to the other rather than a cut, highlighting their connection in space. Yet the whip pan also has an effect similar to the rain in the umbrella sequence, that of momentarily smudging (or dappling, in the case of the rain) the surface of the image, appealing to a tactile sense of motion and texture. Contributing to this textural effect are moments where vehicles pass in front of the lens. A bus glides in front of the sign 'Opéra' before a pan takes us to the façade of the Opéra Garnier. Or a mermaid seen in close-up at 20 rue de Longchamp is momentarily obscured by a blurry flash of vehicular white. The image seems to flicker, but it is the everyday movement of the city, rather than some deterioration of filmstock, that creates the distortion. If petrol fumes have left grey stains on the city's architecture [Fig. 7.2], Varda uses the movement of transport to different ends. Rumbling on the soundtrack and streaking across the surface of the image, these flashes mobilize the statues, creating a dynamic circuit between the past, as evoked in the commentary or music and embedded in old buildings, and the modern city the past inhabits.[3]

In addition to the use of the mobility of camera and city, Varda includes staged set pieces to animate still architecture. These sequences invite an active engagement with the commentary, as the latter does not refer to the action in the scene explicitly, thereby creating a gap between word and image that elicits reflection. So, for example, as we are told that people living in the neighbourhood appear not to notice the huge bas-relief angel at 57 rue Turbigo, we are shown a scene of people standing on the balconies of each floor of the building, using brooms to brush the surface of the angel [Fig. 7.3]. Since there is no obvious improvement in the cleanliness of the angel, the busy activity of sweeping appears symbolic, as though designed rather to slough off the layers of inattention that form a barrier to our gaze. The scene works to repair visually the lack of interest Varda alludes to in her commentary. At other moments the visual gesture that draws our gaze and animates an otherwise still image situates the caryatids as part of inhabited architecture. Such, for example, is the early sequence in which we see an elderly woman, primly dressed in a pink blouse and a grey chignon. As Varda tells us, in the commentary, that caryatids are usually to be found in pairs, the woman opens the shutters of her

FIG. 7.2 (above). Pollution-streaked caryatid, *Les Dites Cariatides* (1984)
FIG. 7.3 (below). Sweeping the angel at 57 rue Turbigo, *Les Dites Cariatides* (1984)

window and shakes out a pink ruffled bedspread over the balustrade. The woman is seen at a distance, framed by a section of the façade of 38 rue du Moscou, with a full-length caryatid on either side of her window. If we scrutinize the sequence, it appears that, in the course of her domestic, yet public, activity, the woman glances first to the left and then to the right of her window, as if nodding to the female statues whose liminal position between home and street she briefly shares. Yet this glance, if indeed there is one, is barely discernible. Most of all it is the humorous incongruity we notice in this scene, between the grand façade and the humble domestic gesture — albeit one that is distinctly bourgeois in its styling (the blouse, the chignon, the ruffle). Varda harnesses incongruity to shock the viewer into seeing the caryatids anew. The most striking instance of this tactic occurs at the very beginning of the film.

Les Dites Cariatides opens with a sequence designed to gain our attention through playful, unexpected juxtaposition. First, a close-up tracking shot unveils the naked body of a female bronze, starting with her feet, placed firmly on a pedestal, and steadily moving upwards to her head, which is shown to support a lamp. This caressing, mobile gaze over the female form is accompanied by the solemn chords of a variation from a piano version of Jean-Philippe Rameau's *Gavotte et 6 Doubles* (1727). With its grave minor key and stately pace, the music indicates a cultural seriousness, perhaps even suggesting the grandeur of a French cultural heritage that includes both eighteenth-century baroque music and nineteenth-century neo-baroque architecture. The link between music and architecture in this shot — an interplay that will be important to subsequent analysis in this essay — becomes clearer if one recognizes this lamp statue as one of many who stand watch outside the Opéra Garnier in Paris. We then cut to a shot of a building, apparently at night time, beside which another female statue holds a lamp, her torso exposed by a gold drape falling from her hips. The opening credits roll across the dark part of the frame. Then, as the music stops, the light brightens, as though day had suddenly dawned, revealing a scruffy, sandy-haired man with a naked torso standing next to the elaborate lamp-post nude and squinting into the light. He glances up briefly at the female figure before walking off into the street. As he strolls away from us, the camera pans to follow him, revealing him to be fully naked [Fig. 7.4]. Towards the end of the shot we glimpse a passing motorcyclist — possibly a police officer — turn his head to stare, slowing down to get a better view.

This surprising sight of a naked man walking through the streets of Paris is accompanied by Varda's commentary on the soundtrack: 'le nu dans la rue est plus souvent en bronze qu'en chair, plus souvent en pierre qu'en peau humaine' [the nude in the street is more often in bronze than in the flesh, more often in stone than in human skin]. These words highlight the incongruity of nakedness in the city, where the contrast between the softness and warmth of human flesh and skin and the cool, hard surfaces of buildings and streets is more usually hidden behind a barrier of clothing.[4] The man has a marked suntan (as revealed by the paler skin of his buttocks), which emphasizes the contrast between bronzed skin and the bronze metal of the statue alluded to in the commentary. With this exuberantly playful opening, Varda cleverly shifts our mode of engagement with both the caryatids

Fig. 7.4. Naked man in the street,
Les Dites Cariatides (1984)

and the film itself. She makes it clear that this film will not be a conventional documentary glorifying French artistic and architectural traditions. Moreover, the unexpectedly naked man makes us realize that these statues are also naked bodies in the street. Even if made from bronze or stone, the juxtaposition reminds us that they embody a human form and that, as nudes, they are brazenly displaying something that is usually kept hidden. In this way, Varda brings them out from their hiding places and into our field of vision.

The gender difference between the man and the lamp women is significant. Varda goes on to mention the lack of surprise we feel seeing 'undressed ladies' decorating the streets: 'on voit sans étonnement des dames dévêtues éclairer des trottoirs ou décorer les immeubles de façon lascive et gracieuse' [we see, without surprise, undressed ladies illuminating the pavements or decorating buildings with wanton gracefulness]. As she says this, a cut takes us to another street scene, in which a group of people pass in front of the camera. The words, 'on voit sans étonnement' coincide with fleeting images of *étonnement* from the group, as first a small child, then a young man turn to stare at the camera. The camera then tilts upwards to reveal a pair of caryatids adorning the large first-floor window. These glances from passers-by at the camera reappear later in the umbrella sequence discussed above. The point is clear. A naked man, a film crew in the street: such things catch the eye and attention, commanding stares. The exposure of female nudity

FIG. 7.5. Illuminated caryatid,
Les Dites Cariatides (1984)

as decoration is merely invisible architecture, part of the everyday fabric of the streets. The gendered power difference embodied in urban space is elaborated more explicitly when Varda briefly turns her attention to the Atlases, male versions of the caryatids, yet markedly different in appearance. While their torsos may be naked, the emphasis is on muscular effort: 'l'Atlante exprime la force and la puissance' [the Atlas expresses strength and power], Varda tells us, while, 'les femmes, quand elles portent le font [...] l'air de rien' [women, when they carry things do so [...] as though it were nothing]. 'Seeing' the caryatids shows how female labour is concealed behind a decorative appearance.

But there is something else about adorned women and women as ornament that Varda wants to bring to the surface when she situates the caryatids historically. In her commentary she explains the supposed origins of the term, taking as her source the Roman architect Vitruvius, author of *De Architectura*. According to Vitruvius the caryatid came into vogue in Greek public architecture after the Greco-Persian wars of 499 BC to 449 BC, when the women of Caryae were condemned to slavery as punishment for collaborating with the Persians and betraying Athens (Vitruvius 1914). Varda is faithful to Vitruvius's brief account but her version highlights two important aspects of the story: the punishment of women and their display. She describes (glossing Vitruvius) how the woman of Caryae were made to parade through the streets like spoils of war, in particular the women of high standing, with their elegant dresses and adornments. As Varda recounts this story, we see a series of examples of caryatids. In this sequence we no longer see nudes; elaborately clothed caryatids take their place. In a visual reflection of the 'édifices publiques' mentioned in her account of Vitruvius's story, these caryatids feature on public buildings, such as the Opéra Garnier and the Conservatoire National des Arts et Métiers. Furthermore, the caryatids in this sequence are carved in static, upright poses in a neo-classical style, making the link with Greek origins visually explicit. At the end of this segment, Varda informs us that, 'l'anecdote a été oubliée: la Cariatide était née' [the anecdote was forgotten, the caryatid was born]. By terming it an anecdote, she discretely points to the subjective, unconfirmed nature of her source. Yet her phrasing also suggests that the caryatid as we know her today was born precisely out of a kind of forgetting. As these words are spoken, we see a shot in medium close-up of a caryatid, one of a pair over a restaurant at 19 rue des Halles, sculpted by Charles Gauthier (who also created a figure for the foyer of the Opéra Garnier) in 1869 (Nebout 1992: 62). A neon light, apparently designed for lighting the façade of the building at night, switches on above the caryatid's head, as if to illustrate the 'birth' of the caryatid [Fig. 7.5]. Recalling the lamp women from the opening scenes, this illumination reinforces a sense of the caryatid's distance from her origins, incorporated now into architecture and the infrastructure, including electric lighting, of the twentieth-century city.

This sequence implies that Varda is less interested in identifying the historically true origins of caryatids and is intent instead upon examining what can be concealed in the re-appropriation of past forms, as well as how these may be brought to light. She reveals a forgotten or hidden connection between the public shaming of women and the decoration of public architecture. This is underscored by her use of the colloquial word *collabo* to describe the women of Caryae. The term calls to mind a more recent public shaming of women in the *épuration* after the Second World War, where women deemed to have collaborated with the German occupiers were publically shorn and paraded through the streets. This public display as punishment ultimately offered, as the historian Fabrice Virgili puts it, 'une fierté retrouvée aux dépens de ces femmes qui n'ont pas compris que, plus que jamais, leur corps ne leur appartient pas' [a sense of pride reclaimed at the expense of these women who didn't understand that, more than ever, their bodies didn't belong to them] (1995: para. 30). Varda lightly reminds us that the female body is politically charged, made to serve not only architecture but also the processing of collective guilt and the memory of conflict. Through the juxtaposition of word and image, this sequence creates connections across time between antiquity, the 1860s, the 1940s and the 1980s, revealing the temporal and ideological strata in the carved stone of Parisian architecture.

Varda situates the 1860s in the context of a renewed enthusiasm for antiquity, citing the *Poèmes antiques* of Leconte de Lisle and the *Cariatides* of Théodore de Banville as examples. She accords even more importance, however, to the wider cultural context of this decade, referring to Victor Hugo, Offenbach's *La Belle Hélène,* Flaubert's *L'Éducation sentimentale*, Marx's *Capital*, the late work of Delacroix and the shocking, early work of Manet. Finally she comes to Baudelaire, whose poetry and life shape the rest of the film. Each of these intertextual references offers the potential for exploration in relation to the caryatids and the historical ideas about women and society embedded within them. I will explore in depth the two that are most prominent in the film: Offenbach and Baudelaire.

The aria 'Dis-moi Vénus', from Offenbach's 1864 operetta *La Belle Hélène*, appears on the soundtrack near the start of the film, just after the opening sequence analysed above. It accompanies beautifully mobile shots of lithe, nude or semi-nude caryatids, over which the camera grazes caressingly, following the flowing forms of arched torsos, limbs, clothing or hair from one caryatid to the other. Offenbach's operetta, like the caryatids themselves, evokes ancient Greece, but in a mode of light-hearted parody. Hélène sings this particular aria before receiving Paris, for whom she is nurturing an adulterous passion. She rails against Venus, whom she holds responsible for her desire, in the well-known refrain, 'dis-moi Vénus, quel plaisir trouves-tu | à faire ainsi cascader la vertu?'. In Varda's version, however, the aria is sung by a man, the singer-composer François Wertheimer, who collaborated with Varda on a number of her films. Just as Offenbach reconfigured Greek mythology, Wertheimer recasts the nineteenth-century song as a lascivious ode to the beautiful 'venus' figures of the caryatids. 'La vertu' becomes a more explicit 'ma vertu', and for a time the words peter out into a sensual humming that seems to express an intoxicated lust for the curvaceous forms seen on screen. Combined with the caressing camera movements that glide over the female bodies, this desiring address to the caryatids brings into view their concealed purpose as an object of sexual enjoyment for the male viewer. Berger highlights this perspective in his analysis of the female nude in European oil painting. For him the 'principal protagonist' in such paintings is 'the spectator in front of the picture and he is presumed to be a man [...] It is for him that the figures have assumed their nudity' (1972: 54). Berger reminds us that the Judgement of Paris is itself a theme that privileges the competitive display of female beauty for a male judge (52). Such representations embody a 'way of seeing' in which the woman is there to be seen and not to look back. Indeed, the nude or semi-nude female caryatids tend to have their eyes closed or their heads tilted so that their gaze is averted.

Of course Varda's film also proffers these forms for our viewing pleasure, and she professes a personal affection for the caryatids in an emphatic 'j'aime', heard in the voiceover as soon as Wertheimer's singing has faded out. In this sense her film functions in a similar way to Siegfried Kracauer's 1937 study of *Offenbach and the Paris of his Time*. In this volume, Benjamin's contemporary explored the revolutionary possibilities of Offenbach's apparently lightweight and popular operettas. According to Kracauer, '[*La Belle Hélène*] allowed the accent to be put on eroticism and the gospel of pleasure' (Kracauer 1937: 234). However, at the same time, 'the mirror was held up to the contemporary regime [...] more unmercifully than ever' (232). The bored Hélène is, he says, 'nauseated by her surroundings' and represents a society 'increasingly filled with a sense of the vanity and futility of things' (232). In Kracauer's analysis the operetta revealed the empty and soulless society of the Second Empire, heading towards its doom, yet it did so in such an exuberant way that soon *le tout Paris* was flocking to see it. Like Offenbach, and indeed like Kracauer in relation to the object of his study, Varda does not deny the pleasure to be had from contemplating the caryatids; indeed she allows us to revel in such pleasure, taking our gaze much closer to the curving bodies and draping fabric of the statues than would be ordinarily be possible. Yet at the same time we are offered a lens through which to see the caryatids in and of their time, as part of a culture that still persists today, in which the commodification of the female body is an everyday facet of the urban environment. Varda has said that, 'chez moi l'information va avec le plaisir d'utiliser de la plus joyeuse et de la plus légère façon possible ce que l'on appelle la culture' (Audé 1988: 2).[5] Varda's use of Offenbach is primarily an audiovisual joke. But it is precisely through such lighthearted playfulness that Varda is able to 'brush history against the grain', as Benjamin would put it (1999b: 248), in a reversal that both reveals and demystifies the appeal of the caryatids.

Of all the cultural objects in *Les Dites Cariatides*, Baudelaire's poetry is perhaps most dear to Varda's heart. In her voiceover she describes him as 'le poète des poètes, celui qui a chanté les femmes et la douleur comme personne' [the poet of poets, he who sang of women and pain like no-one else]. The reference to pain indicates a move to a more sombre, melancholic part of the film, in which Rameau's variations, which we have heard repeatedly on the soundtrack, now sound forlorn and wistful. The use of the verb *chanter* [to sing] with reference to Baudelaire as a lyric poet highlights the continued importance of music, sound and voice in the film. Varda quotes from four of Baudelaire's poems taken from *Les Fleurs du mal*. The first, 'La Beauté', could almost be uttered by a statue, as beauty herself speaks: 'je suis belle, ô mortels, comme un rêve de pierre...' [I am lovely, o mortals, a stone-fashioned dream] (1993: 38–39). Without pause Varda continues from the final tercet of a different poem, 'Que diras-tu ce soir...' ['What will you say tonight...']. Here the words, 'je suis belle' appear again, spoken by the ghost of another commanding muse: '"Je suis belle, et j'ordonne | Que pour l'amour de moi vous n'aimiez que le Beau"' [I am lovely and command | That you will love only the Beautiful] (1993: 86–87). Both poems figure beauty as imperious and distant, seemingly untouched by the desiring gaze and heart of the poet, whilst also appearing to demand complete devotion.

The images we see as Varda reads these extracts from Baudelaire's poems show us more caryatids, mostly revealed by the recurrent camera movement from the feet upwards, but also in close-up on their faces. Some of them we remember from the sequence on the origin of the caryatids and the punishment of the women of Caryae, creating a double impression of these stony-eyed women as both enslaved and commanding. The poems Varda chooses indicate a conflict between strong, beautiful surfaces and fragile, painful hearts and bodies. Thus we have the 'ange plein de gaieté' [angel of gladness] and 'le cœur' [heart] which is crushed and crumpled like paper in 'Réversibilité' [Reversibility] (90–91). Or the breast in a dream of stone and the adoring mortals who bruise themselves upon it in 'La Beauté': 'mon sein, où chacun s'est meurtri tour à tour' [my breast, where you bruise yourselves all in your turn] (38–39). Varda pursues the contrast between impervious ideals of beauty and carnal, human reality when she tells the tale of Baudelaire and Mme Sabatier. The courtesan known as Apollonie Sabatier was rejected by Baudelaire once she

FIG. 7.6 (above). *Femme piquée par un serpent* (1857, Musée d'Orsay, Paris, France), photograph courtesy of Hannah Mowat.
FIG. 7.7 (below). Caryatid at the Dantan family tomb, Père Lachaise Cemetery, *Les Dites Cariatides* (1984)

finally offered herself to him. Varda's commentary quotes from Baudelaire's letter of rupture, citing the dismissive lines in which he proclaimed that, 'a few days ago, you were a divinity, which is so comfortable, so beautiful, so inviolable. And now you're a woman' (cited in Rounding 2003: 144).

The camera's gaze, as Varda's voiceover relates the tale, is on the tomb of the Dantan family in the Père Lachaise cemetery in Paris, flanked by its two grief-struck caryatids. The extract from Baudelaire's letter is read over a slow vertical tracking shot, moving up the draping robes of the right-hand caryatid to come to rest on her face, covered by cloth and her clasped hands. It is an image that, in its relation to Varda's commentary, is both obscure (it bears no direct relation to the tale) and polyvalent. It appears to express both the sadness that one 'might' feel for Mme Sabatier (Varda uses the conditional form of the verb *pleurer*, to cry: 'on en pleurerait' [one could cry]) and the sadness Varda does feel for Baudelaire ('je pleure' [I weep]), as well as figuring Mme Sabatier as both a sculptural, symbolic form and a vulnerable, rejected woman. This combination of real and ideal in one image is all the more apt and striking when one recalls the most famous artistic incarnation of Mme Sabatier: the scandalous 1847 sculpture by Auguste Clésinger, *Femme piquée par un serpent* (Musée d'Orsay, Paris, France). The marble sculpture depicts a naked woman lying with her back arched and head thrown back, supposedly contorted in pain from a snake bite but usually perceived to be in sexual ecstasy [Fig. 7.6]. Many observers at the time considered the piece shockingly indecent, not only because of the pose but also because it was apparently moulded from life, created from casts of the real body of Mme Sabatier (Rounding 2003: 105). The process conserved what Théophile Gautier described approvingly as 'le grain et la fleur de l'épiderme' [the texture and bloom of skin] (1988: 174, n. 3), conveying the dimples on her thighs and the folds of her skin. Historian Virginia Rounding describes it as 'tactile, enticing [...] as though a living, breathing woman is lying or, rather, writhing there' (105). Delacroix condemned it as a 'daguerréotype en sculpture' [sculpted daguerreotype] (cited in Hannoosh 2006: 95).

If Mme Sabatier had been a 'divinité' for Baudelaire, she was one whose stone-fashioned dream already bore a photograph-like, indexical trace of real, womanly flesh. Although absent from Varda's film, Clésinger's figure of Sabatier as a fantasy somewhere between stone and skin haunts *Les Dites Cariatides* in images of caryatids whose tactile forms suggest flesh and whose poses suggest erotic pleasure, such as the mermaids with their arched backs at 20 rue de Longchamp and the semi-naked caryatid at 30 rue Galilée, whose raised arm and tilted back head are seen in close-up as Varda recites from Baudelaire's 'Que diras-tu ce soir'. But as her tale is told, Sabatier is recast in the heavy folds of fabric, covered face and wreath-like hair of the Dantan brothers' tomb sculpture, seen in close-up at the moment when Varda, quoting Baudelaire's letter, exclaims, 'te voilà femme, maintenant' [now you're a woman] (Fig. 7.7). A strip-tease in reverse, the gap between word and image offers the viewer a playful game of hide-and-seek as we try to map one on to the other. But if Mme Sabatier eludes us in the conditional tense of tears we may or may not want to shed, her presence as 'une certaine idée de la femme' still underscores the pernicious objectification of women.

Other than choosing to include his contemptuous rupture with Mme Sabatier in the film's exploration of the caryatids, Varda does not emphasize Baudelaire's misogyny. Infamously, in 'Le Peintre de la vie moderne', he described 'la femme' as 'une espèce d'idole, stupide peut-être, mais éblouissante, enchanteresse' [a sort of idol, stupid perhaps, but dazzling, enchanting] and thought her godlike mystery was likely because she had nothing much to say (1992: 373).[6] Yet, in a film that, as we have seen, exposes the dominant male gaze, Varda is more interested in the relation of Baudelaire to his era, and the silence to which it condemned him in the end. In the poems Varda cites, it is the poet himself who is depicted as fragile and weak. It is his heart, after all, that is crushed, he who is figured as a 'pauvre âme solitaire' [poor lonely soul] (Baudelaire 1993: 84–85). Recounting the poverty, bitterness and illness of his final years, Varda emphasizes his aphasia: 'quelques années plus tard il meurt, toujours muet' [a few years later he died, still mute]. This muteness is all the more striking since it echoes the love that beauty is meant to inspire in the poet, as we have heard in lines read from 'La Beauté': 'un amour | Éternel et muet ainsi que la matière' [So that love will be born in the poet | Eternal and silent as matter is timeless] (38–39). Baudelaire's muteness arises from the fleshly vulnerability of the human body, something that impervious ideals of beauty refuse to acknowledge.

This returns us to the opening of the film: the contrast between the naked man and the graceful nude statues. Moving between the organic and the inorganic, between the human and the artefact, flesh and stone, Varda operates a series of reversals that also cross gender lines. So Offenbach's Hélène becomes a lecherous male voice, while the words of Baudelaire, the mute poet, are intoned by the female filmmaker. Through these shifting relations, the film invites us to read Baudelaire through the caryatids, as much as the other way around. He emerges as a victim of a society that is obsessed with superficial pleasures while hypocritically dressing up commodification as art. Taken from the 'Tableaux Parisiens', it is the last line of 'L'amour du mensonge' that provides the last line of the film: 'Masque ou décor, salut! J'adore ta beauté' [Mask, decoration, hail! Beauty, I worship you!] (200–01). Among the somewhat spiteful missives sent anonymously to Mme Sabatier, this poem pulls away the harmonious and beautiful façade of the woman to whom it is addressed, imagining the over-ripe heart behind her beauty ('son cœur, meurtri comme une pêche' [her heart, bruised like a softened peach]), and the emptiness behind her lovely eyes ('Beaux écrins sans joyaux, médaillons sans reliques' [Handsome, like empty lockets, caskets without jewels]). Yet the last verse restores the façade:

> Mais ne suffit-il pas que tu sois l'apparence,
> Pour réjouir un cœur qui fuit la vérité?
> Qu'importe ta bêtise ou ton indifférence?
>
> [But is it not enough that your appearance can
> Restore to joy a heart that flees from what is true?
> What if you are inane, what if indifferent!] (200–01).

What do stupidity and indifference matter, when the surface is beautiful? Recalling Varda's desire for culture to be 'joyous' and 'light', and as the camera moves upwards from the magnificent angel of 57 rue Turbigo to reveal the rooftops of

Paris, we might be tempted to take this final reference to Baudelaire at face value. By this point of the film, however, we have learnt that although we may adore the beauty of decorative façades, we must also look beyond their surface. Having sloughed off the skin of familiarity, Varda unveils the mystification of the human body also contained in these Parisian monuments. She does this by using filmic layers — commentary, camerawork, music, quotation — to call forth the temporal layers of the city, revealing Paris to be a site still shaped by the forms and ideas of the past, even as those forms and ideas become part of the furniture, vanishing from our immediate view.

Bibliography

AUDÉ, FRANÇOISE, 'Conversation avec Agnès Varda', *Positif*, 325 (1988), 2–5

BAUDELAIRE, CHARLES, *The Flowers of Evil*, trans. by James McGowan, Oxford World's Classics (Oxford: Oxford University Press, 1993 [1861])

—— *Critique d'art, suivi de Critique musicale*, Folio Essais (Paris: Gallimard, 1992 [1868])

BENJAMIN, WALTER, 'Paris, Capital of the Nineteenth Century', Exposés of 1935 and 1939, in *The Arcades Project*, trans. by Howard Eiland and Kevin McLaughlin (Cambridge MA and London: The Belknap Press of Harvard University Press, 1999a [1935–39]), 3–26

—— 'Theses on the Philosophy of History', in *Illuminations*, trans. by Harry Zorn (London: Pimlico, 1999b [1950]), 245–55

BERGER, JOHN, *Ways of Seeing* (London: Penguin, 1972)

BÍRÓ, YVETTE and CATHERINE PORTUGES, 'Caryatids of Time: Temporality in the Cinema of Agnès Varda', *Performing Arts Journal*, 19:3 (1997), 1–10

COHEN, MARGARET, 'Benjamin's phantasmagoria: the *Arcades Project*', in *The Cambridge Companion to Walter Benjamin*, ed. by David S. Ferris (Cambridge: Cambridge University Press, 2004), 199–220

GAUTIER, THÉOPHILE, *Correspondance générale*, III, ed. by Pierre Laubriet (Genève: Droz, 1988)

HANNOOSH, MICHÈLE, 'Delacroix and Sculpture', *Nineteenth-Century French Studies*, 35:1 (Fall 2006), 95–109

HIGONNET, ANNE, MARGARET and PATRICE, 'Façades: Walter Benjamin's Paris', *Critical Inquiry*, 10:3 (March 1984), 391–419

KRACAUER, SIEGFRIED, *Offenbach and the Paris of his time*, trans. by Gwenda David and Eric Mosbacher (London: Constable, 1937)

MCNEILL, ISABELLE, *Memory and the Moving Image: French Film in the Digital Era* (Edinburgh: Edinburgh University Press, 2010)

—— 'Agnès Varda's Moving Museums', in *Anamnesia: Private and Public Memory in Modern French Culture*, ed. by Peter Collier, Anna Magdalena Elsner and Olga Smith (Bern: Peter Lang, 2009), 283–94

MUSIL, ROBERT, *Selected Writings*, ed. and trans. by Burton Pike (New York: Continuum, 1986 [1936])

NEBOUT, JACQUELINE, *Les Cariatides de Paris* (Paris: Éditions Hervas, 1992)

ROUNDING, VIRGINIA, *Grandes Horizontales: The Lives and Legends of Four Nineteenth-Century Courtesans* (London: Bloomsbury, 2003)

PENSKY, MAX, 'Method and time: Benjamin's dialectical images', in *The Cambridge Companion to Walter Benjamin*, ed. by David S. Ferris (Cambridge: Cambridge University Press, 2004), 177–98

VARDA, AGNÈS, *Varda par Agnès* (Paris: Cahiers du Cinéma, 1994)

VIRGILI, FABRICE, 'Les "tondues" à la liberation: le corps des femmes, enjeu d'une réappropriation', *Clio. Femmes, Genre, Histoire*, 1. (1995) Résistances et Libérations France 1940–

1945 <doi: 10.4000/clio.518>
VITRUVIUS, [c.15BC]. 'The Education of the Architect', in *The Ten Books on Architecture: Book 1*, trans. by Morris Hicky Morgan (Cambridge MA: Harvard University Press, 1914), in *The Project Gutenberg EBook of The Ten Books on Architecture by Vitruvius*, EBook No. 20239 <http://www.gutenberg.org/files/20239/20239-h/29239-h.htm> [accessed 22 September 2015)

Filmography

7 p., cuis., s. de b., 1984, dir. by Agnès Varda, on DVD 1 of *Varda Tous Courts*, Ciné-Tamaris Vidéo [on DVD]
Cléo de 5 à 7, 1961, dir. by Agnès Varda, included in *Tout(e) Varda*, Arte Éditions/Ciné Tamaris Vidéo [on DVD]
Daguerréotypes, 1975, dir. by Agnès Varda, included in *Tout(e) Varda*, Arte Éditions/Ciné Tamaris Vidéo [on DVD]
Documenteur, 1980–81, dir. by Agnès Varda, included in *Tout(e) Varda*, Arte Éditions/Ciné Tamaris Vidéo [on DVD]
Les Dites Cariatides, 1984, dir. by Agnès Varda, on DVD 2 of *Varda Tous Courts*, Ciné-Tamaris Vidéo [on DVD]
Les Dites Cariatides bis, 2005, dir. by Agnès Varda, on DVD 1 of *Cléo de 5 à 7 et Daguerréotypes, Édition Collector avec des dessins de Sempé*, Paramount Home Entertainment France [on DVD]
Les Glaneurs et la glaneuse, 2000, included in *Tout(e) Varda*, Arte Éditions/Ciné Tamaris Vidéo [on DVD]
Les Plages d'Agnès, 2008, dir. by Agnès Varda, included in *Tout(e) Varda*, Arte Éditions/Ciné Tamaris Vidéo [on DVD]
L'Opéra Mouffe, 1958, dir. by Agnès Varda, on DVD 2 of *Varda Tous Courts*, Ciné-Tamaris Vidéo [on DVD]

Notes to Chapter 7

1. All translations of Agnès Varda's words from French into English are my own.
2. In this respect my reading of the film here resonates with recent work exploring the significant role of music in Varda's films, exemplified in Phil Powrie and Hannah Mowat's contributions to this volume.
3. Many of the caryatids have been cleaned since Varda made the films. In particular, the final 'angel' of the film at 57 rue Turbigo has now emerged from her veil of dingy grey.
4. Varda's playful deployment the male nude was manifest more recently in an installation at the Gallerie Nathalie Obadia in 2014 (8 February–5 April). As part of the exhibition 'Triptyques atypiques', the piece entitled 'Cinq Bacheliers' (2014) features eight naked male figures standing, statue-like, on tree stumps on the beach, three from the front, five from the back. The photographs are printed onto giant, magnetized puzzle pieces, which could be removed, replaced and rearranged by the gallery visitor. This image resonates with the naked man seen in 'Ulysse' (1954), also part of the exhibition and the photograph at the centre of the eponymous film (1982). In each case Varda reconfigures our gaze upon the naked male body.
5. I am grateful to Hannah Mowat for bringing this statement to my attention, as well as for many inspiring conversations about Varda.
6. My translation.

CHAPTER 8

La mer, la mer, toujours recommencée: A Centrifugal Reading of the Beach in the Work of Agnès Varda

Fiona Handyside

Introduction

> Si on ouvrait des gens, on trouverait des paysages. Moi, si on m'ouvre, on trouvera des plages
>
> [If you were to open people up, you would find landscapes. If you open me up, you find beaches] (Agnès Varda, *Les Plages d'Agnès*, 2008).

The significance and importance of Agnès Varda's 2008 film *Les Plages d'Agnès* (hereafter *Les Plages*) as both the capstone to her sixty-year career as a photographer, film-maker and installation artist, and as a key documentary within the contemporary French cinema landscape, is testified to by the sheer quantity of scholarship already dedicated to it, which is quite staggering considering that the film is less than a decade old. In *Studies in French Cinema*'s special 10-year anniversary edition from 2010, two articles (by Sarah Cooper and Kelley Conway) discuss the film, thus giving this film more attention than any other in this retrospective account of recent scholarship on French cinema, a remarkable signal of its visibility and value.[1] Generally speaking, critical accounts could be placed into two main categories. First, the film has been analysed as a form of cinematic self-portrait, by Raymond Bellour, Cooper, Conway, Stanley Kaufmann, Sophie Mayer and Cecilia Sayad; secondly, as a delicate and careful account of the relation between cinema and grief, by Jenny Chamarette, Kristi McKim and Emma Wilson.[2] Alongside this, I have explained how Varda's film is a complex reflection upon the place of the beach both in her own work and more broadly in French cinematic culture.[3] Rather than repeating my earlier observations about how this film mobilizes the beach site as the critical and creative lynchpin for both her life and work, or commenting on the brilliant work by others discussing this film's place as a reflection on processes of memory and mourning, which can be accessed elsewhere, I want here to take a deliberately eccentric approach (in both senses of the word). Thus I intersperse discussion of *Les Plages* with moves to the margins of Varda's production — a short film, *Trapézistes et voltigeurs*, accompanying the DVD of *Les Plages*; the art installation *La Grande Carte Postale* ou *Souvenir de Noirmoutier*, from her 2006 installation *Île et Elle* at the

Fondation Cartier de l'art contemporain in Paris; and a short film she made in 1982 entitled *Ulysse*. Each of these pieces of marginalia enriches and enhances our understanding of *Les Plages*, giving the latter a status within Varda's filmography of a centrifugal force. Through exploring the 'centrifugal' impact of *Les Plages*, we establish the recurrent importance of beaches to her cinematic philosophy and think through the broader feminist and political resonance of choosing constantly to return to, and make central, a peripheral, transnational location. In her varied and multiple investigations of the beach, Varda examines it as a place of vibrant pleasure, fun and relaxation, and also as the place of hard labour and immense grief. This dual emphasis on the beach enables a reconfiguration of femininity and female-produced art into a rich, outward looking exploration of the self that enables Varda to reflect upon the specificity of her experiences while simultaneously eschewing narcissism and essentialism.

Beach-combing as method

This method, of sorting through assorted marginalia and filmic bric-a-brac to weave together a coherent narrative, borrows from Varda's own approach. Its value is at least two-fold: it establishes the way in which that which seems marginal or unimportant to our view of Varda can be brought to the foreground as originating, essential and necessary; and it also incorporates into the very form of this chapter on Varda processes and ideas she establishes as her preferred working methodology. Furthermore, this methodology echoes that of gleaners or beach-combers, key figures from Varda's latest two feature films, *Les Glaneurs et la glaneuse* (2000) and *Les Plages*, and both of whom search through fragments for objects that have been discarded (whether by accident or design) and that can potentially be re-tooled. The acts of beach-combing and gleaning meet when Varda films people gleaning oysters on the coast at Noirmoutier in a sequence from *Les Glaneurs et la glaneuse* which is worth discussing in some detail, bringing together as it does the two determining motifs of Varda's last decade of film-making.

The sequence announces our arrival at the coast by cutting from the now famous images of Varda using her hand to compose a shot in which she seems to capture the lorries ahead of her on the road she is filming through her car windscreen, to a beautiful shot, taken from a cliff-top, of a blue-grey sea that fills the frame. The camera tracks to a view of the headland with a curve of golden sand hugging the shore. A series of images then links this particular beach to its produce and the labour of beach-combing. We first see people dressed in yellow macs and wellingtons by a seaweed-covered causeway; next a tourist souvenir, in which a postcard image of the causeway is surrounded by transparent plastic, is held over boxes of oysters, so that we can see the oysters from behind the tourist object; then a close-up on oysters moving past us on a conveyer-belt. The music that accompanied the images of the lorries is replaced by a naturalistic sound-track of crashing waves and seagull cries, and Varda's voice-over explains that 'le passage de Gois qui mène à Noirmoutier est célèbre ainsi que ses huîtres' [the causeway that leads to Noirmoutier is famous, as are its oysters]; as the image shifts from the beach itself to the factory production-line, so we hear the faint hum of the conveyer belt and Varda continues: 'il y a deux occasions de glaner: après les grands tempêtes et quand il y a grande marée' [there are two opportunities for gleaning: after storms and during very low tide]. A factory worker, surrounded by the tools of the trade (massive thick rubber gloves, boxes of oysters), explains that during busy periods such as the festive season, they are too busy to collect all the oysters, and the film cuts back from the factory and its mechanical hum to the shore and its natural sounds. We see small clusters of people, with their buckets and spades, collecting oysters at the water's edge. The film cuts between the amateur gleaners and the professional 'oystréiculteurs', all of whom are engaged in the process of farming oysters. Varda combines interviews with thirteen people altogether, working either individually or in small groups, and gathers together (gleans?) a range of information about what exactly would constitute trespassing onto the oyster beds, or how many kilos of oysters taken would shade from gleaning into stealing. Rather than passing judgement on which of these myriad explanations is the correct one, Varda finishes the segment with a close-up on a bucket of oysters, these 'fruits de mer' which have just sustained such heated and contradictory debate and yet in and of themselves are simply an innocent object.

These innocent objects are, of course, embedded in a variety of circuits — commercial, aesthetic, sociological — which Varda's inquiry gently disentangles. As Ben Tyrer explains, the significance of this sequence is not to be found in the rather esoteric discussion of local oyster farming rules in Noirmoutier, but rather in how

> no two gleaners agree precisely on what the restrictions are [...] each gleaner follows their own particular logic and together they show how what is deemed waste by the owners (oysters knocked loose from their beds by the sea) can be considered useful [...] each gleaner is allowed to speak without anyone being considered 'right', each voice throughout *Les Glaneurs* is treated equally.[4]

In other words, this sequence underlines the polyphony and democracy of Varda's methods, and her desire to allow multiple points of view into the frame. Intriguingly however, Varda gives the final word of the sequence to a man who moves the subject on from questions of trespassing and quantities to that of quality. He claims that 'Ils remassent d'ailleurs de petits huitres qui se mangent pas parce qu'ils sont moulés avec la mer et après ils sont plein de sable, quoi. Ils vont au continent et les gens les mangent et après ils disent qu'ils sont malades' [They gather small inedible oysters that are filled with sand. They take them to the mainland and eat them, and then they're ill].

Whatever the validity of this specific claim, it points to a broader cultural truth about the beach and the sea discussed by Jean-Didier Urbain, that is to say it contains threats, menaces and dangers as much as possibilities of pleasure and fun. For Urbain, the history of the beach is one of a civilizing mission, in which 'aquatic, topophilic, large-scale leisure' is now the mass practice associated with this space. But, he asserts, older, more antiquated fears remain.[5] The shark erupting into peaceful waters, so powerfully exploited by Steven Spielberg in *Jaws* (1975), reminds us forcefully that the sea is not a vast heated bathing pool, but 'a giant pit, a menacing gulf'.[6] Furthermore, this more phobic and prudent relation to the sea is expressed in annual calls for caution and vigilance, and here we can find the link to Varda's acknowledgement of oysters' potential danger. According to Urbain, recent years have seen a growing obsession with contaminated shellfish, mussels and oysters in particular:

> One would think that the sea is always ready to trick us with its 'fruits' the way the witch tricked Snow White. There is an underlying layer of anxiety close to superstition here, denoting the marked persistence of an ocean phobia [...] From sharks to contaminated shellfish, from the beach to the table, we find the same anxiety toward what comes from the bottom of the sea — the same nightmare, too, which slips from rawness to cruelty. But after all, the word 'oyster' comes from the Greek *ostrakon*, 'shell', the root that gives us 'ostracism', referring to an attitude of hostility toward another person that leads to that person's banishment.[7]

The etymology brings us back to the persistence of questions of otherness in Varda's work. While the oysters are coveted to the extent they are gleaned in difficult and precarious circumstances, the very fact of working with them (whether legitimately or not) marks their gatherers as other to the mainstream of society, living on the geographical and/or economic margins. Placing a bucket of oysters into the centre of the frame, Varda suggests how the circulation of even luxury/desirable goods depends also on a more peripheral existence, hinting at the paradoxical centrality of the margin.

Rather as Varda's own practice asserts the paradoxical centrality of the margin, so here I seek to problematize a hierarchical approach to Varda's own work, placing her feature films into a far broader and more heterogeneous context that is understood as a polemical intervention into the socio-spatial logic of French (and by extension European/Western) society. As Phil Powrie explains, 'what matters in the films is not the centrality of the subject, but the subject's eccentricity [...] what is central is paradoxically what is always already off-center, marginal, centrifugal, ectopic and [...] heterotopic.'[8] Powrie links then Varda's privileging of the margin with a spatial politics that leads her films to the construction of a heterotopic space, a term he borrows from Michel Foucault. Powrie offers us a summary of the kind of places that could be considered heterotopias, that is to say locations that contest normative social relations, as spaces that are 'the marginal, the imaginary, the festive, the sacred'.[9] As the anthropological and cultural studies work on beachscapes by John Fiske, Rob Shields and Urbain demonstrates, the beach typifies all these categories, being a geographically peripheral and anthropologically liminal space set aside for visiting during holidays and festive periods. As Rob Shields explains, despite attempts to police behaviour on the beach, it remains a space of liminal and carnivalesque encounters 'based on the politics of pleasure and physical senses [...] The grotesque carnival bodies on the beach are thus temporarily outside of social norms and embarked on a liminal project, even if they are in sites commercialised and territorialised in such a way as to control or contain any outbreaks of liminality'.[10] The margin of transition between the safety of the land and the expanse of the sea, the beach is an open field for social innovation and renegotiation. Shields continues: '[T]he beach illustrates the extent of the cultural categorisation of geographic spaces and places. As opposed to being merely a topographic margin, the development of cultural marginality occurs only through a complex process of social activity and cultural work.'[11] The beach becomes then the site par excellence for Varda's spatial politics, as it crystallizes the way that the meanings of space are at once topographically and culturally inscribed, and it exists as a realizable, physically present space that opens out to otherness, festivity, magic, the sacred — as is beautifully illustrated in the sequence of *Les Plages* where Varda fulfils a childhood fantasy and installs a circus trapeze act on the beach.

Circuses and beaches: *Trapézistes et voltigeurs*

Signalling the significance of this sequence, and my first illustration of the importance of paying attention to her marginalia, Varda incorporates a short film — *Trapézistes et voltigeurs* — as a bonus on the Ciné-Tamaris DVD of *Les Plages*. As Ruth Cruickshank explains in relation to Varda's generous incorporation of an hour-long bonus film *Deux Ans après* onto the Ciné-Tamaris DVD of *Les Glaneurs*, Varda harnesses the new technology of the DVD and its different way of communicating to audiences in unusual ways. Rather than simply recycling waste footage, or offering commentary on existing footage (the two usual approaches to offering extra or supplementary material), Varda offers 'gifts' of new films that, nestled into the main attraction, cast new light on it and offer new approaches to it.[12] *Trapézistes et voltigeurs* traces links between the illusion of cinema and the illusion of the circus, as it reveals the work that goes on behind the scenes to enable the spectacular performances we witness. Varda incorporates interviews with Crevette, one of the trapeze artists, and Cecelia Rose, her producer on *Les Plages*. Both women discuss the processes that lie behind what we have seen. Crevette explains how she became a trapeze artist, and how circus performers have to carry all their equipment with them and be ready to install it in all locations (she even owns an HGV licence so she can drive all the material around); Cecelia Rose explains the complex process of obtaining funding for the film and managing the project, commenting in particular on the logistical and financial support provided by the Mairie de Paris as they provided sand from Paris-Plage for the installation of Plage Daguerre (and we see huge machines moving the sand into place, another glimpse of the practical and pragmatic underpinnings of the whimsy of the film). The film holds in tension a desire to show us the material supports of spectacle and allowing us simply to marvel at their beauty as if they have simply effortlessly appeared. In this way, *Trapézistes et voltigeurs* exists in a complex double relation to its originating film, *Les Plages*, working both to extend our pleasure in the wonderful sequence but also to reveal the labour behind it. Perhaps we could almost say it exists as a heterotopic space for the film, as it offers a non-binaristic relation to it, contesting and inversing but also shoring up our initial responses to the trapeze artists on the beach.

In the kind of playful coincidence in which Varda delights, Cecilia Rose has been a trapeze artist for pleasure for twenty years. She gives her interview on the trapeze, often hanging upside down, whereas in contrast Crevette simply talks to camera, unmade-up and in ordinary clothes, reversing their positions from their roles in the main film where Cecilia Rose is in a quotidian, relatively invisible role, and Crevette part of a daring and thrilling spectacle. Cecilia Rose also explains to us that the image of trapeze artists flying over the sea, one of the beach-set 'reveries' in the film, was difficult and expensive to obtain. They had to hire the equipment; pay the team of four trapeze artists; have their costumes made; and set up the entire set on the beach at Sète. As Varda specifically wanted images of flying bodies not simply 'en plein air' [outside] but 'sur fond de mer' [with the backdrop of the sea], 'il a fallu construire une tour de 10 mètres, pour que la Chef Op puisse les filmer dans le bon axe' [a 10-metre high tower had to be constructed so they could be filmed from the right angle]. We are shown still photographs of the crew in the tower filming, before Cecilia Rose concludes 'et voilà', and we cut back to magical images of flying bodies against the backdrop of the deep blue sea topped with cresting white foam and glinting in the sun. Varda then returns to Crevette, who recounts a recurring dream she has had, that she is a bird flying from tree to tree, escaping dangers. A dream she first had as a child, it came back to her when she learnt the trapeze, making her feel that 'c'est en moi, voilà' [it's just in me]. The film then returns to an image of the rigging and trapeze, now empty, the two trapezes swaying gently in the breeze, as the sunset casts pink-orange light into the sky. This image remains for five seconds, accompanied on the soundtrack by a simple, plaintive guitar and the waves crashing against the shore. The music, composed by Georges Delerue, was the opening music to Varda's 1958 film *Du côté de la côte*. This film, a highly personal and quirky account of the Riviera, drawing attention to its overcrowded beaches and bright red sunburned bodies as much as to its natural beauties — all the more striking considering that it was commissioned by the Riviera Tourist Office — is not referenced at all in *Les Plages*, despite the fact that it contains one of the most sustained investigations of beach culture in Varda's filmography. Instead, we find evidence of its existence here, tucked away on a bonus short film, suggestive again of how investigating Varda's work rewards a methodology which privileges gleaning and contingency. Both *Du côté de la côte* and *Trapézistes et voltigeurs* end on rather melancholy notes; the former argues that the Riviera coast is an 'Eden toc' [a false Eden] and that true paradise is to be found on the private gardens of the Riviera. The film finishes with several images of gates being shut in our face, as the gardens are kept empty of people. Similarly, *Trapézistes et voltigeurs* ends with the gentle swinging in the breeze of an empty trapeze. Both images are of a natural space — a garden, a beach — but also provide evidence of human intervention — the shutting iron gates, the trapeze swinging on its rigging. Yet there are no people in the frame, so the traces of their existence point to their past presence and their current absence, creating an undercurrent of melancholy, which chimes with the beach and its geography of absence/presence (with the shifting tides, the beach is a play of presence and absence of sea and land) but also, more precisely, with Varda's use of the beachscape to explore grief and loss in *Les Plages* and in her earlier art installation *Les Veuves de Noirmoutier* (discussed within *Les Plages* as well). In both these short films, Varda explores the beach as a site where people come to play, but equally suggests other resonances of absence, nostalgia and melancholy.

This duality is embodied in the way Varda emphasizes the vastness, expanse, and openness of the beachscape on the one hand, and its associations with home, intimacy and friendships on the other. In the opening pre-credit sequence of *Les Plages*, for example, Varda stresses this vastness and expansiveness through placing mirrors parallel to and perpendicular to the shore, so that the sea, sky and sand are re-reflected and opened up to each other into infinity in a dizzying *mise-en-abyme*.

FIG. 8.1. Mirrors stress the expanse of the sea (© Ciné-Tamaris)

Of course, such an exercise cannot but recall for us the significance of the mirror in Varda's work more generally.[13] Cléo obsessively watches herself in a mirror, and the beginning of *Cléo de 5 à 7* (1962) also features a *mise-en-abyme*, when Cléo's image is reflected by mirrors hanging opposite each other in the fortune teller's hallway. In this sequence, mirrors take Varda back to her childhood, as she informs us that one of them, a mirror on a heavy wooden wardrobe, reminds her of the furniture in her parents' home, and her mother's love of Schubert's *Unfinished Symphony*. As if we are able to enter into Varda's memories, we hear the swelling chords of *Unfinished Symphony* on the soundtrack, so that the past and the present, memory and cinema, Varda's subjective experiences and the objective presentation of the film become blended together. These memories, re-awakened at the beach, are of a childhood home, and her parents, even as we are in a location that emphasizes movement, travel and change.

Homes and Beaches: *La Grande Carte Postale* ou *Souvenir de Noirmoutier*

The coast is located at the very edge of the nation; Varda films beaches from Belgium, France and America, establishing their topographical, aesthetic and cultural similarities across arbitrary national divides. Furthermore, her investment in and sustained reflection on the significance of what Marie-Claire Barnet and Shirley Ann Jordan call the 'key open space of the beach' contrasts with the association within film and visual culture of femininity and art and film production by women with the enclosed (and potentially oppressive) intimacies of the home.[14] Rather, Varda conflates and confuses the home and the beach, such as when she installs a small beach in the rue Daguerre in Paris, the site of home and production office Ciné-Tamaris, for a section of *Les Plages*. This typically ludic installation brings her (largely female) production team outside, onto the street, an updating of Varda's insistence on the right of women to occupy the city street that one can trace back to *Cléo de 5 à 7*'s bold assertion of visibility of the female flâneuse. Here there is a new twist in that the city street itself is transformed, made simultaneously home and beach, a complex interweaving of different locations and meanings — inside/outside, home/office, city/beach — that refuses the long association of femininity with mystery, darkness and interiority.[15] In a fascinating interview recorded with Barnet and Jordan in 2006, when she was in the thick of the creative process that led to *Les Plages*, Varda muses on the very problem that she wants to make an autobiographical film that features beaches. Much of her life has indeed been spent in coastal locations — Belgium; Sète; Los Angeles; Noirmoutier; but 'then I'm stuck. Because I spend so much time in Paris. As for Paris-plages, I'm not sure that works well, so I have to invent something between the beaches, in other words, a home. Maybe beaches are out of homes, and homes are out of beaches'.[16] The solution that Varda finds in her film, to install a beach in rue Daguerre, the site of her home and office, resolves the issue through making the beach and the home the same space, confirming the way in which her representation of beaches breaks up the potentially solipsistic autobiographical exercise into a reaching-out toward and embracing of strangers, colleagues, friends, and family (as illustrated by the sheer volume of interlocutors in the film, from an anonymous Brazilian steel drum player in Avignon to such well-known film personalities as Harrison Ford and Chris Marker). It also speaks to the on-going desire in her work to explore the contradictory resonance of places as sites of both work and leisure, such as the contrast between the fishing community and the young married couple that structures *La Pointe Courte* (1956), although all the characters are in the same location.

The imbrication of home and beach, and the complex cinematic topography this opens up, where places are both personal and public, closed and open, intimate and communitarian, places of leisure and places of labour, is echoed in Varda's 2006 art installation *L'Île et Elle* held at the Fondation Cartier, the witty name-play of its title already hinting at a play between private intimacy (Varda and her relationship with her husband, Jacques Demy) and inviting visitors to explore the broader relations between a place and person (Noirmoutier and Varda). Varda navigates here between the beach as site of isolation, grief and mourning, and place of relaxation, pleasure and holidays. These two elements map onto an understanding of the beach as a highly private, intimate space, and as a place that functions as a place for community, friendship, festivity and fun. One element in the installation, *Grande Carte Postale ou Souvenir de Noirmoutier* offers a complex collage-image of the beach which gestures to its extremely personal significance for Varda, and her willingness/desire to acknowledge the beach as a contact zone and place of reaching out to Others. This is a large image that offers a stereotypical image of a blonde, naked pin-up girl lying on her stomach on the sand, a deliberately flat and cartoonish, picture-postcard image of a woman by the sea. However, the face of this contemporary siren is that of Varda's daughter, Rosalie. Varda added her face onto an anonymous body, inscribing this mythical/clichéd image of beach femininity into her personal universe. Furthermore, Varda literally adds depth to this image by having five rectangles that are in fact drawers to be activated by viewers with remote controls. Each drawer contains either a photograph or a video; and many of these images intimate death, such as that of the a cadaver of a drowned man, a gull covered in oil, or, again in a more personal and intimate register, Jacques Demy letting sand flow through his fingers — an image taken from *Jacquot de Nantes* (1990), Varda's moving account of Demy's childhood and premature death (from an AIDS-related illness we learn in *Les Plages*). But there is also footage of children mooning at the camera, playfully aligned with the pin-up's own bottom. 'Nous avons donc un entrelacement du personnel et du touristique, du plaisir et de la peine. C'est une célébration de l'été à la plage, avec sa promesse de corps ravissants et de jeux d'enfants, à laquelle vient se mêler la présence de la mort.'[17] [We have an imbrication of the personal and the touristic, of pleasure and pain. It's a celebration of summer at the beach, with its promise of ravishing bodies and children's games, which death comes and gets mixed up in.] The beach is coded in a way we would perhaps associate more instinctively with the home, as the site of family relations and intimate losses and grief, and simultaneously explored as a place of pleasure, cliché and myth. In the catalogue that accompanies the exhibition, Laure Adler offers a beautiful rumination on the meaning of the piece, in a piece that is worth quoting at length:

> Agnès, quand tu étais petite, as-tu joué à ce jeu dangereux et pervers où les petits enfants s'éloignaient des parents pour, tour à tour, creuser une tombe dans le sable, décider — généralement c'étaient les filles les plus courageuses — de s'y allonger et accepter que tous les autres vous recouvrent de sable? [...] Ta plage — c'est bien ta plage — je sais qu'elle existe et qu'elle appartient à tout le monde. Tu n'es pas du genre à aimer les choses privées, chères, c'est donc une plage communale, oui, mais c'est tout de même la tienne.[18]
>
> [Agnès, when you were little, did you play that dangerous perverse game where the children ran away from their parents one by one in order to dig a grave in the sand? And then did you decide — it was usually the bravest girls — to lie down in and let the others cover you in sand? [...] Your beach — it's definitely your beach — it exists and it belongs to everybody. You're not the type to like private, expensive things, so it's a communal beach, but it's definitely your beach too.]

Adler's account takes Conway's appreciation of how Varda's beach interlaces play and pain, and sees the intimations of death and burial in the children's game of burying each other under sand. That which seems most far from death — childhood on the beach — is shown here in fact to share uncannily similar rituals (that, Adler goes on to suggest, are both personal to Varda's world view but also have a greater, possibly universal, resonance).[19] This understanding informs a complex sequence in

Les Plages, when Varda decides to reconstruct her childhood games of selling paper flowers and shells on the beach. Two young girls in replicas of period swimming costumes play on the beach. The girls are busy arranging their paper flowers when Varda strides into the frame and stands alongside them, thus revealing rather than concealing the artificial staginess of the historical reconstruction and freely 'foregrounding memory as a site of cinematic play'.[20] As the girls play their games of exchanging flowers for shells, Varda ruminates to the camera about what exactly the purpose of this reconstruction might be. The film then cuts and shows us Varda sitting alongside the girls, all three of them dangling their legs into a large hole dug in the sand. We see a delightful image of the girls and Varda chatting together, and off-camera an unidentified male voice asks Varda, 'Est-ce que tu doutais que soixante-dix ans plus tard tu feras une installation avec des fleurs en papier crépon et des coquillages?' [Did you ever imagine then that 70 years later you would do an installation with crepe paper flowers and shells?]. Varda replies, 'est-ce que t'es obligé de me rappeler l'âge que j'ai?' [do you have to remind me how old I am]? The film cuts to a video image of a kneeling Varda surrounded by flowers and shells, footage from 2006 of Varda's installation *Le Tombeau de Zgougou*, an elaborate homage to her beloved cat (an installation moreover that forms part of *Île et Elle*). The film later shows us Varda scattering flowers in memoriam; firstly, in front of photographs in a chapel in Avignon, at the moment of a retrospective of her work for the theatre festival there; secondly in front of her husband's grave. Flowers are sold on the seashore by Varda as a young girl; scattered in an art installation; placed on her husband's grave. Her film does not ask us to choose between emotion and work, the personal grief and the public artist, but insists absolutely on their co-existence. Is the scattering of flowers by Demy's gravestone an intimate act of love performed by a grieving wife? Is it an artistic gesture that works to weave the loss of Demy into the weft of Varda's film? The answer is that it is both. It is the beach where all of these issues converge, where work and art, love and loss, are to be found and re-found. In a similar vein, *La Grande Carte Postale*'s beautiful woman lying on the sand is an anonymous embodiment of Venus, and also Varda's daughter, bringing together the familial and the mythical into one frame.

Mythologies, vous me faites rêver [Myths make me dream]: *Ulysse*

As Bernard Bastide argues, Greek mythology is a hidden structural element in many of Varda's films. He traces the presence of characters such as Eros, Thanatos, Aphrodite, and Ariane across her films, so that her films come to form 'un creuset imaginare' [an imaginary melting pot] of myth.[21] Several of her films make use of the figure of Venus/Aphrodite, the goddess of love borne ashore from the white foam of her birth on a scallop shell, bringing together Varda's interest in mythology, the beach, and the representation of women in art. Mona in *Sans toit ni loi* (1985) emerges from the sea at the start of her journey. The dominant colour palette is blue and gold, and Mona is naked, glistening, her long dark hair billowing around her head as she embodies a contemporary Venus. The film follows her trajectory from the sea to the earth as she succumbs to Dionysian rituals and is stained by lie de vin during the Fête des Paillaisses held on Ash Wednesday in Cournonterral, a small village in the Hérault. Death follows Mona — the trees are dying of cancer; she meets a prostitute outside a cemetery; she falls, frozen, into a ditch, and in rigor mortis takes on an attitude similar to that of a crucifixion. Cléo's similar struggle with death also sees her as a possible incarnation of Venus. Given the urban setting of the film, the reference is less explicit than that of Mona, but Bastide suggests that the ring she wears, of a toad and pearl, offers a clue that we should see her as a reincarnation of an artistic representation of Venus. Phyrné, a fourth-century Greek courtesan, whose name means toad (allegedly a reference to her sallow complexion) was of such legendary beauty that she was used as the model by the sculptor Praxiteles for his statue of Aphrodite. The reference creates complex links between female beauty, its representation in art, and prostitution, suggesting the awkward parallels between women as sex *and* art objects.

As with Mona, Varda associates Cléo with the mythical goddess of love, but here she also references this myth's representation in art, suggesting that this structural use of myth links her to an artistic heritage and incorporates her films into a broader visual culture history, one that depends on using myth as an alibi for (female) nudity (a reference made explicit in the complex tableau vivant that opens *Jane B par Agnès V.* (1988), when Jane Birkin poses as a composite of Titian's Venus d'Urbino (1538) and Goya's Mayas, clothed and naked). *Nausicaa* (1970), a less well-known film, also reflects on the interplay between cinema, painting, myth, and sex, and here places it into a personal register, as it features a young woman, Agnès, with a Greek father, studying history of art at the Louvre, a clearly autobiographical reference. Nausicaa is a character from the Odyssey — intriguingly, given Varda's identification with her in this film, a character who is sometimes considered to be the person who is actually telling the fantastical stories of Ulysses' voyage — and whose love for him was unrequited. *Les Plages* incorporates a short scene from this film, where Agnès/France Dougnac sits on the quais of the Seine, sunning herself as she reads a book on art history. A young Gérard Depardieu, somewhat anticipating his demeanour and character in *Les Valseuses* (Blier, 1974), comes and steals her books. As Agnès protests, he mockingly replies: 'les jeunes veulent la Révolution mais dès qu'on s'attaque à leur petite possession...' [young people want Revolution but as soon as their own possessions are attacked...]. Clearly, it's a playful and tongue-in-cheek reference but nevertheless Varda points here to the educational and cultural capital needed to appreciate the role myth plays in art and film, but also the physical powerlessness of the young woman in the face of the man's actions.

Bastide makes clear how, for Varda, myth is not only something she has acquired from museums and books, vital though they are, but that it also forms part of an instinctual response to landscapes, especially beaches, nurtured by her family background. 'Un père grec, la lecture d'Odyssée lors d'une enfance Sétoise, un premier film inondé de lumière où évoluent deux personnes hiératiques semblables à des statues hellènes — Varda semble ne jamais départir de sa 'grécitude', au point où son œuvre est parsemée de références à ses origines familiales et culturelles — Uncle Yanco, Nausicaa, Eros, Thanatos, Ulysse, Aphrodite, Dionysius, Ariane.'[22] [With a Greek father, reading the Odyssey during a childhood in Sète, a first film flooded with light with two characters who resemble Hellenic statues, Varda seems never to have abandoned her 'Greekness', to the extent that her work is scattered with references to her familial and cultural origins — Uncle Yanco, Nausicaa, Eros, Thanatos, Ulysses, Aphrodite, Dionysius, Ariadne].

The complex meeting of personal history and myth is explored by Varda in her 1982 film *Ulysse*. It is a short film inspired by a photograph of a naked man with his back to the camera standing at the shore to the left, a small boy in the middle of the frame looking up at the camera, and a dead goat, its eyes wide open, balancing the composition at the bottom right. They are on a rock-strewn beach near Calais. The photograph was taken by Varda in 1954. The title of the film clearly links this beach to the mythical shores haunted by Ulysses on his ten-year voyage to find his home, but it also the name of the young boy in the photograph who lived in the same Parisian courtyard as Varda in the 1950s. The 1982 film undertakes a sustained investigation of the meanings of the photograph, and the memories, opinions and symbolic resonance of its subjects (man, boy, goat), as I discuss elsewhere.[23] As Alison Smith explains, the mythological reference of the boy's name, which becomes the title of the film, seems to take us further from, rather than closer to, any kind of intrinsic, singular meaning the photograph might hold. 'All it does is raise more questions and possibilities.'[24] The title and its provocative naming of a myth only adds to the photograph's range of references, defying any attempt for us to take a definitive reading of its meaning, and resisting the reduction of the myth to cliché. Myth, then, is very important to Varda's world: it multiplies meanings, suggests hidden resonances, fragments stories, and simultaneously conjures up personal biography and the most universal of themes. Furthermore, it does all of this within site of the shore, as the most important recurrent mythological characters in her films come from the sea (Aphrodite/Venus) or wash up on several diverse shores (Odysseus/Ulysses).

Varda does not make any explicit reference to *Ulysse* in *Les Plages* — surprisingly given the importance of the beach to the composition of the photograph. She does, however, provide a very brief gloss on it that can be picked up if one is familiar with the earlier film. As Andrée Vilar recites the opening stanza of Paul Valéry's 'Le Cimitière marin'/ 'The Graveyard by the sea' (a poem set in Sète), 'la mer, la mer toujours recommencée' [the sea, the sea, the sea, renewed forever], we cut to a complex image which digitally superimposes a bright blue, moving sea over the space where the sea would have been in Varda's black-and-white photograph of the man, the boy and the goat. Varda tells us in voice-over that 'tout homme qui regarde la mer est un Ulysse qu n'a pas toujours envie de revenir à la maison [any man who gazes at the sea is a Ulysses who doesn't always want to go home.] The camera moves closer in to the photograph, so we just see a cropped image of the small boy surrounded by pebbles, and Varda says, 'tous les garcons que j'aime, et tous les hommes qui regardent la mer, s'appellent Ulysse' [and all the boys that I love, and all men who gaze at the sea, are called Ulysses]. We then cut back to the bright blue sea of the first image, but this image is now entirely a cinematic colour image, and the naked man is part of this image (the goat and the child have gone). Varda runs up to him, carrying a blanket to cover him; it flaps in the wind and

FIG. 8.2. Varda revisits the figure of Ulysees (© Ciné-Tamaris)

Varda's run is speeded up, giving this sequence a comic feel. The film makes no further reference to, or attempt to explain, this really rather mysterious sequence, perhaps because Varda has already examined the photograph so thoroughly in her 1982 film.

However, what it does do is bring Varda onto the beach and into contact with a man she tells us is Ulysses — 'Tout homme qui regarde la mer est un Ulysse.' In his interpretation of the film from 1991, Bastide states that 'Ulysse le modèle assis sur la grève se metamorphose en héros mythologique rêvant à la belle Penelope' [the model Ulysses sitting on the shore changes into the mythological hero dreaming of his beautiful Penelope].[25] In contrast, in 2008, it is Varda who dreams of Ulysses. As she runs toward him with a blanket, Varda enacts the role of Penelope, waiting patiently on the beach for her lover to return. Even as the film acknowledges that Jacques Demy cannot return to her, Varda has shown how, by assuming the role of Penelope — weaving together the different strands of her films, photographs, art works — she can reanimate memory. Moving away from the gendered tale of Homer, where our concentration is on the man's exciting and adventurous sea voyage, Varda shows us the woman waiting on the beach, exploring the world through her imagination, weaving together different stories from the fabric that is available to her and celebrating life — 'je me souviens pendant que je vis' [while I'm alive, I remember].

Bibliography

Laure Adler, 'La Grande Carte Postale ou Souvenir de Noirmoutier', *L'Île et Elle: Regards sur l'exposition* (Paris/Arles: Fondation Cartier/Actes Sud, 2006)
Marie-Claire Barnet and Shirley Jordan, 'Interviews with Agnès Varda and Valérie Mréjen', *L'Esprit Créateur* [special edition Watch this Space: Women's Conceptualisations of Space in Contemporary French Film and Visual Art], 51:1 (Spring 2011)
Bernard Bastide, 'Mythologies, vous me faites rêver: ou mythes cachés, mythes dévoilés dans l'œuvre de Varda', *Agnès Varda: Etudes cinématographiques* ed. by Michel Estève (Paris: Minard, 1991), pp. 179–86
Raymond Bellour, 'Varda où l'art contemporain', *Trafic* 69 (Spring 2009), 16–19
Dominique Bluher, 'La miroitière: A propos de quelques films et installations d'Agnès Varda', *Agnès Varda: Le Cinéma et au-delà*, ed. by Antony Fiant, Roxane Hamery and Eric Thouvenel (Rennes: Presses Universitaires de Rennes, 2009), pp. 177–85
Jenny Chamarette, 'Spectral bodies, temporalised spaces: Agnès Varda's motile gestures of mourning and memorial', *Image & Narrative*, 12:2 (2011), 31–49
Kelley Conway, 'L'Île et Elle: lieu, temps, écran, récit', *Agnès Varda: Le Cinéma et au-delà*, ed. by Antony Fiant, Roxane Hamery and Eric Thouvenel (Rennes: Presses Universitaires de Rennes, 2009), pp. 209–18
——'Varda at work: *Les Plages d'Agnès*', *Studies in French Cinema*, 10 (2010), 110–19
Sarah Cooper, 'Looking Back, Looking Onwards: Selflessness, Ethics and French Documentary', *Studies in French Cinema*, 10 (2010), 57–68
Ruth Cruickshank, 'The Work of Art in the Age of Global Consumption', *L'Esprit Créateur*, 47:3 (Fall 2007), 119–32
Antony Fiant, Roxane Hamery and Eric Thouvanel, 'Avant-propos', *Agnès Varda: Le Cinéma et au-delà*, ed. by Antony Fiant, Roxane Hamery and Eric Thouvenel (Rennes: Presses Universitaires de Rennes, 2009), pp. 7–11
Fiona Handyside, *Cinema at the Shore: The Beach in French Cinema* (Bern: Peter Lang, 2014)
Stanley Kaufmann, 'Selves', *The New Republic* (July 2009), 22
Kristi McKim, *Love in the Time of Cinema* (London: Palgrave, 2011)
Sophie Mayer, 'Portrait of the Artist', *Sight and Sound* 19:10 (2009), 12–14
Phil Powrie, 'Heterotopic Spaces and Nomadic Gazes in Varda: From *Cléo de 5 à 7* to *Les Glaneurs et la glaneuse*', *L'Esprit Createur* [special edition Watch this Space: Women's Conceptualisations of Space in Contemporary French Film and Visual Art], 51:1 (2011), 68–82
Cecilia Sayad, *Performing Authorship: Self-inscription and corporeality in the cinema* (London: I.B. Tauris, 2013)
Rob Shields, *Places on the Margin: Alternative Geographies of Modernity* (London: Routledge Chapman and Hall, 1992)
Alison Smith, *Agnès Varda* (Manchester: Manchester University Press)
Ben Tyrer, 'Digression and Return: Aesthetics and Politics in Agnès Varda's *Les Glaneurs et la glaneuse*', *Studies in French Cinema*, 9 (2009), 161–76
Jean-Didier Urbain, *At the Beach*, trans. by Catherine Porter (Minneapolis: University of Minnesota Press, 2003)
Emma Wilson, *Love, Mortality and the Moving Image* (London: Palgrave, 2012)

Notes to Chapter 8

1. These articles are Sarah Cooper, 'Looking Back, Looking Onwards: Selflessness, Ethics and French Documentary', *Studies in French Cinema*, 10 (2010), 57–68, and Kelley Conway, 'Varda at work: *Les Plages d'Agnès*', *Studies in French Cinema*, 10 (2010), 110–19.

2. Raymond Bellour, 'Varda où l'art contemporain', *Trafic*, 69 (Spring 2009), 16–19; Stanley Kaufmann, 'Selves', *The New Republic* (July 2009), 22; Sophie Mayer, 'Portrait of the Artist', *Sight and Sound*, 19:10 (2009), 12–14; Cecilia Sayed, *Performing Authorship: Self-inscription and corporeality in the cinema* (London: I. B. Tauris, 2013); Jenny Chamarette, 'Spectral bodies, temporalised spaces: Agnès Varda's motile gestures of mourning and memorial', *Image & Narrative*, 12:2 (2011), 31–49 ; Kristi McKim, *Love in the Time of Cinema* (London: Palgrave, 2011) ; Emma Wilson, *Love, Mortality and the Moving Image* (London: Palgrave, 2012) .
3. Fiona Handyside, *Cinema at the Shore: The Beach in French Cinema* (Bern: Peter Lang, 2014).
4. Ben Tyrer, 'Digression and Return: Aesthetics and Politics in Agnès Varda's *Les Glaneurs et la glaneuse*', *Studies in French Cinema*, 9, (2009), 161–76 (p. 170).
5. Jean-Didier Urbain, *At the Beach*, trans. by Catherine Porter (Minneapolis: University of Minnesota Press, 2003), p. 33.
6. Urbain, p. 283.
7. Urbain, pp. 283–84.
8. Phil Powrie, 'Heterotopic Spaces and Nomadic Gazes in Varda: From *Cléo de 5 à 7* to *Les Glaneurs et la glaneuse*', *L'Esprit Createur* [special edition Watch this Space: Women's Conceptualisations of Space in Contemporary French Film and Visual Art], 51:1 (2011), 68–82.
9. Phil Powrie, 'Heterotopic spaces', 70.
10. Rob Shields, *Places on the Margin: Alternative Geographies of Modernity* (London: Routledge Chapman and Hall, 1992), p. 95.
11. Shields, p. 4.
12. Ruth Cruickshank, 'The Work of Art in the Age of Global Consumption', *L'Esprit Créateur* 47:3 (Fall 2007), 119–32. In a similar vein, Antony Fiant, Roxane Hamery and Eric Thouvanel argue that in 'son travail autour de l'exploitation DVD de ses films [...] elle est l'une des rares à considérer aujourd'hui comme travail de création à part entière et non comme démarche purement commercial. On peut y voir une manière de faire dialoguer les/ses images par les rencontres occasionnées entre les films — notamment les longs métrages et les courts proposés en boni qui en soulignent la complémentarité — et d'impliquer le spectateur dans un réseau de correspondances' [in her work on the DVD version of her films, she is one of the few people to see this as a work in its own right and not a purely commercial exercise. She brings her images into dialogue by drawing films together — notably feature films and shorts which are included as bonus in order to underline their complementary natures — and implies the viewer in a network of correspondences]. 'Avant-propos', *Agnès Varda: Le Cinéma et au-delà*, ed. by Antony Fiant, Roxane Hamery and Eric Thouvenel (Rennes: Presses Universitaires de Rennes, 2009), pp. 7–11 (p. 9).
13. For an excellent general account of mirrors in Varda's films, see Dominique Bluher, 'La miroitière: A propos de quelques films et installations d'Agnès Varda', *Agnès Varda: Le Cinéma et au-delà*, pp. 177–85.
14. Marie-Claire Barnet and Shirley Ann Jordan, 'Introduction', *L'Esprit Créateur* [special edition Watch this Space: Women's Conceptualisations of Space in Contemporary French Film and Visual Art], 51:1 (Spring 2011), 4.
15. Furthermore, as Cecilia Sayad points out, the film's line, 'si on m'ouvre, on trouvera une plage', part of Varda's opening dialogue as she walks backwards along a beach and reproduced in the beautiful booklet that accompanies the DVD and which I have used as this chapter's epigraph, aligns a sense that the film will open us to Varda with the openness of the beach. An examination of the self and of the beach are both promised as exercises in transparency (a posture the film considerably complicates and plays with). *Performing Authorship*, pp. 45–46.
16. Marie-Claire Barnet and Shirley Jordan, 'Interviews with Agnès Varda and Valérie Mréjen', *L'Esprit Créateur* [special edition Watch this Space: Women's Conceptualisations of Space in Contemporary French Film and Visual Art], 51:1 (Spring 2011), 186.
17. Kelley Conway, 'L'Île et Elle: lieu, temps, écran, récit', *Agnès Varda: Le Cinéma et au-delà*, pp. 209–18 (p. 211).
18. Laure Adler, 'La Grande Carte Postale ou Souvenir de Noirmoutier', *Île et Elle: Regards sur l'exposition* (Paris/Arles: Fondation Cartier/Actes Sud, 2006), p. 26.
19. This association of childhood play on the beach and death can also be found in François Ozon's *Le Temps qui reste* (2005).

20. Kristi McKim, *Love in the Time of Cinema,* p. 96.
21. Bernard Bastide, 'Mythologies, vous me faites rêver: ou mythes cachés, mythes dévoilés dans l'œuvre de Varda', *Agnès Varda: Etudes cinématographiques* ed. by Michel Estève (Paris: Minard, 1991), pp. 179–86.
22. Bernard Bastide, 'Mythologies, vous me faites rêver', p. 180.
23. Fiona Handyside, *Cinema at the Shore*, pp. 177–84.
24. Alison Smith, *Agnès Varda* (Manchester: Manchester University Press), p. 48.
25. Bernard Bastide, 'Mythologies, vous me faites rêver', p. 184.

CHAPTER 9

Still Varda: Photographs and Photography in Agnès Varda's Late Work

Shirley Jordan

Agnès Varda's installation exhibition *L'Île et Elle* [*The Island and Her*][1] (Fondation Cartier, Paris, 2006) included two companion studies based on a colour photograph of the same Noirmoutier seascape.[2] Coldly monochrome, with soft gradations of grey and silver bands marking off sea, sky and beach, the photograph is illuminated by shafts of light reflected on the water and the work of the waves can be seen in the rippled sand. The studies occupied walls at right angles to each other, setting up a dialogue about modes of visual representation. With the same determination as the mid-nineteenth-century marine photographer Gustave Le Gray, whose technical accomplishment and palette they evoke, both focus on the challenge of freezing this restless motif. The larger study, *La Mer immense* [*The Immense Sea*] (2003) is a double digital image whose huge size (3.40m × 6.0m) evokes the sea's resistance to containment. Here a version of the seascape printed onto canvas is hung on top of a slightly larger one, printed on polyester paper and pasted upon the wall, its flatness evoking a screen and alluding to projected images. This pasting thus constitutes a frame or margin of the same motif. *La petite mer immense* [*The Little Immense Sea*] (2003) (0.34m × 0.60m), a tiny echo of its companion, is a silver print from the same digital file, carefully mounted and presented inside the kind of heavily ornate, status-endowing frame that connotes a fine art image. A playful reminder that photography has found its way to the cutting edge of contemporary art, this image poses in condensed form the array of questions currently asked by critics about the status of photography and its overlapping with, or usurpation of, the functions of painting.[3] Both seascapes defy categorization. Accompanied in the installation by the murmur of the sea (the looped soundtrack of the nearby triple-screen video piece *Triptyque de Noirmoutier* [*Noirmoutier Triptych*] (2004–5)) whose allusion to motion and time further counterbalanced their immobility, the pair declined the seascape in formats which conjured and unsettled the regimes of the photographic, the cinematic and the painterly. Between them, they stood as sharp illustrations of how Varda, often referred to as the *grand-mère de la Nouvelle Vague* [grandmother of the New-Wave] seeks to release the still image from its moorings.

The title of this chapter is a deliberate misnomer, for little in Varda is ever truly still: witness the slowly sprouting potatoes of her *Patatutopia* installation,[4] surely one of the most intelligent of recent dialogues with the genre of still life. My subject is how Varda will let neither the still nor the moving be. Intent on the temporal and spatial expansion of the still image, she fragments it, frays it and teases it into movement; intent on the moment, she slows or halts what moves. While this aspect of Varda's work is not new, it is increasingly foregrounded as she experiments with innovative installation formats and devices, engages in intermedial adventures in what we might call 'curating' the world, and focuses ever more intensively on temporality. An explicit purpose of recent exhibitions such as *Agnès Varda — Y'a pas que la mer* [*Agnès Varda — Beyond the Sea*] (Musée Paul Valéry, Sète, 2011–12) or *Triptyques atypiques* [*Atypical Triptychs*] (Galerie Nathalie Obadia, Paris, 2014) was to further explore this preoccupation with the mobile and the still; not, I would argue, as part of what Raymond Bellour calls a 'querelle des dispositifs' ['quarrel of devices'][5] but rather in a spirit of cooperation, an investigative coaxing of each away from what appears intrinsic to it.[6] Focussing especially on photography, this chapter examines some of the things that are at stake in the aesthetic of interruption which I see as the hallmark of Varda's late period.

The ongoing moment

While Varda began her career as a photographer, she has taken few 'stand-alone' photographs in recent years, insisting instead on inserting them into a variety of mobile contexts. In this section I explore how she is increasingly concerned less with what Henri Cartier-Bresson famously referred to as the 'decisive moment' in photography than with what Geoff Dyer has called the 'ongoing moment', and with opening photographs up afresh to time.[7] In the first of her 2011 five-episode television series for ARTE, *Agnès de ci de là Varda* [*Agnès Here and There Varda*] which charts her connections with the contemporary art world, Varda lingers over numerous stills: for instance, a found family photograph from the era of the First World War taken by a soldier on leave. She notes how the technological requirements of the day involved complete stillness and enjoys seeing this confirmed by the smudge — a kind of ectoplasm — left by a woman who moved during the lengthy exposure. It is precisely this indicator of temporality, this interruption of the still that makes Varda value the photograph. Similarly, she singles out a self-morphing video portrait by her artist friend Christian Boltanski which defies portraiture's temporality by reversing time and returning the adult artist back to childhood. Elsewhere in her extended musings she produces what amounts to a visual essay — 'une digression qui me tient à cœur' ['a digression on a subject close to my heart'] — on slippages between still and moving images.[8] Arriving in Portugal during a downpour, she films the streets through the rain-smeared car window. Later, on the cutting table, she takes pleasure in freezing the figures that cross the road at the traffic lights as they leap (balletically in the freeze frame) from road to pavement or pavement to road, umbrellas aloft, legs outstretched, held above the stream of gushing water. The suspended body appeals to Varda: her 1955 photograph of an exuberantly leaping Alexander Calder — maker of mobiles — springs to mind (surely a forebear of John Swannell's leaping John Gielgud (1991)). A yet more irresistible connection is struck

FIG. 9.1. Unpicking the decisive moment.
Agnès de ci de là Varda [*Agnès Here and There Varda*] © 2011 ciné-tamaris

up with Cartier-Bresson's famous photograph of a man making a wide leap above a puddle in a water-logged yard behind the Gare Saint-Lazare, his body mirrored in the reflection beneath him (1932). Varda's new stills become, by association with this photograph, mini-meditations on the decisive moment. Tellingly, she momentarily offers us a cunning triptych by splicing Cartier-Bresson's photograph into the centre of her own film still, supplanting her leaping figure with his and creating an original art work. Thus a supremely self-referential exemplar of analogue photography — one in which physical and temporal suspension are redoubled and caught in dialogue about their own medium — is re-contextualized among the new spaces, technologies and formats of Varda's art practices. The triptych (with a still image in its centre panel) has indeed become emblematic of her late period, favoured precisely for its ready incorporation of diversity, of dialogue between still and moving images and of technical innovation.[9]

Varda's essay goes on to highlight some of her own early decisive moments: a man descending a mountain of salt, his feet precisely level with an adjacent roof; a barefoot woman in a Lisbon street, caught in mid-stride beneath a poster of Sophia Loren.[10] She reminds us too of the syncopated five-per-second stills of Benny Moré which she propelled into rhythmic sequence in *Salut les Cubains* [*Hi Cubans*] (1963), a photo-documentary which is perhaps one of the clearest harbingers of her recent interweaving of the moving and the still. I want now to contrast two further photographs featured in Varda's essay, both of which give rise to determined exercises in temporal expansion some years after they were taken. The first has compelling intellectual appeal, the second a powerful affective draw. In each case I am interested in what happens when Varda makes of the still an ongoing moment.

The first photograph was taken by Varda in Marseille in 1956 at Le Corbusier's

Fig. 9.2. *Les Gens de la terrasse* [*The People on the Terrace*] © agnès-varda

Cité Radieuse. It features six people dispersed among the setting's clean architectural lines: a mother, father and toddler in the right-hand foreground; a photographer with a box camera who is about to take (or has just taken) their portrait; and two background figures, a woman and man, the former beginning to climb the steps of a stage-like construction that creates a curiously theatrical space within the image field, the latter sauntering upon it. Not only does this impromptu shot exemplify the fascination of street photography, capturing individuals in mid-action and appealing for supplementary narrative,[11] it is also sharply self-referential, containing a photographer setting up her shot and also what seem to be two cuts into space-time, with the inner stage-like space marking off its own discrete field (reminding us in turn of the edges and the materiality of the larger image). The trio of figures animating the inner field (the strolling man, the climbing woman and the photographer who anchors the whole) express an idea of circularity, as if they were caught in an eternal loop walking into and out of the central composition.

So inexhaustible is the fascination of this photograph that Varda devises a brief sketch, *Les Gens de la terrasse* [*The People on the Terrace*] (2007) to supplement and animate it, stretching it out within a fictional chain of causality to imagine both the moments before the shutter closed and something of the post-snap story. Here the individuals 'unwittingly' edging into place for the click of the shutter are imagined as an extended family group gathered for a reunion, the meticulously choreographed scenario proposing one further photograph as the man in the background descends the steps to join his 'daughter' (the mother of the infant) for another portrait. Varda's ARTE programme shows not only the sketch but the labour involved in indulging her fantasy (reconstructing the scene in Sète; creating a replica of the stage-like edifice; ensuring 1950s period detail). This kind of playful reanimation is a staple device in Varda's epic autobiographical compilation *Les Plages d'Agnès* [*The Beaches of*

Agnès] (2008) where memory work involves an elaborate aesthetic of expanding and unravelling frozen moments. This photograph's opening to time is, however, a kind of purely intellectual play, a formal experiment belonging with inventions such as Varda's recent *Portraits brisés* [*Shattered Portraits*].[12] By contrast, the exploration of our second photograph as an ongoing moment relates to another impulse that receives concentrated expression in *Les Plages d'Agnès* and one which is followed through in the remainder of this chapter: that of sharing photographs (as well as other traces of the past) in processes involving emotion, dialogue and enhanced attentiveness to materiality and touch.

Varda's return to the photograph entitled *Ulysse* [*Ulysses*], taken in May 1954 at St Aubin sur Mer, gives rise to a 22-minute-long film (*Ulysse*, 1982) which aims to 'situer cette image dans ma vie et dans son époque' ['situate this image in my life and in its era'].[13] If we accept Laura Marks's powerful metaphor of the 'skin' of the moving image,[14] we might argue that the photograph is a scar; a thickening in the skin of time, memory and emotion. *Ulysse* prompts Varda to scratch at it as if to open it up in what becomes an 'enquête presque douloureuse' ['almost painful investigation'].[15] Such an obsession is reminiscent of Roland Barthes's response to selected photographs, yet where Barthes is interested only in his own intense responses Varda, characteristically, is interested in eliciting the responses of others and using the image to rekindle shared memory. The film records her attempts to 'connect' as she gathers the original participants and interrogates them about what the photograph means to them now.

The photograph in question is an enigmatic, almost mythical image of three figures on a beach. It is arranged in a powerful diagonal from top left (where a naked man stands looking out to sea) to bottom right (where a dead goat lies on the pebbles, a stake and tether still attached to its leg). Beside the man a naked boy sits awkwardly, looking to camera. Varda's film will not let this photograph be still. It unsettles it, zooming in on the goat, the man or the boy; reconfiguring, re-cropping, duplicating and setting up collages in ceaselessly renewed compositions. Varda probes the origins of the image and the context (both personal and socio-historical) of its making. Most importantly, she sets the photograph in circulation and requests that others respond to it; that they touch and are touched by it. First Varda approaches the man from the photograph, Fouli Ellia, visiting him in his office. She has asked him to undress for the conversation. She offers him the photograph to touch and explore along with a clutch of pebbles, which he discards (see Fig. 9.3). There ensues an encounter with the image that amounts to a memory test: Ellia remembers the boy, his own impatience to put his clothes back on and the type of photograph Varda was making at the time, but little else. Further photographs from the period, including portraits of Ellia, exchange hands. He recalls items such as sweaters and shoes but, to Varda's consternation, not who he was: 'Je ne me souviens pas de cette personne-là'; 'Je ne veux pas; je ne veux pas me souvenir' ['I don't remember that person'; 'I don't want to; I don't want to remember'].

The child in the photograph, now owner of a book shop in Paris, is still less responsive to Varda's exercise in photobiography. We are shown portraits of the boy and his parents, Spanish political refugees who shared Varda's courtyard in the

Fig. 9.3. Fouli Elia untouched by Varda's photograph. *Ulysse* [*Ulysses*] © agnès-varda

rue Daguerre, and we are brought through the tenderness and intimacy of these photographs to feel Varda's love for them. This affect is still vivid for Varda and she offers it to us. But for the adult Ulysse this ongoing moment is problematic. He stands awkwardly in his shop, responds minimally to Varda (who remains off camera) and looks haplessly at the photograph, of which he claims no memory. Varda hands him a Matisse-like painting that as a little boy he had produced in response to the photograph, evidence to her of the impact both the image and the event of its making had had on him. Again, he cannot recognize it. Disappointed at the adult's unresponsive reaction to vestiges of his childhood, Varda reproaches him: 'tu n'y crois pas, tu n'en veux pas!' ['you don't believe in it, you don't want it!']. The most emotionally present in this film is the boy's mother who hovers behind her adult son as he gazes at the photograph and later weeps as she recalls his frailness and her fears for his health at the time. The scrambling of the past and present which Varda seeks to provoke around this photograph brings disappointing results. In stubborn and somewhat bathetic literal-mindedness (she must open the moment to all who figure in her photograph) Varda finally presents it to a goat, which chews and then abandons it, as indifferent as were Ellia and Ulysse. Finally, Varda hands both photograph and painting over to a group of children, creative strangers with no initial investment in the images and who pass them around with great interest (they observe that of the two, the photograph is more 'real', 'human' and 'truthful'). Ultimately what strikes us as we watch Varda's attempt to make of this still image an ongoing moment is the way in which photographs are touched, held and shared.

In her book *Touching Photographs*, Margaret Olin explores how the difficulty of disentangling touch and sight has played an important role in the phenomenological thinking that has helped form our appreciation of photography.[16] She speaks of the many ways in which touch remains associated with the photographic image, both through the residual interconnectedness of touch and vision, and through the materiality of photographs themselves. Further, her study investigates gatherings around photographs and the ways in which photographs 'participate in and create relationships and communities'.[17] Such ideas are useful for considering Varda's concern with community, recorded and also brought about in her late work not only by shared visual experience but by enhanced attentiveness to materiality and the interconnected senses. They are playfully at work in her triptych *Cinq bacheliers* (2013), conjoined photographs of naked boys poised on posts on a Noirmoutier beach (alluding deliciously both to classical sculpture and to the photograph *Ulysse*) which Varda has turned into a vast magnetic jigsaw of 167 pieces. In the Galerie Nathalie Obadia, it was this invitation to touch, play and intervene in images that greeted the visitor. To compound the invitation, three of the giant jigsaw pieces were removed and placed on the wall outside the triptych proper, spilling out beyond its edges. More sombrely, the desire to come together around the image that drives *Ulysse* is present again in, for example, the complex installation on widowhood and mourning, *Les Veuves de Noirmoutier* [*The Widows of Noirmoutier*] (2006). Here, notable in the video portrait of each widow is the way in which she not only alludes to the tactile dimension of loss but also holds up for the camera a framed photograph of her missing husband — the image a magical fetish, both index and icon — that now stands in his stead. There is here a strong ethical dimension to sharing and opening the image together, which is sensitively accounted for in the installation's physical invitations to involvement (its configuration of chairs and headphones, permitting intimacy and attentiveness). I turn now to analyse how Varda's second major memorial installation harnesses still images to create powerful intersubjective experience.

Hommage aux Justes de France [*Homage to the Righteous of France*]

Varda's acceptance of a request by the French Ministry of Culture that she produce a commemorative installation for the occasion of a major ceremony in the Panthéon in 2007 was courageous since the risks and responsibility involved were immense. The occasion was the unveiling within the Crypt of a marble plaque dedicated to the 'Justes de France', the numerous non-Jewish individuals who assisted in the survival of Jews, protecting and sheltering them during the years of Nazi occupation.[18] Varda's highly-charged companion piece opened the day after the ceremony of 18th January. To refer to it as an 'exhibition' is inadequate: it was, rather, an event; a reflective space destined to be part of the national narrative about its past and to draw in the visitors as they walked up the Great Nave. In this part of my chapter I explore how Varda works skilfully within the confines of this solemn event and august setting to overcome the challenge of the context and to create something quite extraordinary: a homely space in the Panthéon; a space emphasizing intimacy

Fig. 9.4. *Hommage aux justes de France* [*Homage to the Righteous of France*]
© Mémorial de la Shoah — SCDJC (dont ph. E. Finkiel) — Yad Vashem — USHMM — Centre des Monuments nationaux, MONUM. — INA

and touch which seeks to open up memory, fleshing out the near-abstraction of the simple plaque.[19] Once again, Varda demonstrates in this installation a special care for the still image — particularly, but not only, the portrait. I shall argue that stills and stilling are central to her sensitive contribution to France's ongoing collective memory project concerning this period of the national past.

Varda's installation, a combination of photographs and fictional and documentary-style film, was contained within an arrangement of temporary walls which cushioned the Pantheon's immensity, creating a smaller, immersive environment. Chairs invited the visitor to linger. The apparatus included four elevated screens, organized in pairs, each pair simultaneously showing two interconnected nine-minute films on a loop, one of them black and white and characteristic of news broadcasts of the Occupation period, the other in colour. Projected on a further, larger screen was a colour photograph of a majestic tree in full leaf set against a blue sky, its stillness dominating the installation space. On the floor, upon a circular plinth, stood some 300 photographic portraits derived from various archive sources, including the Mémorial de la Shoah in Paris, and intended to represent the 2,693 'Justes de France'. Each black-and-white portrait had the name of the subject written upon it. There were also colour photographs of the actors from the short fictional reconstruction films shown on Varda's screens. Around the circumference of the plinth was a text, hand-written in appearance: 'Au temps de l'Occupation, ces hommes et ces femmes, n'écoutant que leur cœur et leur conscience au péril de leur vie, ont accueilli, protégé et caché des Juifs par milliers, dont beaucoup d'enfants, les sauvant ainsi de l'extermination' [At the time of the Occupation, these men and women, heeding only their heart and their conscience and putting their lives in peril, welcomed, protected and hid Jews in their thousands, including numerous children, hence saving them from extermination']. There was no further text in this quiet and unassuming installation. Instead, background murmurs infiltrated the space: snatches of dialogue; simple violin music based on a Yiddish song; sounds of the countryside; and fragments of noise associated with bureaucratization and terror: the heavy tread of boots, a distant train, a telephone, a typewriter, the small thud of a stamp as it leaves its irrevocable mark on a document.

Analyses of this installation have focused in particular on the moving image, notably on the intricate dialogue between the two separate yet interwoven films which mirror and circle around each other, sometimes affording different perspectives on the same event and through which Varda creates, as Bellour observes, 'un véritable montage [...] d'un écran à l'autre' ['a veritable montage [...] from one screen to the other'].[20] Varda's interlinked films show fictional evocations of episodes which, rooted in historical fact, partake of the typology of everyday, intimate acts of courage in the period: hiding, feeding, sheltering and caring, very often for children. As if to underscore the complexity of memory, the films seem to remember differently. While the black-and-white film observes a realist aesthetic, privileges narrative and shows complete episodes, the colour film privileges small details, insisting on gesture, objects and materiality. More importantly, this close-grained investigation is periodically stilled for us to engage with its magnitude. A mother steers her children across a dangerous zone in the countryside and the vulnerable group is abruptly held in a freeze frame. A door opens and we hold our breath. The camera holds still for a close-up of a yellow star sewn on a garment, evoking not only the dreadful symbol but the fabric and the grimly intricate labour of stitching it in place. The knot in the tie of a Vichy official suggests the hands that tied it.

In a brief text about her work, Varda highlights her concern to isolate resonant moments and hence to awaken 'des sensations fragmentées, des moments d'émotion liés à l'Histoire et à des images-clés de nos mémoires collectives' ['fragmented sensations, moments of emotion linked to History and to key images from our collective memory'].[21] A vignette of a nun hiding a child in the fold of her garment as a family is abducted nearby is supplemented by several arresting stills: one of the woman alone; one with the child held close to her body; a portrait of the 'Juste' in question, sister Marie-Paule; and a portrait of the actor who gives us an insight into her courage. In this way, the film suggestively proposes 'des attitudes, des gestes, des idées, concretisés l'espace d'un instant' ['attitudes, gestures, ideas, given concrete form for an instant'],[22] before connecting them to given individuals. Each of the thirteen vignettes developed by Varda concludes in this way, on the projection of two photographic portraits: one of the *Juste* in question; another of the actor who rekindles their past.

Bellour observes that stilling here foregrounds 'une pensivité du film' ['a pensive quality in the film'][23] but I want to argue that Varda's insistence on hovering, waiting and holding does much more than make us think. Laura Mulvey's comments on the relationship between stillness and the (digitalized) moving image are somewhat nearer the mark, underlining how cinematic images can be 'stretch[ed] out [...] to allow space and time for associative thought, reflection on resonance and connotation' thus ensuring that '[k]ey moments and meanings become visible that could not have been perceived when hidden under the narrative flow and the movement of film.'[24] Even here, the word 'visible' feels limiting: Varda is not merely stilling or fixing visual images but, more profoundly, uncovering image-impressions and drawing them to the surface in a congealing of sense and affect which connects with memory in specific ways. In deliberate contrast to the abstraction of the Pantheon's memorial plaque, Varda provides textured close-ups which re-create embodied experience, not only offering 'une vision touchante' ['a touching vision'][25] of the 'Justes' and of those they saved — many of whom were children — but also determinedly restoring touch. And in contrast to her moving images whose narratives propel us forwards, she suggests how memory is often condensed to single imprints that endure, just as scars on the skin contain their own complex and intimate back story. In *Les Plages d'Agnès*, a protracted exercise in autobiographical and collective memory, Varda briefly recounts her own memories of war-time camping trips in the Alps with the *Éclaireuses* [Girl Guides]. With the aid of several group photographs fleetingly animated by the sound track of a crackling camp fire, she recalls in her voice-over how the party would sometimes split as leaders took Jewish children to safety over the border with Switzerland. It is on more elaborate experiments with the power of re-animated documentary fragments that Varda's entire installation to the 'Justes' will later be based.

Hommage aux Justes de France is not the first time that we have seen the quiet authority of private photographs enlisted to great impact in work concerning the Holocaust: Varda's much admired friend Boltanski uses them in his own installation pieces, harnessing their affective charge and metonymic power. Boltanski's use of photographs is disquieting and alienating: they are rendered unfamiliar by blurring and are wrenched from domestic circulation to be attached to supports with archival or commemorative evocations, as evidence of the erasure of humanity that the Holocaust entailed. The profusion of photographs in Varda's installation is instead a celebratory factor. The manner of their display is very different from that in Boltanski, or indeed from most other memorials commemorating large numbers of people, which most habitually use perpendicular supports. Here the photographs are arranged on the floor not, to my mind, like stela (Bellour's suggestion)[26] but drawing on a much more domestic trope. Not only are the framed portraits themselves intimate artefacts of the kind we like to touch and which touch us; the manner of their display is also quietly emotive, redolent of those piano tops or sideboards that effectively become shrines to family, that invite touch as portraits are picked up and brought close. As a concession to their surroundings the portraits are enlarged in scale so as not to be entirely dwarfed, but the implications of homeliness are nonetheless strong; we might be in a family *salon*. Varda's recreation of such a domestic corner amid the chilly materiality of the Pantheon's marble and stone is a considerable achievement. The gap between the fragility of the photograph itself, humble in dimension and ephemeral in medium, and the pomp of the context astonishes. It is, then, largely due to the distribution of photographs that Varda creates such a productively incongruous space within this national monument.

I want to return here to the call to touch in Varda. Olin's study of 'touching photography' speaks of touch as a creator of community around photographs. Her interest lies especially in displays of American photographs related to 09/11, but her comments on the spectators' own experience of being present at (not just of viewing) these displays has relevance for Varda's installation. With reference to the post- 09/11 photographic project exhibition *Here is New York*, Olin speaks of a 'therapeutic connection' between viewer and image and observes that creating community was indeed one of the exhibition's goals: 'The emphasis [was] on contact between people and contact with photographs standing in for people.'[27] Further, Olin suggests that the particular kind of seeing in which visitors were engaged is aptly described as 'basking': '[we] bask in an image to obtain what we need from it, much as we bask in the sun or under a sunlamp, to obtain the benefits of light.'[28] Basking is immersive. It unifies people. It is a phenomenon produced especially when the image is generic. It does not entail close examination or intellectual scrutiny: basking is about seeking not knowledge but reassurance. I borrow Olin's idea of basking in the photographic image not to apply it wholesale to Varda's installation, but precisely in order to problematize it as it might apply to experiences of visiting *Hommage aux Justes de France*. True, it is only a step from the idea of community created around the installation to the uncritical, even sentimental notion of the nation as 'community', even as 'family'. In this regard, the term 'basking' might concern us. It seems to resonate with ideas about the easy consensus criticized by those who have, in recent years, quite rightly approached the obsession with memory through a critical lens; thinkers such as Todorov whose thesis on 'abuses of memory' provides an important counterpoint.[29] 'Basking' appears to imply a completely uncritical reception of the way in which art mediates history. Conversely, as it gathered people around photographs and fulfilled the commemorative role for which it was commissioned, Varda's *Hommage aux Justes de France* also brought participants to consider precisely such questions. The entire installation, with its appeal to the senses, its complex relay between still and moving images, its invitation to stillness as well as its deliberate halting, back-looping, reiterative quality, constituted not only a call to memory, but an observation upon it. Most notable is the significance derived from the disjuncture between the installation and its physical context. Arguably, Varda fractured the national monument with her emphasis on touch and touching, shifting perspective and historical discourse within a monument that engenders awe and aggrandisement; that connotes what is too large, sanctified and distant to touch. Instead Varda domesticated heroism, bringing it to a human scale and giving the Pantheon an airing. The vast, still tree projected on the largest screen and the close, child's-eye focus on aspects of the countryside where fine-grained everyday experiences of hiding were commonplace, help to ensure this.

Finally, Varda's installation had the great merit of feminizing this daunting national space. It confirmed, within the very embodiment of a particular idea of History (great men, great events, eternal monuments) the important shifts in historiography that have taken place over the past seventy years, emphasizing the everyday, domestic, grass-roots events that also make history; the small scale and the small acts that have at last become the legitimate focus of historians. In an essay on 'enfant caché' [hidden child] accounts in recent French women's writing, Lucille Cairns notes the multiplication of female-authored testimonies on the subject in the first decade of the 2000s;[30] Varda's choice to emphasize women and children in her installation is consistent with this development. The contrast between the installation and its setting could, then, scarcely have been greater. Their conjunction provided a model lesson or *mise en abyme* of the struggle over history that has taken place and in which micro details, ordinary people, women and history from below have re-established their place. Arguably, this is attained in large measure not just by the way still images were set back into motion (Flitterman-Lewis notes that the installation allowed Varda to 'animer les portraits des Justes et de leur époque d'une manière exceptionnelle' ['animate in an exceptional way the portraits of the Righteous and their era'])[31] but by the very stillness of images which are closely attentive not to the flow of narrative but to details that might otherwise have been overlooked. Varda's frozen micro-gestures contribute a new kind of collagen to the fabric of national history.

Concluding remarks

As Varda's interrogation of both still and moving images escalates, what strikes us is her energetic thrust to the future as well as her refusal to allow photographs to recede from the present. Varda's restlessness repeatedly sends her back to set stills in motion, to open up what was (provisionally) fixed and to remind us of that very provisionality. We have seen that in *Les Justes* such a strategy makes a powerful contribution to national memory. I want to end this chapter on a quite different example of returning to the past. Perhaps the most arresting of Varda's *Triptyques atypiques* are not her conspicuously mixed-media experiments but two pieces each composed of three stills taken from the 1985 film *Sans toit ni loi* [*Vagabond*]. These 'belong' to the sequence in which Mona (Sandrine Bonnaire) is attacked and covered in wine lees in a grotesque and terrifying folk ritual. Suddenly in these original stills the film congeals into something newly vital: blurred, frenetic, extraordinarily kinetic. These close-ups evoke the fluidity, drama and struggle of bodies in a birth scene, their strange beauty approaching abstract painting. Here the still image is clearly hesitating at the juncture between the indexical (although a trace, in this instance, of a film) and the independent, non-representational art object. These new stills, neither decisive moments nor ongoing moments, yet so clearly in dialogue with film, photography and painting, seem to promise a further, as yet untested exploratory route for an artist whose experiments with interrupting both the moving and the still are the defining feature of her late work.

Notes to Chapter 9

1. Translations in the text are my own unless otherwise stated.
2. For further analyses of this exhibition see Marie-Claire Barnet and Shirley Jordan (eds), *Watch this Space: Women's Conceptualisations of Space in Contemporary French Film and Visual Art*,

L'Esprit Créateur, 51:1 (Spring 2011), as well as chapters by Handyside and Mowat in the present volume.

3. See Michael Fried, *Why Photography Matters as Art as Never Before* (New Haven: Yale University Press, 2008).
4. Varda's first art installation, shown in the 2003 Venice Biennale. See Perry in the present volume for further analysis.
5. See *La Querelle des dispositifs. Cinéma — installations, expositions* (Paris: P.O.L., 2012) and especially 'Ce que peut une installation', pp. 412–17.
6. For further analysis of Varda's *Triptyques atypiques* installation see Barnet in the present volume.
7. Geoff Dyer, *The Ongoing Moment* (New York: Vintage, 2007).
8. See 'Portugal. De la photographie au cinéma'.
9. See the elemental triptych *Marie dans le vent* (2014) for a powerful recent example. Here the wind's animation of stately turbines captured in high-definition video film and projected on the outer panels feels seamlessly connected to the central silver print still of a girl whose hair and toy windmill are blown into movement.
10. This photograph was used in Franz Villier's *Portugal, Petite Planète* (Paris: Editions du Seuil, 1957). For discussion of the photograph's significance in this particular context, see Susana S. Martins, 'Between Present and Past: Photographic Portugal of the 1950s', in Jan Baetens, Alexander Streitberger and Hilde Van Gelder (eds), *Time and Photography* (Belgium: Leuven University Press, 2010), pp. 85–102.
11. 'Je me suis souvent demandée', comments Varda in the voice-over to her essay, 'qui étaient ces gens, et ce qui s'était passé avant cet instant et après' ['I often asked myself who these people were and what had happened before and after this instant'].
12. The recent *Portraits brisés* are further evidence of how Varda readily resists the smooth completeness of photographic portraits by breaking them up temporally and physically. Among them is her *Autoportrait morcelé* (2009), a photographic version of a Cubist portrait wherein small overlapping mirrors of different dimensions are superimposed upon each other, reflecting fragments of the artist's face from different angles. In *Agnès de ci de là Varda* we witness her pleasure in smashing a mirror before asking her subject to gaze into it for his portrait.
13. *Ulysse* is discussed in Agnès Varda, *Varda tous courts* (Ciné-Tamaris, ARTE France, 2011). See also McNeill in the present volume.
14. See *The Skin of the Film. Intercultural Cinema, Embodiment and the Senses* (Durham and London: Duke University Press, 2000).
15. See 11.
16. Margaret Olin, *Touching Photographs* (Chicago and London: The University of Chicago Press, 2012).
17. *Ibid*, p. 15.
18. The title (in full, 'Juste Parmi Les Nations' ['Righteous among Nations']) is attributed by the Yad Vashem memorial in Jerusalem, created in 1953.
19. The installation was shown again during the Festival d'Avignon (2–27 July, 2007) but it is the iteration in the Pantheon that interests me here.
20. Bellour, p. 415. See also Sandy Flitterman-Lewis, 'Varda, glaneuse d'Histoire(s) (*Hommage aux Justes de France*)', in Antony Fiant, Roxane Hamery and Éric Thouvenelric (eds), *Agnès Varda: le cinéma et au-delà* (Rennes: Presses Universitaires de Rennes, 2009), pp. 221–28.
21. Varda's text in the programme accompanying the Avignon installation (p. 7).
22. See Flitterman-Lewis, p. 225.
23. Bellour, p. 430.
24. See *Death 24x a Second: Stillness and the Moving Image* (London: Reaktion Books, 2006), pp. 146–47.
25. Edouard Launet, 'Entre fracas et emotion, Varda honore les Justes', *Libération* 26 January 2007 <http://next.liberation.fr/culture/2007/01/26/entre-fracas-et-emotion-varda-honore-les-justes_83030> [accessed 20 September 2015].
26. Bellour, p. 414.
27. Olin, p. 188.
28. *Ibid*, p. 197.

29. Todorov, *Les Abus de la mémoire* (Paris: Arléa, 1998).
30. See 'Vichy, Jews, *Enfants Cachés*: French Women Writers Look Back', in Amaleena Damlé and Gill Rye (eds), *Women's Writing in Twenty-First-Century France* (Cardiff: University of Wales Press, 2013), pp. 47–59.
31. Flitterman-Lewis, p. 223.

CHAPTER 10

Les Cabanes d'Agnès

Gill Perry

'Mais ces maisons sont des palais'
(Le Corbusier, *Une Maison, Un Palais*, 1926)[1]

'Bien sûr, ce n'est pas une cabane, mais un palais'
(Jacques Drillon, *Agnès Varda L'Île et Elle, 2006*)[2]

Le Corbusier's 'palais' was a primitive cabin or hut *(hutte)* inspired by the fisherman's huts he had seen in Archachon in the south-west of France. These basic wooden dwellings, nestling under the pine trees in the sand dunes which separate the Basin d'Arcachon from the Atlantic, influenced some of his earliest architectural writings and encouraged the development of his own 'hut myth'. He identified a basic simplicity in shacks conceived without historical pretensions or fashionable taste – compact dwellings built from available local materials.[3] Eighty years later the writer and critic Jacques Drillon used the term 'palais' to describe Varda's *Cabane de l'Échec* (subsequently renamed her *Cabane de Cinéma*) of 2006 (Fig. 1). This structure presents the shack or *cabane* as a more imaginary space, with walls made of 35mm film strips from *Les Créatures* that according to Varda was a 'flop'.[4] Drillon's *palais* then speaks of the film-maker's rich archive. It provides tangible evidence of the laborious process of film-making, and of an art that can disappear with time. As the viewer scours each stop frame from *Les Créatures*, the faces of Catherine Deneuve and Michel Piccoli are constantly repeated. Both subsequently became iconic figures within the French film world and beyond; yet here their repeated (and here forgotten) faces are part of the structure of the walls. With its sloping roof, also made of film strips and corrugated plastic, its old reclaimed wooden door and window openings, this is also a compact architectural form made entirely of recycled objects, of *récup*. Like Corbusier's hut, Varda's *palais* speaks of autobiographical experiences and musings, metaphorical simplicity, nostalgia and available, recycled materials. Stripped of its regal associations, *un palais* can become a complex cultural and architectural metaphor, used to suggest the hidden riches of deceptively simple dwelling structures, their personal resonances and creative possibilities.

At home and *chez soi*

The theme of the *cabane* features prominently in Varda's oeuvre (both films and installation art) to provide a multi-layered, sometimes humorous and self-referential

FIG. 10.1. *La Cabane de cinéma*, 2006, mixed media and strips of 35 mm film

leitmotif. It dominated her substantial exhibit at the Lyon Biennale of 2009, titled 'Les Cabanes d'Agnès'.[5] The caption to a group of three separate hut installations opened with the (now much quoted) words 'Agnès Varda is, to use her own description, "an old filmmaker and a young artist".' The exhibit comprised her *Cabane de Cinéma, Cabane de Plage* (2009) and *Cabane aux Portraits* (2006) (Figs 10.1, 10.2 and 10.3). After a career confronting issues of poverty, feminism and political activism, she has appropriated a domestic cliché — a shack or space of 'dwelling' with immense personal and metaphorical relevance to her own history as a woman, an artist and filmmaker. In various interviews Varda has identified the house *(la maison)* as both a symbol of bourgeois repression and desire for ownership, and a haven or retreat, an intimate space of rêverie,[6] encapsulating some of the contradictions that weave in and out of artistic engagements with the idea of 'home' in the twenty-first century.[7] She says she came from the 'rejecting bourgeoisie. We all become bourgeois when we have a house. I have a house now, a bathroom — two bathrooms! We become bourgeois in terms of the way we live — but it terms of spirit, that's another thing'.[8] Her *cabanes*, then, might be seen as literal and metaphorical 'homes' that are infused with Varda's notion of 'spirit'. And as Le Corbusier acknowledged, the hut or shack can be conceived as a modest dwelling that can condense — or simplify — the idea of 'home'. His famous *cabanon* at Roquebrune-Cap-Martin on the Côte d'Azur was built in 1952 as a holiday house only 15 metres square. This compact wooden structure has entered French architectural history as an iconic motif for paired-down living by the sea. It self-consciously embodies some of those contractions implicit in the 'hut myth'; it straddles that mythical gulf between modern design and rustic fantasies.[9]

The hut or shack still functions as a 'home' within many globalized cultures today, not to mention its associations with idealised or 'pure' forms of dwelling, as adopted by many modern theorists and philosophers, among them Martin Heidegger.[10] And the 'hut myth' is most often appropriated and identified by male architects and philosophers (among them Le Corbusier and Heidegger) as spaces with predominantly masculine identities (fishermen, hermits, writers). Although women and mothers are often the most visible occupants of primitive huts, they have rarely carried the iconic significance of the 'hermit' or the fisherman/architect/writer. Varda re-appropriates and curates this mythical space for a feminine practice of both art-making and film-making.

Many social and cultural associations of the simple hut or 'dwelling' are related to our acculturated notions of 'home', belonging and growing up. And 'home' with its historical associations with domesticity and the 'private' labour of 'homemaking', is often gendered feminine.[11] That said, 'home' is a complex concept that can denote a multi-layered physical, social, gendered and ideological space. Evolving definitions of 'home' have enriched debates within the spheres of cultural geography, anthropology, sociology, architectural and design history, art history, among others.[12] Although 'home' is usually a site where we live, it is also an idea or 'spatial imaginary', which according to Alison Blunt and Robyn Dowling, is 'a set of intersecting and variable ideas and feelings, which are related to context, and which construct places, extend across spaces and scales, and connect places'.[13] Given these fluid, variable and intersecting possibilities, 'home' emerges as a concept with great potential for aesthetic re-workings and re-framings. As I argue, Varda's *cabanes* are rich in spatial, gendered and autobiographical confusions and explorations; they can even evoke some of the 'nomadic gazes' identified in her films.[14] But in making such claims, I am also aware of the semantic issues that surround attempts to translate the English concept of 'home'. In many European languages to say that one is 'at home' often requires the use of several words, often with the 'house' as a metonym. Thus one is *à la maison* in French, or *zu Hause* in German or *en casa* in Spanish.[15] In French, the term *chez soi* is also used, denoting a personalized, intimate connection, a form of belonging.[16] *Chez soi* denotes much more than being in a house; it can evoke a cultural and physical identity, an active form of inhabiting. Such semantic equivalents can contribute to the complexity of meanings that circulate around the idea of 'home'. Varda's films and writings seem to acknowledge this complexity; they are full of references to both literal and metonymic houses, associations reinforced and extended in her photographic and installation works in which the shack or *cabane* often signifies a haven or retreat, an intimate space of rêverie. In her autobiographical film *The Beaches of Agnès* (2009) (see chapter 8 — Fiona Handyside) the beach or fisherman's hut is one of several leitmotifs that frame Varda's mischievous role-playing and cinematic story-telling, a narrative that ends with Varda inside her *Cabane de Cinéma*. Exhibited in art galleries as installations, such personal havens are also physical spaces of display. She simultaneously evokes, and undermines, any idea of intimacy, reconfiguring her huts as public spaces to be entered and experienced. Thus *chez soi* is re-conceived as *chez nous,* a participatory strategy that is at the heart of modern installation art.

Kristine Stiles has described installation (together with video and performance) as a 'living art' that can interact with social practices, environments and technologies.[17] Claire Bishop makes a similar point when she describes installation as invoking an experience in which the viewing space is 'a living area'.[18] The literal presence of the embodied viewer is now widely seen as a defining characteristic of installation art. It presupposes a viewer who may also be invited to deploy her/his senses of smell, touch and sound. The descriptor 'living' suggests the active communication of social questions and considerations of everyday life, not to mention the labels 'participatory' and 'relational' that are increasingly applied to this genre.[19] Given these concerns, it is hardly surprising that assemblages of household objects and architectural constructions that evoke the spaces and traces of 'home' are much repeated points of reference within contemporary installation art. Varda's *cabanes* consistently invite her audience to enter her space and engage: to watch a film (as in her *Cabane de Plage*), to review a montage of portraits (as in her *Cabane de Portraits*) or to decipher her film archive, deliberately conflated with the architectural structure (as in her *Cabane de Cinéma*).

As intimate spaces of reverie, opened up for public viewing, Varda's *cabanes* reveal a strategic use of 'public intimacy'. Here I am appropriating a term that has been used by theatre historians and sociologists to describe a quality of celebrity culture, the feigned intimacy that is suggested and projected by the endless media representations (both visual and written) that cluster around and help to mythologize modern celebrities.[20] Although I am not suggesting that Varda uses such forms of dissemination to promote her own mythical status or fame, I see her *cabanes* as complex constructed spaces which encapsulate some of the contradictions inherent in this oxymoronic concept. As Joseph Roach has written: 'Public intimacy' is paradox-ridden, conveying 'contradictory qualities simultaneously: strength *and* vulnerability, innocence *and* experience; singularity *and* typicality among them'.[21]

Varda's intimate enclosures echo such contradictions. They are all viewing spaces — for her photographs, film strips or films; the basic simplicity of recycled materials that make up their architectural structures is thus reconceived as part of that sophisticated viewing space. At a distance her *Cabane de Cinéma* appears almost monumental, imposing, and even architecturally ambitious for a *cabane,* with its corrugated, sloping roof and heavy wooden door. On closer inspection and when displayed in a light-filled space, it appears ethereal, semi-transparent, as if floating. From some angles the multiple strips of celluloid combine to convey a fragile, elusive structure, in which inside and outside are merged. Similarly, the expanse of wooden *récup* that seems to promise the simplicity of a fisherman's hut in her *Cabane aux Portraits* is transformed into a public space of display in the sixty portrait photographs of inhabitants (30 women and 30 men) of the island of Noirmoutier that line the interior walls (Fig. 2). As Marie Claire Barnet has suggested, Varda uses this form of installation art to create 'a privileged space of encounter and *partage* with others, as well as a dreamscape'.[22]

FIG. 10.2. *La Cabane aux Portraits*, 2006, wood and mixed medid including 60 photographic portraits and two videos

Beaches and Beach Huts

Varda's *Cabane de Plage* included in the Lyon Biennale of 2009 (Fig. 3), was intended both as a fisherman's shelter (unwittingly, perhaps, echoing Le Corbusier's idealized fisherman's huts at Arcachon) and as a projection booth. Inside, the viewer could watch her film *La Mer Mediterranée, avec deux r et un n, entre Sète et Agde*. Inspired by the fishermen's shelters she observed on the Mediterranean coast and on her beloved island of Noirmoutier, in *Cabane de Plage* she used sheets of coloured canvas stretched with rope. The seascapes, beaches and salt marshes of Noirmoutier provided her with a rich and varied library of *cabanes*, recorded in photographic form in her preparations for her show *L'Île et Elle* at the Fondation Cartier in 2006. In a booklet accompanying a collection of photographs and postcards gathered to inform her ideas for that show, she wrote of the Noirmoutier shacks:

> CABANE:
> le mot même renvoie à des désirs d'enfance, à des désirs, toujours, d'un abri rustique. Dans l'île, à part des minuscules maisons en dur au milieu des marais salants, il y a des cabanes faites de matériaux de récup. Celles en tôle sont les plus belles.[23]

As her photographs suggest, this *tôle* — or corrugated metal, which appears (sometimes in plastic form) on the roof of her *Cabane de Cinéma* and on the walls of her *Cabane aux Portraits*, is a recognized symbol of the *cabane* or makeshift shack. Le Corbusier used it on the roof of his cabanon at Roquebrune.[24] And across different global cultures the simple shelter made of recycled junk and corrugated iron is also a signifier of slums, poverty and favelas. But on the beaches of Noirmoutier, such structures speak to Varda at least of the value of local culture and its defences against the westerly winds that batter the island.

La Cabane de Plage reworks evocative leitmotifs that run throughout Varda's film and installation work: the beach and the fisherman's cabin. Her directorial debut, *La Pointe Courte* (initial release 1955), set in a fishing village on the lagoon of the Mediterranean port of Sète, features views and tracking shots that are framed by, or take place within, wooden fishermen's *cabanes.* Simple shacks without modern amenities are represented as both the living spaces of family life, but also as fishermen's havens — their separate, ramshackle, working spaces or 'dens' on the edge of the lagoon. Here they repair their nets and tackle, hide the fruits of their illegal fishing trips to areas deemed out of bounds by government inspectors, and share their tales of love, jousting and family tensions. Weathered wood, wooden structures and *récup* are everywhere in the black and white visual montage of *La Pointe Courte.*

But Varda has deliberately modernized and confused such references in her *Cabane de Plage.* Although inspired by those fisherman's huts that weave in and out of her filmic and photographic oeuvre, her sheets of brightly coloured canvas, folding beach chairs and added sand, speak of the modern leisure culture of the beach. The weather-beaten *récup* of Sète and Noirmoutier is transformed here into a more mischievous engagement with the twenty-first- century beach, and the colourful, often kitsch commodification of play objects that signify that leisure culture, an approach that is taken to colourful extremes in her installation *Ping-Pong, Tong et Camping*, 2006.[25] Here rows of brightly coloured flip-flops, spades, buckets and plastic containers suggest a phantasmagoria of modern consumerism 'on the beach'. As Fiona Handyside has pointed out, the beach has been reclaimed as a 'modern rather than an Arcadian space', another site expressive of modernity, comparable with those of the modern city.[26] Moreover, in *Les Plages d'Agnès* Varda re-configures the modern beach as a fragile and shifting space that can be reclaimed for a feminist project.[27]

She produced a literal and playful enactment of this reworking of the Arcadian or pastoral space in her notorious staging of her own 'Paris-Plage' or 'Daguerre-Plage', when multiple truckloads of sand were deposited in the rue Daguerre, in front of her home and office headquarters at Ciné Tamaris. Women office staff, dressed in beachwear, worked at the desks, conveniently placed on the sand, with Varda herself seated at the head of this pseudo *bureau.*[28] Conceived both as a local event/installation and filmed for a sequence in *The Beaches of Agnès*, 'Daguerre Plage' referenced multiple associations of the beach, but provocatively re-instated it as an urban space of female labour. As such, it turned upside down the motif that has often featured in French art of the late nineteenth and early twentieth century as a pastoral or Arcadian site of leisure for the display of the nude (often female) body, adopted by artists from Puvis de Chavannes to Henri Matisse, among so many others.[29]

Beaches are perpetually changing and profoundly liminal sites. They can also mark boundaries between nations, cultures and geographical identities. No surprise

Fig. 10.3. *La Cabane de Plage*, 2009/10, canvas, ropes, projection booth

then that for Varda, as for many other contemporary women artists, the beach is deployed as a leitmotif, metonym and framing space that enables discursive, playful and 'cosmopolitan' forms of aesthetic intervention and reverie. John Mack has written eloquently on this liminal status:

> The beach is an ambiguous place, an in-between place. It is a place where for much of the time nothing much seemingly happens: the tide comes and goes; people arrive to pass time in leisure activities; occasional ships anchor there. But at the same time, the beach is a place where everything transformational in the cultures of coastal peoples begins and ends. The tides create a shifting boundary between sea and land. Their effect is to emphasize the liminality of the beach as parts of it are successively revealed and then swamped by tidal action. The boundary between sea and land alters on a daily basis. It is a neutral space, neither properly terrestrial nor yet thoroughly maritime, awaiting a metamorphic role.[30]

Positioned on such ambiguous sites, beach huts can carry some of these shifting and transformational associations. They are part of that changing landscape, vulnerable to being weathered by the sea and its fluid boundaries. They offer potential for both artist and viewer to assume marginal, imaginary, feminist or even nomadic positions. Rickety beach huts positioned on shifting sands can add ambiguity and flow to the idea of a local identity. The 'nomadic' gaze of Varda's films[31] is referenced more obliquely in her *cabanes*. In her *Cabane de Portraits* the ever-changing seascapes and beach landscapes of the island of Noirmoutier are used to frame, or to form, artificial backdrops to each of the portrait studies displayed inside the shack. Thus individual portraits appear as if double-framed by their surroundings, confusing the specific geographical contexts of each. Female and male subjects are distinguished from each other by part of their montaged backgrounds; both men and women, young and old, are presented as the distinctive yet changing inhabitants of the island, reinforcing her frequent claim: 'I love the sea and those who live near the sea.'[32] Small islands like Noirmoutier, that are entirely defined and altered by a sea that is always visible, offer sites loaded with metaphorical possibilities of travel, the power of the ocean, and fluid boundaries.

Along with Varda's love of beach huts, the island offers rich spaces for imaginary contemplation and creation. Such themes have seized the imagination of several other contemporary women artists whose work can also be seen to evoke a 'nomadic' gaze. The liminal possibilities of the hut at the water's edge have inspired the British Caribbean painter Lubaina Himid in her written and painted reflections on the beach house (Fig. 4).

She has used the imagery of the sea and the beach house to chart a nomadic personal history, from her birth place near the beach in Zanzibar, to memories of beaches in Lancashire, the Isle of Wight, Havana, Blackpool, Brighton, Santa Monica, Malibu, Dieppe and St Ives, among others coastal sites. In her exhibited works in *Beach House*, 1994 (Rochdale Art Gallery), and her evocative writings,[33] she uses the literal and metaphorical status of the beach house, shack or dwelling-place to reference obliquely issues of colonization, childhood memory, slavery, trans-national identity, gender, play and dreamy pleasure. She describes arriving in England on Christmas Eve, 1954, flying into Blackpool, a chilly seaside home in the north of England where summers were spent making sand castles on the beach at Lytham: 'The sea was wet and good for basic architecture. The shapes were crisp and crunchy. The windmill stick entered the bucket shape perfectly its plastic sails pink, green, yellow and orange whizzed in the brisk air from the Irish Sea' [sic].[34] Colourful buckets and spades, like those that appear in Varda's installations, haunt Himid's memories. And her sandcastles push the liminality of the beach house to extremes; partly made of the sea (sand) they are short-lived architectural structures that disappear with the movement of the sea. Himid is inspired by those same 'holiday' huts that haunt Varda's *cabanes*. As Himid recalls:

> ...Brighton: an endless row of beach huts pale pink, deep magenta, lilac, purple, salmon, apricot, sky, lemon, orange, banana, violet, pale green, turquoise; small and ready for flasks of tea with iced buns or white wine with chicken sandwiches...
> ...At Wells-next-the-Sea in Norfolk in front of a pine wood, in which nestles the queen of England's beach house, is a huge and flat expanse of pink grey sand, [sic] it swells and floats up to the horizon. Five of us walked up and then down that beach; a famous five arguing parrying displaying conceding, collaborating and isolating. All on a theme of women painting women. I looked out towards the sea and wished I could stay a year. The beach huts there are sturdy serious small wooden buildings on stilts with wooden steps leading up to the door and down the sand. The owners (one day I hope to be one) sit a careful distance apart on a platform.[35]

Himid's poetic descriptions of the beach huts she has encountered — and inhabited

FIG. 10.4. Lubaina Himid, *Metal/Paper*, 1995, acrylic on canvas, 153 × 213 cm. Photograph courtesy of the artist

— offer countless metaphors of the 'house' or dwelling, including its potential as 'a place of refuge', without telephone, and as 'on the edge of time, a woman's place of contemplation'. The hut is figured in her work as a potential feminine space of reverie and leisure — a haven. But she also describes the beach house as a site of conflict with potential to represent a troubling colonial history of invasion and departure; she describes the slave companies' barracoons: 'Some captains preferred to build a makeshift house of the upper deck — in these houses, constructed between the masts, their roofs thatched with mangrove branches and reeds, their walls made from woven bamboo shoots, were penned terrified Africans, many of whom had never seen the sea.'[36]

Himid's beach house, then, is another site of contradiction — a palimpsest rooted in her nomadic, colonial history, but appropriated as a woman's space. Like Varda, she reworks an architectural form with multiple symbolic possibilities, and weaves it into to an ever-changing spatial imaginary. While Himid's slave shacks and the post-colonial references that are embedded within them (both visually and through association), are rather different from Varda's huts inspired by those of fishermen and island salt farmers, both artists draw on aspects of their own nomadic lives and interests to inflect and inform their representations, both architectural (Varda) and painterly (Himid).

Mobile Homes and a 'Cosmopolitan Imagination'

In 1967 Varda shot a short twenty-two-minute film, *Uncle Yanco*, filmed in the houseboat community of Sausolito Bay, north of San Francisco. With her husband Jacques Demy, who was awarded a production contract by Columbia pictures, she spent three years in California from 1967 to 1970. Sausolito Bay became one of the centres of the American 60s counterculture, or as she called it a 'centre intellectual et cœur de la bohème',[37] where Alan Watts, Allen Ginsberg and friends gave regular poetry readings. It also became a site of pilgrimage for European architects intrigued by these extraordinary floating constructions.[38] *Uncle Yanco* is focused on her long-lost Greek uncle,[39] the bohemian painter Jean Varda, who lived and sailed his boat at Sausolito. The film features many visual sequences that describe and explore these fascinating mobile homes, as the camera pans around various houseboats and their 'homely' details and scavenged architectural features.[40]

In *Uncle Yanco*, Varda quotes a passage from Henry Miller's book *Remember to Remember* of 1952 which includes an account of Jean Varda's life and concerns. Miller describes his fight against waste and his 'plundering of the refuse heaps and from the plunder creating veritable mansions of light and joy. One of the first things [Henry Miller] was instructed in, on coming to stay with him, was never to throw away tin cans or empty bottles — nor rags, nor paper nor string, nor buttons, nor corks, nor even dollar bills'.[41] Agnès Varda's passion for *récup* and salvaged materials then had its own cultural and familial legacy, within the Californian counter-culture of the late 1960s. Moreover, that culture actively embraced the idea of nomadic homes and identities that seem to have informed her later *cabanes*. In her voice-over Varda describes the appeal of a 'maison flottante. Ma racine flottante'. The discovery of Jean Varda seems to have confirmed a sense of her own fluid, nomadic identity, albeit one (ironically) with family roots. The floating homes of *Uncle Yanco* are replete with some of those contradictions that haunt her installations and *cabanes*. These houseboats are both personalized, intimate, yet also mobile and un-rooted or *déraciné*, encapsulating some of the contradictions at the heart of installation art that can be both designed to relate to the site of display, yet also infinitely mobile and subject to different iterations in different international sites.

For her recent exhibition in Beijing China in 2012, Varda reconceived a *cabane* for a Chinese site. First designed in model form as a passage or portico that enters a house, *Chinese Portico* was conceived to encapsulate a global or 'trans-national' model of artistic inspiration and exchange. Made in Beijing workshops from her model, Varda described the project as follows:

> A door, a portico, is a passage to enter a house or universe, but here on exterior walls hang my photographs, as if at the entrance to the cinema. It all started with child's play, making models using pieces of wood, adding clothes-pegs for the roof.
> I built a mock-up gantry intended to look like a pagoda and painted it red. It's the year of the dragon and I, myself, am a dragon...
> ... It is an invitation to share our points of view, mine in 1957 of a China under construction, and those of Chinese visitors today, in 2012. How will they see their elders, people from the same era as their grandparents, whose children met in Guangzhou or Yunnan... who are now in turn grandmothers and grandfathers?[42]

Varda's comments reinforce the rich metaphorical possibilities of her *Chinese Portico*, and its potential to encourage trans-cultural exchange and reverie. Alongside the pseudo-Chinese, pagoda-like elements of the structure she displays her own photographs, both personalizing and distancing herself from the intimate, 'homely' associations of the shelter. 'Home' is thus constituted at a geographical distance. Like most contemporary artists, Varda of course inhabits a global world, but it is a world with which she seeks some form of critical dialogue. Her *cabanes* self-consciously position ideas of dwelling and sheltering within worlds that she (sometimes mischievously) seeks to interrogate and reframe: her cinematic history, her passion for beaches, her love of the people and spaces of Noirmoutier, for example. Each project evokes an embodied yet open form of dialogue, or what the art historian Marsha Meskimmon has called a 'cosmopolitan imagination'. She has identified art works that 'constitute a form of "being at home" that is simultaneously marked by movement, change and multiplicity'.[43] Meskimmon re-appropriates a notion of 'cosmopolitanism' that is rooted in imaginative engagement and interconnections, rather than the 'brutal exclusions' of some identity politics.[44] She argues that art can participate in a critical dialogue between a 'cosmopolitan imagination'-embodied ethics and locational identity. Moreover, this is a concept that, as she claims, is indebted to some of the insights of feminism, especially transnational feminism.[45] While Varda has not espoused any specific brand of feminist theory, her constant engagement with gender, gender politics, marginalized feminine subjects and feminine spaces in both her film and installation works, enable a kind of mobile vision (locational and aesthetic) that Meskimmon envisages.

And another more literal form of (aesthetic) mobility has characterized Varda's recent engagements with the theme of the hut or *cabane*. As if to remind her audience that these are essentially portable, mutable and changing structures, made up of tactile, functional materials, she has also used the form of the assemblage to signify the beach shack and its contents. Her exhibition at Musée Paul Valery in 2011 included a carefully arranged (yet seemingly random) pile of objects used in the construction of fishermen's beach huts. Her *Dépot de la cabane de pêcheur (Fisherman's Storage Hut)* included nets, tarpaulin, poles, crates and fishing tackle, echoing the piles of fishing debris and wooden poles and planks scattered around the port in *La Pointe Courte*. But this is a work that also invites an 'affective' turn, a form of participation.[46] As if to remind us that a *cabane* (or installation) is made up of specific material elements that the artist must construct or sculpt, Varda's *Dépot de la cabane* is a gallery piece with some clearly defined viewing positions, for this assemblage includes a projection of the video *La Mer Méditerranée avec deux r et un n (The Mediterranean Sea with two 'r's and one 'n')* against the corner wall of the gallery, which according to Varda 'nous présente une plage qui est possible...'[47]

Varda's beach huts and *cabanes*, like her films, can conflate notions of public and private, object and subject, to evoke nomadic and imaginary spaces. But as forms of installation art they are also complex material objects, replete with the traces and signs of both art-making and 'living'. They carry social and aesthetic histories and meanings, and invite an embodied viewer to enter and/or engage physically with the space. The public intimacy of Varda's *cabanes* is also related to their mobility — their tendency to migrate, to transmute, and to weave in and out of an autobiographical journey. As metaphors of home, they are also rich in contradictions and oblique references, deploying deliberate slippages between the media of film and installation art. Varda's *cabanes* invite a critical dialogue on 'home', belonging, gender, creativity, work, space and place — in search of '*une plage qui est possible*'.

Bibliography

K. H. Adler and Carrie Hamilton, eds, *Gendered Histories of Domesticity and Return* (Chichester: Wiley-Blackwell, 2010)

Marie-Claire Barnet and Shirley Jordan, eds, *Watch this Space: Women's Conceptualisations of Space in Contemporary French Film and Visual Art*, special issue of *L'esprit créateur*, 51:1 (Spring 2011)

Claire Bishop, *Installation Art: A Critical History* (London and New York: Routledge, 2005)

Alison Blunt and Robyn Dowling, *Home* (London: Routledge, 2006).

Agnès Varda L'Île et Elle, exhibition catalogue (Paris: Foundation Cartier, 2006)

Agnès Varda: Y'a pas que la mer, exhibition catalogue (Sète: Musée Paul Valéry, 2011–12)

Agnès Varda, The Beaches of Agnès Varda: 1957–2012 (Beijing, CAFA Art Museum and Hubei Museum of Art, 2012)

Gill Perry, *Playing at Home: The House in Contemporary Art* (London: Reaktion Books, 2013)

Notes to Chapter 10

1. Le Corbusier, 'Une Maison, Un Palais' 1928, cited in Gill Perry, *Playing at Home: The House in Contemporary Art* (London: Reaktion Books, 2013), p. 136.
2. Jacques Drillon, catalogue essay for exhibition *Agnès Varda L'Île et Elle* at the Foundation Cartier, 2006, p. 6.
3. Perry, *Playing at Home*, p. 136.
4. See Drillon, p. 6.
5. Exhibited on the top floor of La Sucrière in the 10th Lyon Biennale (2009), curated by Hou Hanru.
6. 'Disons que c'est une cabane de ciné récup, une cabane de rêverie'. Agnès Varda, quoted in the dossier *La cabane de l'échec, devenue la cabane de cinéma*', Archive Ciné-Tamaris, Paris.
7. See Perry, *Playing at Home*, p. 138
8. Quoted by (among others) Jonathan Romney, 'Step into My Office: Agnès Varda's New Career as an Installation Artist', *Independent*, 4 October 2009.

9. For a fascinating discussion of the significance of this *cabanon,* and its relevance to a growing leisure culture of the seaside, see Claude Prelorenzo, 'Le cabanon et les unités de camping ou les vacances en Méditerranée selon Le Corbusier', in Claude Prelorenzo (ed.), *Eileen Gray — L'Etoile de Mer — Le Corbusier* (Paris: Archibooks, 2013), pp. 92–121.
10. While the hut or shack can signify extremes of global poverty in the contexts of, for example, South American favelas or South African townships, the idealized notion of the primitive hut, reformulated in Le Corbusier's *hutte,* was taken up by the German philosopher Martin Heidegger (1889–1976) who explored the idea of the hut as a dwelling that could signify both a physical building and a 'home'. In his essay 'Building, Dwelling, Thinking' (1954), he argued that dwelling (in the sense of making a home) is a basic characteristic of consciousness, directly opposed to 'homelessness'. He believed that the latter condition, a symptom of modern life, was susceptible to alienation and existential homelessness, a view that encouraged his romanticized ideas of 'primitive' homes, provincialism and the German homeland. Heidegger's famous 'hut' (*die Hutte*) that he built in the Black Forest Mountains in 1922 was his response to this perceived alienation and an embodiment of the 'hut myth'.
11. For a discussion of some of these issues see Perry, *Playing at Home,* 2013, p. 17ff. See also K. H. Adler and Carrie Hamilton, *Gendered Histories of Domesticity and Return* (Chichester: Wiley-Blackwell, 2010). For an exploration of gender, domesticity and space see Beatriz Colomina (ed.), *Sexuality and Space* (Princeton: Princeton University Press, 1996).
12. For a useful overview of the discipline of Cultural Geography see Alison Blunt and Robyn Dowling, *Home* (London: Routledge, 2006).
13. Blunt and Dowling, p. 2.
14. See Phil Powrie, 'Heterotopic Spaces and Nomadic Gazes in Varda: From *Cléo de 5 à 7* to *Les Glaneurs et la Glaneuse,* in Marie-Claire Barnet and Shirley Jordan (eds), *Watch this Space: Women's Conceptualisations of Space in Contemporary French Film and Visual Art,* special issue of *L'esprit créateur,* 51:1 (Spring 2011), pp. 68–82.
15. For a fuller discussion of these semantic issues see Adler and Hamilton, p. 4.
16. Isabelle McNeill has also referenced the semantic differences between notions of 'home' and *chez soi* in her chapter 'Virtual Homes: Space and Memory in the Work of Yamina Benguigui, in Barnet and Jordan, p. 13.
17. Kristine Stiles, 'I\Eye\Oculus: Performance, Installation, Video', in *Themes in Contemporary Art,* ed. by Gill Perry and Paul Wood, (Newhaven and London, 2004), pp. 183–229 (p. 185).
18. Claire Bishop, *Installation Art: A Critical History,* (London and New York: Routledge, 2005), pp. 11, 81.
19. Nicholas Bourriaud's influential essay *Relational Aesthetics* (London and Paris: les presses du réel, 1998, English translation, 2002) has generated wide-ranging debates about the nature and function of installation art, its 'relational' potential and the 'culture of interactivity' that it can involve.
20. See, for example, Joseph Roach, *It* (Ann Arbor: University of Michigan Press, 2007).
21. Ibid, p. 8.
22. Marie-Claire Barnet, '*Elles-Ils* Islands: Cartography of Lives and Deaths by Agnès Varda', in Barnet and Jordan, *Watch this Space,* 2011, p. 99.
23. Agnès Varda, *L'île et Elle: Raconter l'île de Noirmoutier en imaginant et la réalité,* 2006, p.38
24. See Prelorenzo, 'Le Cabanon', 2013, p. 101.
25. Exhibited in her show at the Foundation Cartier in 2006.
26. Fiona Handyside, 'The Feminist Beachscape: Catherine Breillat, Diane Kurys and Agnès Varda' in Barnet and Jordan, *Watch this Space,* 2011, p. 84. Handyside also cites Alain Corbin's useful book *Le Territoire du vide: L'Occident et le désir de ravage (1750–1840)* (Paris: Flammarion, 1990; translated as *The Lure of the Sea; Discovery of the Seaside,* Penguin, 1995) in which the author charts the history of the modern concept of the beach as a site of leisure and modernity.
27. See Fiona Handyside, 'The Feminist Beachscape', 2011, p. 90ff for a development of these arguments.
28. For a discussion of this 'Daguerre Plage' and its role as part of Varda's 'playful mapping', see Marie-Claire Barnet, in Barnet and Jordan, *Watch this Space,* 2011, pp. 98–100
29. See for example, Puvis de Chavannes, *The Happy Land,* 1882 or Matisse's famous *Bonheur de*

Vivre, 1904–05. Interestingly Puvis de Chavannes also produced one of the most iconic images of impoverished French fishermen in his *The Poor Fisherman*, 1888 (Musée d'Orsay).

30. John Mack, *The Sea: A Cultural History* (London: Reaktion Books, 2011), p. 165.
31. Phil Powrie has explored the 'nomadic gaze' in some of Varda's films in his essay 'Heterotopic Spaces and Nomadic Gazes in Varda: From *Cléo de 5 à 7* to *Les Glaneurs et la glaneuse*' in Barnet and Jordan, *Watch this Space*, pp. 68–82.
32. Agnès Varda, Introduction to exhibition catalogue *The Beaches of Agnès Varda: 1957–2012* (Beijing, CAFA Art Museum and Hubei Museum of Art, 2012), p. 25.
33. Lubaina Himid, *Beach House* (Rochdale: Rochdale Art Gallery, 1994). Her written piece 'Beach Houses' was included in Griselda Pollock, ed., *Generations and Geographies in the Visual Arts: Feminist Readings* (London and New York: Routledge, 1996), pp. 149–55.
34. *Ibid.*, p. 150.
35. *Ibid.*, p. 50. I have quoted at length from Himid's vivid account to emphasise the similarities in the rich potential seen by both artists in the motif of beach hut.
36. *Ibid.*, p. 155.
37. Cited in Caroline Maniaque-Benton's fascinating book: *French Encounters with the American Counter Culture* 1960–1980 (Farnham: Ashgate, 2011), p. 27.
38. See Albert Garvey, 'The Houseboats of Sausolito', *Architectural Forum*, 126, no 2 (March 1967), and Varda's voice-over to *Uncle Yanco*.
39. Varda was born in Belguim in 1928 to a Greek father and French mother.
40. Her film and photography from this period, along with some more recent installations have been celebrated in an exhibition at LACMA Los Angeles, titled 'Agnès Varda in Californialand', 2013.
41. Henry Miller, *Remember to Remember* (London: 1952).
42. *The Beaches of Agnès Varda in China*, 2012, p. 46.
43. Marsha Meskimmon, *Contemporary Art and the Cosmopolitan Imagination* (London: Routledge, 2011), p. 5.
44. Meskimmon cites Kwame Anthony Appiah's thinking on 'cosmopolitanism' that explores the relationships between 'conversations across boundaries' that begin with forms of imaginative engagement. *Ibid.*, p. 7.
45. *Ibid.*, p. 7.
46. Meskimmon discusses the role of the 'affective turn' within a 'cosmopolitan imagination' in *Contemporary Art and the Cosmopolitan Imagination*, pp. 8–9.
47. *Agnès Varda — Y'a pas que la mer*, exhibition catalogue Musée Paul Valéry, Sète, 2011–12, p. 67.

CHAPTER 11

Out of Sites: Art Matters, Contemporary Activism, and Public Encounters with Agnès Varda

Marie-Claire Barnet

'Qu'est-ce qui vous inspire? Ce qui ne m'expire pas. Des spectacles minimaux de la vie des autres. Plus c'est inattendu, plus l'imagination vagabonde [...] Le presque pas vu, le non-dit.' [*What inspires you? What doesn't make me expire. Other people's lives, seen as minimal spectacles. The more unexpected these are, the more they catch the vagabond imagination[...] The barely seen, the unsaid*] — Agnès Varda[1]

'Can One Lead a Good Life in a Bad Life?' — Judith Butler[2]

'I like to bear witness to anti-violence by moving around the media at my disposal: photography, cinema and video. Black-and-white and colour... Paper, wood. Metal and cardboard, everything can be made into a proposition.' — Agnès Varda[3]

This chapter considers how Agnès Varda's enduring and experimental artistic practice extends far beyond celluloid and the conventional museum space into site-specific installations in public spaces, reconfigured as private spaces and spaces to reflect upon the visual arts, memory, and other key concepts such as political engagement, socio-cultural margins, and supposed *lieux communs*. In order to see where, and why, Varda's forever 'vagabond imagination' was taking her various audiences, I selected (as I had to for the purposes of this essay) two different exhibitions, arguably far less visible or visited than other major retrospectives or Biennales. The two installations I visited were in two separate locations, on quite different scales, and with apparently contrasting themes, offered as deceptive first impressions: the first, part of a vibrant major regional arts festival that has become a big touristic success in the Loire-Atlantique since its creation in 2011, and the other a solo exhibition in a quieter but key contemporary Parisian gallery.[4] The dual analysis of, first, Varda's summer 2012 double installation for *Le Voyage à Nantes*, 'Des Chambres en ville et des téléviseurs' and 'La Chambre occupée, paroles de squatteurs' (15 June-19 August 2012) with its downstairs-upstairs effect, and, second, the puzzling portraits and triptychs she reunited and deconstructed for her Spring 2014 exhibition at the Nathalie Obadia Gallery in Paris (*Atypical Triptychs*, 8 February-5 April 2014) show her continuously exceeding both viewers' expectations and the confinement of the potential 'white cube' of the art gallery. Drawing on work by a range of scholars and theorists such as Claire Bishop, Judith Butler, Naomi Klein, Phil Powrie, Kaja Silverman, Emma Wilson, and Slavoj Žižek, among others, or bearing in mind many essayists, activists, poets, artists, such as Noam Chomsky, Maggi Hambling, Jackie Kay, or Sally Mann, my key focus and objective in examining, firstly, this split into two (floors or public/private spaces), with its ambivalent approach to an 'exhibition', and secondly the two re-cut as a split into three for her take on the classic triptychs of religious art, is to explore Varda's recurrent political agenda in the twenty-first century, and to assess in its wider sense how her work engages with renewed debates about the artist's contemporary role in our communities. My analysis will strive to revisit and offer new twists in the overall and persistent reflection brought about by Varda's recent mixed-media work on cinema and in her varied artistic practices, including her re-creations of Demy's world. I will also re-examine their vital role and relevance today for reassessing her 'artistic language' — if one can qualify as such her famous '*cinécriture*' involving a further exemplary development of her ongoing interdisciplinarity, implying much more than the creation of deceptively 'fun' titles and linguistic puns. How is it deployed and applied in these experimental installations, and why could one consider that this constitutes not quite a new phase, but a key part of Varda's undeniably and richly diverse work over the past six decades?

Revisiting the past, the deeply loved one(s), the self and its autobiographical representations, will be touched upon. Encounters with others, as we will see — other artists, as well as sought-out outcasts, migrants, and more perfect 'strangers' on a beach met by chance, or the 'ordinary but extraordinary' general public that Varda always pictures as personal and distinctively individual — seem to me very high up in the list of objectives or affect of Varda's creations.[5] However, it is equally important to remember that that Varda also insists repeatedly on the inevitable and complex 'risk' taken in art, 'the wager' a filmic experience entails — on both sides of the screen — as she eloquently comments on in the interview in this volume.[6] As Claire Boyle points out in her luminous essay on the uneasy genre of 'filmic autobiography', Varda does 'not attempt to hide the missed encounters' in *Les Plages d'Agnès*. Far from it, she suggests there is even a necessary failure of the *face à face* encounter in this 'not recording', for 'art does not record, it creates'.[7] Claire Bishop's reflections on the overall history and challenges of installation art also accompany my lines of thinking on Varda's engagement with the practice itself and my analysis of the representation of 'community'. Reflecting that 'not new characteristics, but key questions [remain] still to be asked about the types of experience sought, the types of participating viewers envisaged', Bishop puts her subtle finger on the heavy and ongoing debates about what 'addressing' gallery visitors — through a specific spatial and web of multi-sensory experiences — looks like and entails, looking further into what 'interactivity' and 'installation art' may stand for, and speculating on the degrees and values of 'relational aesthetics' which has been relying on a 'collective elaboration of meaning' from the start.[8] As mentioned in the preface, Varda talked about 'risk' involved in installing art, and we can see that involving various audiences, reaching out, or even creating a sense of our 'communities', is far from another readymade idea or ideal. I will also consider, in the second part of this chapter, the recurrent themes but also the new types of audiences that Varda's installation work seems to address, bearing in mind (as Bishop lucidly states) that the very concept of installation art, even if it has had an 'increasingly canonical history' since the 1960s, proves to stand on highly slippery postmodern territory and has become a notably 'contested term' — and probably not only because all our virtual relationships have been expanded via technological innovations, the internet and globalization.[9]

Rooms with Interactivist Views: From Demy's Dreamworld to Varda's *Sans toit ni nantis*

Nantes as a privileged cinema location for Jacques Demy is well known, and one may also recall that he advocated our right to go through material walls, see beyond appearances, and to dream wide awake, what he called, 'to lead a double life'[10]. As a commissioned artist and guest of honour for the *Voyage à Nantes* festival in summer 2012, Agnès Varda went back to build and transfer her own haunted dreams 'visually', transporting the public to unexpected places by revealing the darker sides of this French city — alluding less, though, to its notorious past of eighteenth-century human trafficking and slavery than to our contemporary society haunted by relentless and increasing waves of migrating people who have little space and few shelters to rest or dream. She created two site-specific installations (a closer look revealing, actually, three parts), located right next to the majestic, renaissance-style staircase in the legendary covered shopping arcade, the Passage Pommeraye of Jacques Demy's youth and artistic visions, where he visited the former local cinema club hidden in its heart. Film buffs will recall that he shot his iconic star, the seemingly abandoned but hopeful, or hopelessly romantic, Anouk Aimée, as light as the dreaming and restless female butterfly of *Lola* (shot in 1960). Varda's installation alludes to other images and ideas and her choices are revealing: the intallation includes two sets of symbolic 'rooms' on two levels of the passage, one open as a fake boutique on the commercial side, the other hidden from public access, separated by a further hidden service and defunct staircase. The third element in that architectural collage was a whole property letting-agency which many passer-bys may have missed. Attention to 'le presque pas vu' and 'déjà vu' filmic references, or tiny details can help: the agency called Une Chambre à soi [A Room of One's Own], was represented by just a classic A1 poster, but with potentially strong Virginia Woolf echoes (1929) and a list of curious contact names. Hidden or, rather, coded references to Jacques Demy's cast in his arguably less remembered musical film, *Une Chambre en ville* (also shot in the Passage Pommeraye, 1982), offered a list of available lodgings outside one of the two 'big' installation rooms downstairs, Le Magasin des téléviseurs, the very same type of old fashioned TV shop where the madly jealous husband, Edmond, and distraught wife, Edith, played by Michel Piccoli and Dominique Sanda, clash and meet with tragedy, with the memorable staged death of Piccoli. Half-hidden coded messages therefore trigger darkly funny reminiscences about the lead characters, as names seem to come straight out of Demy's film, i.e., read 'please contact Mme

Fig. 11.1. 'Le Magasin des téléviseurs' (photographed in August 2012)

Edith' (Sanda), 'Mme Langlois' (Danielle Darrieux), or 'be prepared to do school runs with little François' (the first name of Guilbaud, Richard Berry). It may have appeared like a marginal addition, not very conspicuous outside, especially to the long queues by the door, until, perhaps, visitors started to connect the two installations and traced their foosteps in various different mind-walks, trying to decipher where exactly Varda had just taken them, on and off the 'touristy' or artistic tracks, looking for delights or derelict places (to which I will return): symbolic stairways, entre-deux vagueness, and a flagrant upstairs-downstairs effect, except that Varda put the squalid squat in the upper floor, above the reconstitution of Piccoli's television shop in *Une Chambre en ville.*

As Phil Powrie had shown us regarding Cléo's meaningful meandering and awakening while wandering, what is presented and visible is far from being the end of the dual story Varda was telling us with her (walking) installation, which I would also qualify as 'autrement itinérante'.[11] My analysis will focus further on Varda's curious configurations of *city rooms* where visitors were invited to pause, participate by their presence and perception, ultimately passing through as flickering images of themselves shown on many old television sets. Firstly, looking at echoes of Demy's *Une Chambre en ville* — grief and drama implied, mixed media, motions and emotions intended — my reflections are here influenced by Emma Wilson's analysis of interconnected themes in *Love, Mortality and the Moving Image.*[12] Secondly, my study will revisit Varda's own 'revised' squat or *cabinet de curiosités* and other potential connections, in order to show that more than food as a surrealist prop pops up, with unexpected places involved: further hybrid symbols, distorted dreams, or neglected voices of the poor will prove to be less exhibited than re-installed, challenging visitors' expectations on the (always hard to define) 'artistic encounter'. Varda's temporary *installation nantaise* in two rooms (and the three elements remind us irresistibly of her triptych leitmotif) thus offered both continuity and discontinuity, as in matters of life and death, so that one had to go in and out (or pass by), while all along, she (mis)led us from an apparently colourful/harmless fantasy world (*Le Magasin des téléviseurs*) to the harsh realism of social exclusion (*La Chambre occupée, paroles de squatteurs*). This very title may be read as anti-'empty premises', but I cannot help seeing a timely nod to the Occupy movement of protestation against capitalism and its discontents, whose growing popularity coincided with the art project.[13] I would also argue that both rooms eventually mirrored each other in their perfectly unnerving and uncanny mix of fiction and reality, fiction as reality or reality as fiction. After all, there was to be no such fine line between easy/uneasy viewing, as I concluded when witnessing a few people refusing to climb up the delapidated staircase.

'Double lives' or interconnected universes: *Demy Monde* & Varda's World

Serge Toubiana coined the jokingly *louche* phrase 'Demy-monde' to celebrate the ambiguity of the filmmaker's creation at the cinémathèque retrospective, which greeted visitors with a clever hall of mirrors to reconstruct a Passage Pommeraye with a maritime feel. Captain Demy was seemingly up on deck greeting us and our passing reflections, leading us to many interwoven connections with Calder and Nikki de Saint Phalle, as seen in the 'puzzle' of orchestrated encounters of the *Demoiselles de Rochefort* in the art gallery — with Cocteau, Duffy, Leonor Fini and Hockney appearing, among other artistic influences.[14] On Varda's Nantes reconstitution of Demy's cinema world, Alexis Campion saw an invitation to meditate — out of place in a shopping centre, doubled by a sense of wonder — that greeted visitors in *Le Magasin des télévisieurs*: if familiar with Demy's films, they would have the privileged sensation of stepping into a cinema set, while being bombarded with more or less dated images shown on a loop on further old television sets.[15] Location, location and reconstruction are key, and several stages explained might demystify but will not erase the 'wonder effect' (or the darkness and horror behind the wonderful staging). I have learnt that the so-called 'TV shop' had been used as an art gallery for years, and after the 2012 festival was used as an information kiosk for the overall renovation of the Passage Pommeraye planned for 2013–2014.[16] If not a Nantes resident, one may not have realized the other mirror effect of the change from 1982 to 2012: indeed, the television shop had been reconstructed opposite the actual Demy film set, on the other side of the staircase. Proximity, at least, must have been a priority for 'Agnès la miroitière', as nicknamed by Dominique Bluher. Indeed one recalls the importance Varda has given to walls before, not only in *Mur murs*, but also in *Jacquot de Nantes*, insisting on using the exact location of the family garage: 'Je crois trop aux murs, à la matière, à tout ce qui reste d'un lieu' [I really believe in walls, material, everything that remains of a place].[17] Perhaps Demy himself would not have minded having to use a substitute again, highlighting as he did the dream value, above all, for the garage location and transcending walls, and similarly referring to and defining Passage Pommeraye, and not just the cineclub located there, as a fundamental dreamspace: 'Là j'ai tellement rêvé dans mon adolescence' [as a teenager, I dreamt so much there].'[18]

What did these revamped and reinvented walls by Varda contain, as far as surprises are concerned? At first glance, and on one level, 'the TV shop' is '*un 'hommage au 1er degré*', as Varda explains in the Nantes exhibition notes handed out to visitors; it is devoted to and clearly related to Demy's world thirty years after *Une Chambre en ville*. We have the TV sets, the echo of political unrest (strikes in the film are echoed by shots of elections scenes in 2012 on Noirmoutier island), the dark green walls, the abandoned mink coat and the suitcase, and (in the back room) an extract from the film: the sequence when Sanda and Piccoli argue so fiercely and fatally — a foreshadowing of the tragedy, the horror of death, being hinted at. This 'shop' functions therefore as dark room, a chamber of echoes, to reanimate, reveal and connect memories; and more than that, since it can also function as *Une Chambre à soi* with a twist, or *une chambre pour lui/elle* (Demy/Varda), or a room for them/others (actors, viewers, all of us). Indeed, looking again at the list of lodgings, one notes the nod to the Ciné-Tamaris production headquarters and combined home, with the iconic Zgougou cat label drawn under the pointed lines of a roof. Varda stated that she intended a 'salut nostalgique et décalé', as she plays with linguistic, visual tricks or pushes back the 'durs murs' or any walls that might constrain our great expectations about her installations as *cinéma exposé* [exhibited cinema], as Dominique Païni cleverly observes.[19] 'Who knows,' asked Varda, 'as they lie petrified and staring out with such intensity, for which reality cats are our clairvoyants?'.[20] One may wonder what the bogus TV room could also be, if not a bigger picture (à la David Hockney) of reality and cinema, another version of *la maison du cinéma*, the cinema as home.[21]

Agnès Varda included a now well-recycled so-called cabin of failure, with strips from her film with Piccoli and Deneuve, *Les Créatures* (1966). The humble shack was reappropriated simultaneously and forcefully as the cinema cabin and home *par excellence* in 2006 at the Fondation Cartier: rebaptized her 'palace', Jacques Drillon muses on this assemblage which he also sees as a 'cow in her field', 'very proud of its status of 'work of art'. He also queries the relative artistic nature and value of these 'found again objects', turning to the (personified) editing table right nearby which, he imagines, 'was not destined to end up as a work of art', adding with humour that it wants nothing to do with 'horrifying' Duchamp's readymades.[22] A mixed 'failure' transfigured into a resonant success, is this a two-part composition that perhaps people do not put together, and which paradoxically leads to further mixed feelings? And whose? We may also remember that Demy's *Une Chambre en ville* was 'a beautiful film which was absolutely unsuccessful', as François Ozon put it tactfully.[23] It was the 30th anniversary of Demy's film, giving it back to us as a home and hommage to Demy, with, instead of the forever dreamy and luminous Lola forever rushing in the passage Pommeraye, we have a new version of this dark

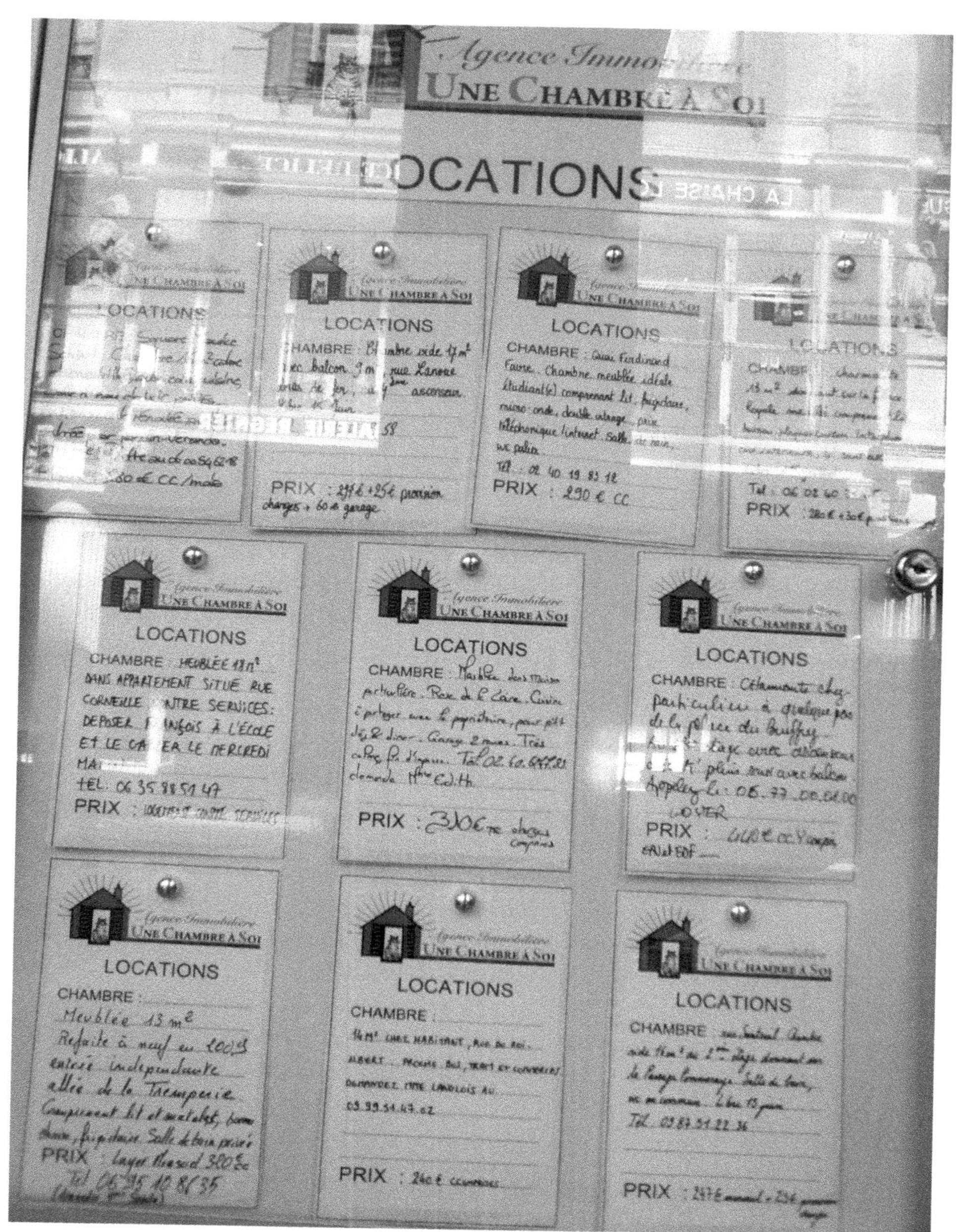

Fig. 11.2. 'Une Chambre à soi' (photographed in August 2012)

'opera en-chanté décalé' about strikers in 1955. More sociopolitical unrest was on Varda's mind (as seen in the 'Occupied room' upstairs). But there is also a different concern at stake, namley that cinema is always reinvented by viewers and goes far beyond critical judgement, four dark walls, or the corners of the changing screen of all sorts of projections: we have so many TV sets or 'filtres de la réalité' filtering the real, as Varda puts it; so if we add one huge cinema screen at the back, which one do we look at longer? Are we facing another collage or a zapping mode of modernity?[24] Where did we think we would end, entering the fake shop of horribly nightmarish Edmond/Piccoli, slicing his own throat: with all these discarded props looking like toys, the cardboard scenery will be most uncanny for some viewers. Portaits, as seen in *Les Plages d'Agnès*, make Varda laugh with mischievous mirrors, Isadora Duncan scarves, in a hide-and-seek game.[25] I would like to suggest we were perhaps in another 'drama' in Nantes, and right in little Jacquot de Nantes's feverishly inventive brain, as seen in Varda's biofilm, with his own focus on the violent stuff of dreams, how to catch a thief or survive airplane bombing, the animated experiments in the 40's, *Attaque nocturne*, *Le Pont de mauves*. Therefore what we could acess here, differently, is a renewed 3D representation of Demy's imagination as 'reality'.

What did one potentially get in the TV shop or *Demy-monde* on a loop? The recent black and white shots of boats in China (Spring 2012) did not look very different from turn-of-the-century archival footage of strolling figures along the Loire river. Varda commented that she actively fought off nostalgia, including therefore the recorded presence and invasive flow of 'the present' to enter this (made up) studio set, which could so easily turn into a stuffy museum with dated scenery.[26] It did look frozen, a perfect crime scene, after all, for the film it precisely evoked. An uncanny sign again, of creative repetitions: Varda used that teasing trick of the dizzying collage of film extracts, superimposed on the exclusively exterior shots of a big staircase when filming another hommage, the celebration of (the former) Cinémathèque de Chaillot (*T'as de beaux escaliers tu sais*, 1986), the 'inside' of which we never got to see but entered differently via the filmic collage. In Nantes she added shots from 'real' passers-by going down the passage staircase outside — blending in, so to speak, with *France 3* live coverage, or superimposed even onto a broken TV set: an obvious paradox, which arrested 'time' and movement via the blunt symbol of the broken machine. Therefore I would stress that Varda's installations here are not products but other types of interactive spaces; or someone else's words, invitations to step in, see and sense differently. I think of Christian Boltanski's adamant desire to have active minds and footsteps from his visitors, no longer facing but entering the space of the art not 'displayed' but to be played with/'created', even stepping perhaps into the (uncontrollable) mind of the creative process itself.[27]

Sans toit in Nantes: 'on n'habite plus, on squatte.' On the afterlives of ghosts[28]

Another type of 'local' *Nantais* interested Varda; not only the visitors or visible shoppers in the elegant passage turned busy shopping arcade (the '*nantis* or rich (enough) people'), but also the (arguably hidden from view) poor, mostly illegal immigrants, homeless, paperless, and voiceless. Another floor of her installation therefore leads to 'virtual' squatters in former student rooms, a dilapidated (and well-named) *hôtel des colonies* fallen from grace. The realism of the installation made me research the history of that building thoroughly. As clearly shared by other

Fig. 11.3. 'La Chambre occupée, paroles de squatteurs' (photographed in August 2012)

visitors, there was an 'uncanny' sensation lingering in the air, beginning at the bottom of the staircase. Initially, one did and did not know what was represented. In other words, not quite trusting one's eyes, one felt this creation could be/have been a 'real' squat with broken sinks, mirrors, and peeling walls covered in graffiti. On one level, this is déjà vu, another political message and a reinvented version of her famous marginalized 'poor' and outcasts, the immortal/mortal Mona in *Sans toit ni loi*, the gleaners, and the whole range of social outcasts who appeared as early as 1958 in her *Opéra Mouffe*. Further links and echoes emerge. Their worlds may have seemed divided (the bourgeois universe of consumerism par excellence and the hidden occupied squat for excluded soon-to-be *expulsés*), but the inextricably tangled sense of tension, semi-emptiness and repressed violence represented the split world that Varda chose to make us see again, at the very heart of the symbol of *luxe et calme* (forget the *volupté*) in this passage for flâneurs à la Baudelaire. The TV messages were subverted below, and upstairs the repressed violence of Piccoli or strikers exploded through newspapers cuttings, with threats from the police and the city hall, all the quoted news representing stark facts from the lives of hopeless *sans-papiers, sans abris*. As read and posted on the walls upstairs in the lobby at the exit: 'not enough hot beds; back to the bleak, cold streets; police uses brutal force; 38-year old mother sets herself on fire out of despair.' An extract from the law about gleaning and abandoned/found objects resurfacing in the collage of articles shows us that Varda is not rewriting but remapping the real, not only reappropriating the

Fig. 11.4. 'La Chambre occupée, paroles de squatteurs' (photographed in August 2012)

old Surrealist collage technique, but carefully zapping, cutting and pasting together daily papers to give us another type of 'cutting-edge news'.

Discussing her filmed food items (a tin shot and shown in a microwave stuck in a shopping trolley) or interviews with *squatteurs*, reframed and broadcast in symbolic furniture (a shelter where to eat, sleep, get warm, reduced to a mattress and a stove), Varda dismissed them as 'not that original', claiming that these elements are simple visual tricks (Duchamp-style readymades), showing basic and common needs to all.[29] What to select for this show and (re)tell is nevertherless more complex than one might think. The displacement à la Magritte she operates on symbols, matching the forced exclusion of people, I would argue, is not that easy to represent, as poignant details could easily become 'déjà vu', potentially losing their raw bleakness, or even like an oversentimental, sensationalist piece of news on TV. Where are the thin frontiers between (non-)intervention and showing one's deep care and serious concerns? Varda is well aware of the uneasiness of affect, leading to interpreting her 'good/suspicious' intentions, and the limits of 'representation', and other 'wagers', or even dangers of these voices she makes almost tangible, paradoxically emerging 'differently' from an old mattress, or a wood stove: 'Je ne voulais pas faire un documentaire social, j'essaie de trouver des choses réelles qui facilitent l'émotion [...] Sans me transformer en assistante sociale ou infirmière sans frontières, on est en souci pour ce qui se passe' [I didn't want to make a social documentary, I am trying to find real things to make it easier to connect with emotionally [...] Without turning into a social worker or a Nurse Without Borders, one is deeply concerned by what's happening].[30]

How to match the outside with the inside, Varda's query goes further than this dichotomy. 'I need images, I need representation which deals in other means than reality. We have to use reality but then get out of it. That's what I try to do all the time'.[31] The general degraded state of walls, ceilings, lobby, spiralling and condemned staircase, reminded visitors at least and at last that these voices were from unseen and unheard citizens of the world, if not officially of France, or again, that they were the displaced dreams, hopes, hidden faces of thousands of people. Varda mixed lives and fiction; she gave back visibilty to the invisible squatters, paradoxically becoming quite close to the disappeared/the dead, in the way they vanish from our field of vision. Extraordinary people are to be found in Varda's unflinching gaze at the so-called 'ordinary' (to add a twist to Bluher's terminology), or poor, or illegal, as testified by her political interventions/installations. One may think of what Varda said about the fundamental need for a desire to see, seeing differently and deeply, or what Maggi Hambling said about art's function, against all odds and clichés, that its power is 'to make us pause in the midst of our busy world'.[32]

What can one make of it all? Varda herself has always been aware that a key part of installations is the possible total lack of people's reactions/non reactions, as viewers are free to roam, leave and comment or ignore. But for '*La Chambre Occupée*', solutions might start by activating further queries about what and who is right next to us, and without wishing to provide model 'repesentations' or answers, she clearly aimed at asking again, at asking us aloud via others' voices, how 'unlivable' such a type of clandestine and silenced life could be.[33] Moreover, I would like to suggest her rooms are fundamentally engaging, interactive, even *interactivist* as she always seems to go beyond the apparent boundaries of technique, modes of expression, language itself, even, visibility. What and who she gives us to encounter rather than 'see', glance at, pass by, seem to expand our outer fields of vision while stretching our inner elastic levels of imagination and capacity to go beyond appearances: her installations are invitations to revisit all kinds of preconceptions and insights. If representing the dead is to inflict a wound (in the sense of Kaja Silverman), then were we wounded or touched in Nantes by the representation of the disappeared, the invisible and the almost hidden from our fields of vision?[34] Emma Wilson notes that despite us gazing at images of our dead and imagining them still wanting our love, 'the dead, remote, may turn away from us, no longer seeking love'.[35] To answer such a disturbing idea of a potential rejection from the dead, or to ask again, 'What do the dead (or the poor) want?', to paraphrase Freud with Emma Wilson, is surely not so easily for us to say. Yet where they might be is perhaps a little less problematic according to Jackie Kay's suggestion to Julia Darling in *Darling*, 'the dead don't go till you do, loved ones. / The dead are still holding our hands'; or if one thinks of Bill Manhire's 'darker furniture' such as old TV sets, radio waves and booming boxes (bearing in mind the displaced use of ovens and beds by Varda too): 'I don't know where the dead go, Kevin. / The only far place I know is inside the heavy radio./ [...] They are mothers and fathers [add partners, strangers], Kevin, whom we barely know. / They lift us. Eventually we all shall go into the dark furniture of the radio.'[36] One may also recall the more than bizarre, darkly humorous and uncanny effect that Slavoj Žižek's reconstructed film sets triggered, by bringing them 'back to life', so to speak, and by putting himself (and his viewers) inside them.[37] A much obvious (perverse or predictable, à la Žižek?) transfer and a consciously-made visible projection seem involved in *Le Voyage à Nantes*, from the creator (Varda) who pays homage to another very special and fellow artist (Demy) — or what else does she want here, splitting her exhibition in so many parts and contrasting moods ? — and it seems to me that the alchemy of artistic references, influences and interferences is, as always, actively and ambivalently porous, fundamentally hard to pinpoint as a one-way process with one clear objective. In any event, Demy never left the Passage Pommeraye.[38]

'Everything can be made into a proposition'

Let's turn again and briefly to images via a (temporary) triptych of propositions about the potential processes involved. The much celebrated and controversial American photographer Sally Mann recently revisited archives of her own, endless boxes of pictures and papers, while examining her life's beginnings and assessing her husband's upbringing. Via a parallel analysis of her phenomenally innovative work, mixing a range of techniques, and with a wide-angle focus on the complex 'immediate family', interwoven with intimate portraits of other dead or living ghosts, Mann came to the conclusion that photographs do not simply erase but replace — and 'corrupt' — memory.[39]

Kaja Silverman, when rethinking the uncontrollable 'kinship' and radical fluidity of so-called 'fixed' photographs, 'mov[ing]through time, in search of other 'kin', some of which may be visual, while others may be philosophical or literary', proposes that photos are endlessly happening or co-'developing' 'with us': 'Not only is the photographic image an analogy, rather than a representation or an index, but analogy is also the fluid in which it develops. This process does not begin when we decide it should, or end when we command it to. Photography develops, rather, *with us*, and *in response to us*.'[40] I cannot help recalling, in another context, as pointed out above, Drillon transposing/seeing/imagining a cow where a Varda cabane stood (was he looking at a picture of the exhibition when he wrote for one of the catalogues?); images, textual or visual, are tricky that way. Comparing while selecting is also part of the artistic process, which Varda herself explains soberly in terms of an uneasy 'exclusion': 'To choose one image means to shut others away'.[41]

Creating Others/'Ourselves as a Work of Art', and the Value of Other Portraits[42]

Susan Bright suggests a further most fruitful and masterly review of where the ever-popular portrait can emerge from and what it might stand for, as part of a complex (post)contemporary art practice:

> Laden with ambiguity and uncertainty, the portrait is perhaps the most complex area of artistic practice. Used by contemporary artists to explore issues of identity — national, personal or sexual — the portrait has moved away from its commercial roots to become a powerful encounter or exchange between artist, sitter and spectator. Motivations and desires are never really clear and reactions to a portrait can vary enormously. To one it can be exploitative, engaging, or ethically uncertain, and to another tender, informed and noble. These tensions make portraiture one of the most compelling of artistic genres and also one of the most popular.[43]

Toujours Provence, anyone? An interesting departure (in all meanings of the word, as this is an 'on the road' project for the summer of 2015) is the recent encounter between Varda and the visual artist, 'JR Artist' (as self-called on his Facebook page), which promises (see JR's Instagram) to lead to series of 'new' portraits, as seen in their intended reciprocity to shoot each other, to produce also double 'funny' portraits in the vein of 'the artist shot and photographed by the other artist', and take more shots of 'local' people (read, probably the ones standing out, typical or atypical, as you wish) in the Lubéron region — again, in the vein of the rue Daguerre series of portraits, for instance, one will recall, except this time, Agnès V. 'aka AV' is to be a co-creator, 'comrade', an 'accomplice', accompanied by 'JR aka JR', all identities or egos joyfully blended in a collage of capital letters from the start. Self-centred selfies are not on the cards, and this textual portrait of the duo is therefore revealing of these multiple aims and objectives focusing on provocative encounters with 'people', and keeping an eye on each other's practice:

> — JR: I also had Agnès pose on a Solex in front of the photobooth truck. The adventure continues...
> — AV: So that's the project. We're going to be truckers.

— JR: Yep! And when you're not driving, you can catch trucks as you did in The Gleaners!!
— AV: We'll go to the Lubéron region in Provence for an adventure of encounters sparked by this wonderful truck. I've noticed that people with cell phones, 'ay-phones' or otherwise, always want to take self-portraits, the recent and notorious 'selfies'!
— JR: So while we're at it, we'll invite them into the truck, take their portraits and offer them enlargements of themselves. But the main thing we'll be doing is improvising art installations in the region.
— AV: I want to film the locals, the people of the region, their gestures, their houses, their children... and evoke their concerns.
— JR: I want to photograph Agnès while she's filming.
— AV: And I want to film JR while he's taking photographs![44]

And what else do they, or we, want from a work of art?[45] This might be a neat pendant — or typically Vardian triptych — to the dialogue above, focusing on the key role of the audience, bearing in mind the explicit participation actively sought from the public in the latest 'art on the go' installation by Agnès Varda with her 'co-conspirator' JR. Unfortunately, and irresistibly, a mix between Freudian echoes and feverish failures to answer, or worse, the entropy of endless endgames à la Beckett, immediately seems to unravel. Art does matter; art means a lot to a great deal of different people. Or does it? Should we simplify, perhaps try another question: 'Does a work of art always mean something?' This deceptively simple and startling 'national' philosophical essay question asked to all 17-year-old baccalauréat candidates ('bacheliers') in France in June 2015 reminds us that concepts of 'art' and 'meaning' never mix that well (and let's not mention the vast Pandora's box of 'to whom it may concern' and other 'subjects involved in that type of interweaving and (mis)matching). It also tells us that art is always put (back) at the forefront of philosophical enquiries and thrown back on the younger generations as an essential part of an ongoing reflection upon what and who we are. New locations, locations, pluridisciplinary points of view, and a firm grip on 'representation' versus 'reality': would that help at all to reconsider art alongside rather confusing terms of 'value', 'impact', or perhaps 'affect'?

What is clearly in the foreground and at stake in the 'artistic' productions over six decades by Agnès Varda, I would claim, is that she has always embraced and engaged with seminal debates about socio-political issues and art practices of her times, her/our present, with a sharp eye on the future (and, as seen above, other omnipresent forms of (self-) expression via iPhones).[46] Cinema needs more visibility and support for women directors, and more money: these two factors were repeatedly underlined and intertwined by Varda when she was covered with lifetime achievement awards and the most prestigious honours and titles at different festivals.[47] What does art need? Shall we dare ask firstly about basic budgets involved, or quote Varda on the subject?[48] As for cultural value, it is still surprisingly under-studied, according to a leading report on culture and inequality led by the British Arts and Humanities Research Council, even if inequality is officially claimed to be an integral part of both the production and the consumption of culture, and the further understanding of our communities.[49] International art shows evolve, meanwhile, with both enthusiastic and cynically negative audiences.

Let's not forget that the Fondation Cartier pour l'art contemporain, a vibrant and eclectic hub initiated in the mid-1980s which held a major exhibition of Varda's installation art in the summer of 2006, still aims to 'be a reflection of our times, embrac[ing] all creative fields and genres of contemporary art, ranging from design to photography, from painting to video art and from fashion to performance art', with a commitment to 'open up contemporary art and render it more accessible'.[50] Raising awareness about the heterogeneity of 'contemporary art' still stands out as a precious factor for many institutions and not a given fact, as one can deduce from echoes between contrasting examples, such as prominent regional galleries offering discussions 'aimed at those who find contemporary art intriguing, baffling or confusing';[51] the Venice Biennale (where Varda got her first 'proper' taste of recognition and popularity as an artist in 2003) being patronizingly branded as a mixed bag of basically 'bad art' and 'non-art? Most of it';[52] or even one of the latest reviews of Anish Kapoor's monumental commission at Versailles (a brilliant interpretation and re-creation of violent political unrest and ambiguous sexual politics, interwoven into the supremacy of the Sun King and his unplanned legacy of the French Revolution), warning visitors to avoid the whole installation as degrading 'ugliness and incongruity', a pure disgrace 'wrecking' the untouchable, 'sublime' Le Nôtre vistas and Louis XIV visions, three centuries on.[53]

But is it art? This is the telling and popular question that permeates minds as much as galleries and their floors, or (non)hanging walls bounced back up on the mouldy patches of the ceiling in Agnès Varda's home filmed in *The Gleaners*.[54] It is after all arbitrary and not that easy to distinguish between celebrated frescoes and the domestic sphere, once reconsidered and recaptured by the camera. And the worth of both is arguably not that dissimilar, but just as relative, since Varda precisely brings forward the underlying question of 'beauty', as we will see in a further section. What she personally finds 'beautiful' clearly matters, but the artistic question is how to translate and connote a potentially shared sense of beauty; because for all its socio-cultural codes and corsets, the concept can be opaque, '*presque pas vu*', or a perfectly elusive, intimate preference that others may not perceive or remain blindly immune to. Is that such a bad thing? Bearing in mind what Emma Wilson elucidates about Varda's portraits of another filmmaker, the thoughtfully 'felt and feeling' re-creations of 'close encounters' with Jacques Demy's body (and soul), I would like to suggest that exchanges between artist and viewers will be better off refraining from a desire for certainty, and could happily remain in complicated but uncharted territories: 'Varda's images encourage us to feel, as well as to look, with our eyes [...] [She] courts this suspension of judgement by bringing us so close to Demy's skin and its markings, while we remain uncertain of what we see and know. This uncertainty has implications for thinking accompaniment and love'.[55]

Close encounters of another type, but in the same (mine) field of art, come to mind. Since the filmic arrival of the iconic moving train at La Ciotat staged by the Lumière Brothers (1895) and the legend of a phenomenal reaction of the audience moving away from the screen fearing for their lives, one could argue that artistic encounters have a long tradition of not merely showing and (falsely) reflecting our (equally non-static) lives, but triggering confusion, and consciously provoking, in all senses, further fits, stops and starts in our enduring debates about artistic creations and responses. *Glenn Ligon: Encounters and Collisions* is an exhibition title promising 'clashes', as selected by one of the key American contemporary artists at Nottingham Contemporary, Spring 2015, and Tate Liverpool, Summer 2015.[56] Not put together by chance, I would argue, or simply because both Glenn Ligon and Varda were significantly showing in Los Angeles at the LACMA in successive years, this conversation as a confrontation between art pieces could indicate more than a revealing selection, as it also shows us what Ligon thinks an art piece can look like: in his 'personal museum', of 'archives for his 'inspiration', the American artist notoriously favoured by Barack Obama to bring art into the private wing of the White House, has put next to Varda's *Black Panthers* (1968) works by Andy Warhol, Jean-Michel Basquiat, Jackson Pollock, Franz Kline, Cy Twombly, and Lorna Simpson, among others.[57]

In any event, the Ligon-Varda conjunction calls into question the separation of the visual arts and cinema. This is in fact demonstrated by the entire career of Agnès Varda, 87, 'the young plastic artist' who detests the label 'plastic'.[58] Ten years ago Varda's work became part of the international collections of both the Cartier Foundation in Paris and MoMA in New York, featuring her curious Noirmoutier 'puzzles' as refashioned triptychs — frames of moving images of 'her' island and portraits of Breton widows, with her own self-portrait included with graceful delicacy in a series strongly emphasizing communal voices and lives. As Varda herself puts it, she has three lives: photographer, filmmaker and visual artist — 'artist for short'. Over the last six decades she has produced a remix of images and media that gives us the latest news from her visual, political and poetic world about our own arguably media-dominated world. In this chapter I will analyse how she takes on, in a surreal vein, the challenge of re-enchanting perspectives that seemed out of date, which we may also link to Barthes's critique of the frame of representation, namely how to escape the frame placed around yourself and others, as in *Les Glaneurs et la glaneuse*, 2000. In other words, in the manner of the defeat that the other can inflict on us, as Judith Butler argues in *Undoing Gender* (2004), and which can paradoxically be seen as a fortunate transformation and opening of the self, I would argue that Varda has been surely and steadily undoing everyone and everything, including herself, as in the unusual self-portrait presented in her series of encounters with artists. Affirming her intention in *Agnès de ci de là Varda* to give up making feature films while at the same time proposing to film in a different way, Varda reinserts herself into a dynamic and developing community of artists, among her own 'encounters and collisions'.

Subjects to (ex)change

My focus in this section will be on the Nathalie Obadia Gallery *Triptyques atypiques* exhibition (2014), part of the recent series of broken portraits: reframing and recycling, and the mixing-up of old and new photos. Have we seen this before?[59] Puns are omnipresent and clues ultimately only lead to one's own associations. And there

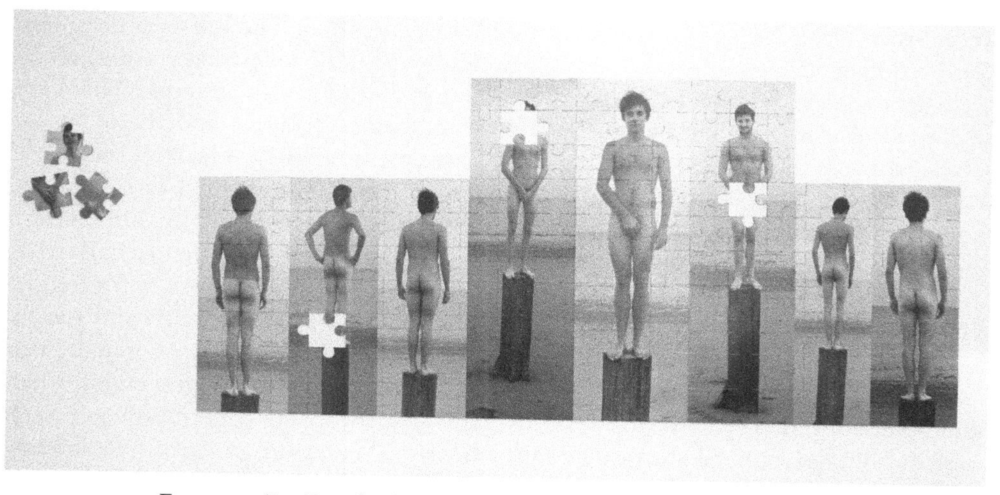

Fig. 11.5. 'Le Puzzle des cinq bacheliers' (2013) © agnès-varda

is a title that rhymes — with a mobile Y thrown in — *Triptyques atypiques*. Question: which visions and whose crises of identity appear hanging on or against the white walls? We will return to how Varda pushes the boundaries too with specific installations. How could we miss that her different kind of triptych — of mobile and sometimes tactile film screens (a puzzle after all is a game to be handled) — summons us to find ourselves there too? Mirrors that Varda broke for her subjects of 'portraits brisés' were highly visible, hence probably turned back in the viewer's direction, and in a different way from Rebecca Horn's *Spirits* (a hall of mirrors hiding skulls, Madre Museum, Naples, 2005), they produced a shattering *vanitas* effect, with similar unsettling reflection on the precarious nature of our lives.

Different visual tactics and 'analogical' effects (in Kaja Silverman's sense) are deployed here to puzzle viewers further. Varda directs and sharpens our gaze by 'undoing' or breaking apart very young men (into 167 pieces of a puzzle, like fragments of seagulls perched on posts); she tints a double portrait of her daughter Rosalie, 'marking the passage of time within time'; and alludes to the fragile nature of our ecosystem via a graceful Marie (definitely 'full of grace'), artificially animated with mighty wind turbines; and through such a juxtaposition of panels, the harassed Mona of *Sans toit ni loi* resurfaces.[60] Remix is in order: these uncanny broken and glued-together mirrors haunt her work. Just as the young men can be interpreted as new, naked versions of the Beach Boys, recto verso, the mirroring effect of the videos framing a still photograph can also be a renewed version of the seaside reflections of many mirrors displaced, and replaced in *The Beaches of Agnès*.

Masculinity as nudity: graceful figures, high winds of vulnerability

Agnès Varda undoes stereotypes with a magic feminist touch, or so it seems. Robert Mapplethorpe's iconic male nudes, among others, have already made us rethink masculinity, the erotic gaze and a certain sado-masochism. Here we are seeing unclad men differently and voyeurism may not be intended. The isolated figures on these wooden poles might evoke chaste nudes, and their broken state would make them potential St Sebastians, if they didn't look so full of life and energy. There are all the usual visual tricks: the mismatching number of bottoms and fragments of torsos: frontal shots, backs, heads and feet. These are nevertheless broken images of young *bacheliers*, high school leavers, on the verge of change in their lives. Playful innuendos abound on a deadly serious topic — smiles are visible but broken. Sexual organs are hidden, broken, erased by their hands, a detail that gives them a collective identity at the end of their lycée years. Varda may have in mind a reconfiguration of the representation of Adam, and to me, the male subject highlights and recalls by contrast the tradition of female nudes of 100 years earlier. As noted in the description of the piece, there are words and pieces missing (or fragments of other bodies added?). In any case, the 167 pieces do not constitute a harmonious entity either with five (could one as easily count parts from six?) young men all of a sudden interrupted, by the pose they are making. What we are facing is another type of lacuna, and as not intended in Varda's 'beautiful beach shot', this could also be read an ongoing revision and viewing of what Susan Faludi has pointed out as a severe breaking down of wholesome and self-assured male identity.[61]

Accessory with fans, umbrellas, sewing machines: dissecting the déjà vu

Varda's enquiry into aesthetics is as classic and serious as it is hard to miss: what is Beauty? The question takes over the whole Obadia Gallery when one considers her careful reconstruction and staging of Lautréamont's definition of beauty as 'the chance encounter between a sewing-machine and an umbrella on a dissecting table', a comparison famously quoted by André Breton in *Nadja*. Varda's explicit homage is a curiously vibrant installation, unmistakably uncanny, with dreamlike and deadly clinical effects: she put together another trio with a 'real' and imposing 'iron' dissecting table, a large black umbrella in tatters and (as a nod to Magritte's iconic signs and another tangible sign of represented death) an old-fashioned sewing-machine complete with wooden flap, drawer and pedals. This 3D embodiment of a timeless reflection on beauty is developed and shared further by a pile of small pieces of folded translucent paper which function as invitations to visitors to take them and read the carefully transcribed phrase from Lautréamont. Varda's comment is that this definition influences all readers of surrealist authors and one can therefore deduce that the staged installation activated by participating and willing readers of her mini-pamphlets aim to make them think again about what beauty can and might look like. A punctum stands out for me as I note the traces of the broken words inside that corner of the gallery and the rampant ivy on the ground which climbs up on top of that curiosity table, so that I cannot help thinking of two visual echoes: firstly Jacques Demy's decors and vegetable props for the royal chambers of Jean Marais's Blue Kingdom in *Donkey Skin* when it is invaded by greenery (as seen when the set was recreated for the Paris Médiathèque's Jacques Demy exhibition); and secondly the use of other types of 'broken walls', as seen before in her reconstruction of a squat in Passage Pommeraye in Nantes.

Aesthetics but also ethics are visibly at the heart of this multifaceted exhibition, *Atypical Triptychs*. One can think of Judith Butler's concept of 'ecstasy' when confronting life. Reactions to Varda's moving images or seemingly fixed assemblages will vary uncontrollably (as Susan Bright reminds us) but I would like to suggest that Varda's endless play of media oscillating between fixed images and moving video panels, with the visitors' gaze animating the death scene, their hands reaching for the folded messages on the adjacent table, seems to translate into visual (and visceral) terms her intention to make us think again about movement as instability and fragility — the same factor of undercurrents Varda associates with the sea and the beach (which may rule over our senses, sensations and variable perceptions of self and overall, never whole, identity).

Varda's optical tricks are her clear tracking of the ebb and flow, the in-between or the more than ambivalent creative 'developing' process of pictures, as highlighted above by Kaja Silverman. What viewers come face to face with are 'atypical', as in harmonious but discontinuous triptychs, which consistently connect *and* disconnect 'broken' panels, with mirroring effects as the double-sided panels also echo each other. Varda claims she placed photography and video put side by side to see if they work together or not. We can infer that the whole side effect can trigger deeper ramifications for her intention to move us. Does she want to shake up frames and disturb conventions? A mere suggestion: we are probably never meant to be quite 'still' ourselves in front of triptychs by Varda, even if other installations did provide and include chairs to pause and be still. If we are moved from within and see the splitting of ourselves — as 'strangers to ourselves', in Kristeva's sense of inner alterity — we could picture Varda's atypical triptychs (bearing in mind the constant reflection on 'others' art work she interweaves and her own glance sideways at the fringes of society) as putting us, simultaneously, paradoxically and literally, out of the frame.[62] We would therefore not be in a static passive position facing them, but as potentially 'ex-static' viewers — beside ourselves — out of ourselves, beyond norms in the sense ascribed and expanded by Butler regarding a self that becomes communal, in a community of marginalized others living in dissonance. We could think of Butler's explicit question that such a notion of an ex-static position of the subject entails, which also seems reflected by Varda's meaningful 'art' objects, subjects, and the intended, problematic affect on viewers: 'the predicament is to understand what kind of community is composed of those who are beside themselves'.[63] The question is bigger than our fragile or broken, multifaceted selves; as retold by Varda's fragmentary, or even restless, installations, it does also concern an impossible wholeness.

In other words, and in view of Varda's previous extensive filmic and artistic work on marginal outcasts or 'broken portraits', one can clearly see that these 'atypical' triptychs are in fact typically Vardian visions of the complicated community she has relentlessly represented in many series of echoes and fragments (from *Opéra Mouffe*, *Black Panthers* and the squat in *Le Voyage à Nantes* to the latest mosaic-like broken portraits). I find the choice of a 'broken' and split structure most insistent and revealing. In that sense, these fragmentary 'triptychs' resonate deeply with what has been and still is at the heart of her reimagining of our societies and ourselves, paradoxically, if not increasingly, bound together (or 'broken') by various degrees of 'crisis'. *Atypical Triptychs* therefore offered visitors another glance at what and who seems to inspire, to amuse, as much as concern and worry, this formidable advocate for freedom and compassion.

How can one communicate, or better, act upon, such visions? This very ethical concern and key injunction, as passionately articulated by Butler in *Precarious Life: The Obligations of Proximity*, seems to me strongly and vividly expressed by Varda. Fragments or multiple points of view have more than a double edge; they are still unavoidable and impossible to pinpoint as a 'fixed' sense, as we saw in *Sans toit ni loi*, and Varda keeps her/our gaze open and mobile, susceptible to being affected by multiple projections and emotions. In Varda's worlds, we are always asked, I would suggest, to look and think outside the single square, the classic rectangular frame.

Pause and rewind on the wind

Marie in the Wind, one of the *Atypical Triptychs*, reveals a similar hybridity of refined artistic creativity and subtle artistic achievement. Could viewers only think of the 'obvious' challenge displayed, i.e. how to counter the controversial 'ugliness' of the gigantic wind turbines and make them more than nice-looking/aesthetically pleasing. One cannot quite fail to notice, by more/mere juxtaposition, the dual strategy of 'trompe-l'œil' and the splitting of images into two. The 'green' energy powerhouses or giants of our contemporary landscapes are contrasted with the miniature windmill Marie is holding thoughtfully in her clasped hands as if holding a precious candle, thus procuring a variable sense of comic disproportion but again triggering a potentially serious sense of responsibility towards the environment and ecosystems. I would suggest that it is probably unlikely that many visitors today would not think of the ongoing disputes which have dominated our global conversations about the industrial and human impact on climate and the environment.

These infamous NIMBY objects of contention are perhaps not here to stay (think of 'old' windmills) but are worth reconsidering from another angle. As Naomi Klein said when Bill Gates rejected cute solar panels as merely inefficient, one can suggest that Varda's tripartite remapping of today's skies, nature's fields and the air is probably not only to draw attention to their 'cuteness' value, but also to offer multiple layers of a burning political issue. What do we do with/without these alternative sources of energy? The question becomes translated visually by Varda into a potential answer: by putting them in *her* background, foreground, focus and bringing them forward, right back into our field of vision, at the forefront of our reflections, Varda's *Marie in the Wind* tells us that we cannot escape them and I would like to suggest that there is no denying their dream-like presence and quality when set against Varda's expansive skyscapes. She makes us keep in mind the tiny garden wheels and the old windmills, too, with all that is implied when comparing tools from one century to the next. In other words, Varda's triptych creates a dream vision of a pure 'NIMBY' nightmare and a timely politically charged (re)vision about the uncertain bad time we are facing — with enormous ecological challenges.

Furthermore the use of 'new' technologies used worldwide shows that Varda's

FIG. 11.6. 'Marie dans le vent' (2013) © agnès-varda

play on our old style/ new style technologies and her own remix of media (photo/ film) can produce just as energizing conversations. When shared live video streams from iphones seem to bring us closer to all the breaking news (major accidents, social unrest, minor incidents), a similar sense of intimacy and immediacy about global warming seems activated by Varda's *Atypical Triptychs*. They are not an impromptu captured view of 'real life', but carefully crafted revisions of real-life issues, just as deep, all shown in the art gallery. They are showing us everyday objects in a new light, bringing an uncanny sense of false familiarity and comfort, I would argue, before one sees the works as 'broken up', split into different panels, changing images. Our eyes are not certain as to what they see, as Emma Wilson reminded us previously.

Humour and a light touch can also be Varda's deadly weapons. Skies and clouds shot in the two films vary in colour, shades of light and texture. One notes that the visual passage from daytime to dusk brings a Baudelairean echo with his 'wonderful clouds', but who is this Marie? A hippy iconic figure with 60s hair floating in perfect synchronicity with the wind turbines appears at the corner. Does that make her a muse to the green movement? What can one tell from her miniature windmill echoing the giant turbines? And there is also her fixed gaze. Is she silently asking us to figure out these puzzling discrepancies or is she dreaming of a green future? Why wear a woolly jumper if you want to use a cooling mini-fan? Out of synch elements, a self-centred sense of comfort can jump out of the screens. There are also two portraits of Marie, with open and with closed eyes, on the gallery website archives, and one chosen for the exhibition provides a full engagement with the reciprocity of glances. In any case, what we do see is unclear, since the difference between the images of a warmly clad Marie and the young naked *bacheliers*, whose pose is ambiguous at best (between showing and hiding), is ultimately blurred or blinding on account of its sharp contrast in gender, state of (un)clothing, skyline versus seafront.

One way to rethink Varda's carefully crafted composition of her triptychs is through the human figure — the academic painter's composition exercise *par excellence*. Marie's long hair moves perfectly. It stands still in the captured shot but we can infer that it moves and mimics these big so-called 'unnatural eyesores'. It is up to us to decide if these fixed and moving elements — yesterday and today's mills — when placed together, work together or not. Varda is not only putting old tricks from a surrealist hat onto the dissecting table. She brings back wonder into our material world, arranging and mixing up everyday objects to show us how symbolic and symbiotic they can be and how (surreal) our world can look. For some viewers who left the Gallery Obadia in the Spring of 2014, it is also possible to conceive that Mme Landier's (quiet and steady, if not peaceful) fight for a 'green' cause, made famous by Macha Méril's incarnation of the specialist in diseased plane trees in *Sans toit ni loi* three decades ago, may have also found old fans who remembered the film, caught by surprise by its unexpected reinterpretation as a 'violently shaken' style of strip of images. These are glued again in an arrested/arresting triptych, with a curiously calm 'Marie in the wind' caught up herself and surrounded by mighty reminders of important environmental issues that still prevail, and which one can indeed imagine might even have gained new advocates and supporters.

Looking back at Varda looking back at herself?

JR's recent double portrait of Varda irreverently thumbing her nose at her own 'old' self-portrait as a Bellini procession figure is another characteristic and classic visual pun associated with both Varda and her 'accomplice' who took her back on the road to interview and capture people as extraordinary subjects in the South of France.[64] One should bear in mind that the autobiographical-fictional self-portraiture and on-the-road adventure pictures in *The Beaches of Agnès* are a relatively late 'autobiographical' exercise in Varda's prolific and ongoing career, as if she had previously felt a resistance to self-scrutiny. Varda's *Beaches of Agnès* (2008, aged 80) is therefore reminiscent of Nathalie Sarraute's own reticence about a lifelong retrospective or backwards glance in *Enfance* (1983, aged 83).[65] 'Freezing films' can happen: three 'little pieces' of *Sans toit ni loi* torn from her film, as Varda puts it, forcefully form another Vardian triptych as it can also stand for a deliberate visual device to remind viewers that Varda the Artist — Bellini or Marcel Duchamp style — is also a filmmaker and a virulent feminist voicing the undesirable status (quo) of women marginalized or forced to live at the margins of society. The three shots of a badly treated Mona (Sandrine Bonnaire) are equally hard to see at first sight: simply a sense of familiarity will enable viewers to recognize the deformed and fuzzy forms and face of Bonnaire, as well as the grim participants in the wine festival. The actress's agitated movements trying to tear herself away from her drunken assailants are chosen as the three parts of this triptych. Out of all possible elements of the puzzle that her film adopted with its multifocal points of view and structure, Varda selected male violent and sexist behaviour towards women. This shows what Varda had in mind when she selected her collection of Triptychs. A new Mona emerges, which can be read as an 'unlimited' Varda resisting labels.

Uncertainty reigns once more when having a closer look at certain details: are there 3 or 7 digital photos in the triptych? Varda renews 'old' films and old photos (dog at Parisian street corner, 1950s) but clearly reaffirms her commitment to a wide range of socio-political issues, with her activism equally visible on her own website at Ciné-Tamaris, her production headquarters and 'home'.

Who is Varda? 'I am Charlie' was the headline on her site for several months after the Paris attacks in January 2015. Her own Facebook page will also show and tell many surprising tales and portraits: instead of a self-portrait/selfie, Varda is opening up her virtual space to others, including fellow artists with whom she clearly feels an affinity, as seen in *Agnès de ci de là Varda*, with its moving portrait and homage to Manoel de Oliviera. A lasting and last impression: Manoel Cândido Pinto de Oliveira's names as a triptych, his surfacing portrait and joyful reappearance, in his prolonged 'afterlife', as a superb parody of D'Artagnan or Zorro, on the virtual Face(filled)book of his friend and fellow artist, his walking stick frozen in the air like a sword.

Notes to Chapter 11

1. Agnès Varda, interview with Anne Diatkine, 'J'ai horreur du gâchis', *Libération*, 18 August 2006 [my translation]. See also her definition of anticonformism today: 'As before, to wear two socks of different colours. Maybe to visit France rather than far away countries. And to be without a TV, a mobile, or a driving license.' <http://www.liberation.fr/Cahier special/j-ai-horreur-du gachis>[accessed 21 July 2012]
2. See Judith Butler on all precarious, unliveable states, and degrees of being alive, in *The Adorno Prize Lecture*, 11 September 2012, Frankfurt.
3. A. Varda's presentation text. See Galerie Nathalie Obadia website archives for full details of the press release of the exhibition, *Agnès Varda: Triptyques atypiques* [Atypical Triptychs], Paris, February 8-April 5, 2014. <http://www.galerie-obadia.com/show> [accessed 24 September 2015].
4. See Shirley Jordan, Hannah Mowat and Gill Perry's chapters in this volume for discussion of many more art connections and installations.
5. See A. Varda, interview in *Lisières*, 13 (19 October 2000), pp. 5–28: 'I tend not to think of the audience as a big crowd but as individual people. The public are not an amorphous mass boosting box-office ratings, they are people I turn to. Saying that, afterwards, everyone, every man or woman, turns to be nearer to the film and to approach me' [my translation], 5.
6. See preface and Q&A in the volume.
7. Claire Boyle, 'La Vie rêvée d'Agnès Varda: Dreaming the Self and Cinematic Autobiography in Les Plages d'Agnès', in Fabien Arribert-Narce and Alain Ausoni, A. (eds), *L'Autobiographie entre autres: Écrire la vie aujourd'hui* (Bern, Oxford: Peter Lang, 2013), pp. 149–66, 165.
8. Claire Bishop, *Installation Art* (London: Tate, 2005), pp. 6, 8.
9. Bishop, p. 116.
10. Jacques Demy: 'Tout le monde a le droit de rêver. C'est ma double vie' [Everyone is entitled to dream. This is my double life] (my translation), in interview for *Chronique Cinéma*, bonus material, *Model Shop* (1969), in *Intégrale Jacques Demy* (ARTE Éditions: DVD box set, 2008). N.B. TV viewers of *Agnès de ci de là Varda* (ARTE, 2011) knew that Varda had already been and shot her hommage trip, 'Voyage en perm à Nantes' (pour Jacques Demy), a title with a nod and echo, sung by Jacques Perrin, the 'other' *Jacquot de Nantes*, *aka* Maxence from *Les Demoiselles de Rochefort*. This was part of the official commemoration of Jacques Demy and restoration of his *Lola*, Varda commenting with a dry sense of humour on the funky decalcomania which transferred and transformed Demy's bigger-than-life image into a bus.
11. Phil Powrie, 'Heterotopic Spaces and Nomadic Gazes in Varda: From *Cléo de 5 à 7* to *Les Glaneurs et la glaneuse*' in M-C. Barnet and S. Jordan (eds), *L'Esprit Créateur*, 51: 1, Spring 2011, pp. 68–82.

12. Emma Wilson, *Love, Mortality and the Moving Image* (London: Palgrave Macmillan, 2012).
13. See Noam Chomsky, *Occupy* (London: Penguin, 2012), on the 'Occupy' history and legacy, and all its complexity since the 2011 protest movement in New York became international, and discussing how socio-economical inequality could be re-addressed by 'active' civic participation, and more personal and global engagement with civil rights.
14. See <http: > [accessed 24 September 2014]. Serge Toubiana, 'Jacques Demy ou le rêve éveillé', in 'Le Monde enchanté de Jacques Demy' (catalogue of the exhibition, curated by Matthieu Orléan with Rosalie Varda-Demy, Paris, La Cinémathèque de France, 10 April-4 August 2013) (Paris: Skira, Flammarion, 2013) pp.10–11. Demy's notes on *Les Demoiselles de Rochefort* were part of the retrospective.
15. Alexis Campion, 'Nantes 'renversée' par l'art', *Le Journal du dimanche*, 28 June 2012. <http:www.lejdd.fr/.../Le-Voyage-a-Nantes-un-periple-dans-l'art-contemporain> [accessed 30 September 2012].
16. All my thanks to Marie Dupas, Chargée de production artistique, *Le Voyage à Nantes* art festival, correspondence with the author, 18 September 2012.
17. Dominique Bluher, 'La miroitière: À propos de quelques films et installations d'Agnès Varda', in *Agnès Varda: le cinéma et au-delà*, pp. 177–85. See Varda in her bonus interview for *Jacquot de Nantes*, in *Tout(e) Varda*, preface.
18. Varda, *ibid*.
19. See Dominique Païni, 'Hommage au Festival du Film de La Rochelle', <http://www.cine-tamaris.com/actualites/hommage-au-festival-du-film-de-la-rochelle> [accessed 24 September 2015]
20. A. Varda: 'Qui sait de quel réel les chats sont les médiums dans leurs aguets pétrifiés', in *Regards sur l'exposition* (Paris: Fondation Cartier pour l'art contemporain, 2006), p. 44.
21. See Gill Perry's chapter in this volume.
22. Jacques Drillon, 'La cabane de l'échec', in A. Varda, *Regards sur l'exposition*, pp. 6–7.
23. François Ozon, 'François Ozon on Deneuve and Demy', interview with David Jenkins, 16 June 2011, <http:www.timeout.com/.../Francois_Ozon_on_Deneuve_and_Demy> [accessed 10 July 2012]
24. A. Varda with François Busnel, 'Grand Entretien', France Inter, 5 November 2012, <http:www.franceinter.fr/emission-le-grand-entretien-agnes-varda> [accessed 24 September 2015]
25. See Fiona Handyside's chapter in this volume.
26. A. Varda, interview with Elsa Daynac, 'Des chambres en ville avec Agnès Varda', in 'Regard Rhésus', *France Inter*, 27 June 2012. See <http://www.franceinter.fr/podcasts>.
27. See C. Boltanski with Tamar Garb in the preface to this volume.
28. See 'the man with the artichoke', a Georges Moustaki lookalike, 'we don't live in homes any more, we just squat', in the sequel to *Les Glaneurs et la glaneuse, Two years later* (shot in 2001–2002), in *Tout(e) Varda*.
29. A. Varda, Correspondence with the author, 18 July 2014.
30. A. Varda, interview with Eric Loret, 'Trouver des choses réelles qui facilitent l'émotion,' *Libération*, 28 June 2012, <http://www.liberation.fr.cinema/2012/06/28/trouver-des-choses-reelles-qui-facilient->. She insists on her non-invasive process of 'listening' to the interviewed *sans-abris*. On the other hand, as a visitor/spectator, one becomes keenly aware that the freedom of choice, that is, precisely the choice of not listening (total blindness towards the recorded messages from the interviewees is not an option, one is confronted with different monitors in the space), is also at the heart of her installation. I would suggest that Varda also invites visitors to choose, whether they want to drop by and listen in, or turn a blind eye and move on: 'Here, I put these recorded voices in a different situation, heard differently when right next to a mattress. This is not about representing them, but putting them inside. It's a bit dreamlike but not too much. I don't even know if these voices will be heard. They're inside little TV sets, this is not aggressive. You don't have to listen to them if you don't want to' [my translation].
31. Varda, Agnès with Liza Béar, interview in *Interview Magazine*. 2009, <http://www.interviewmagazine.com/film/agnes-varda> [accessed 24 September 2015]. See also A. Varda with François Busnel, 'Grand Entretien'.
32. Maggi Hambling with Jackie Kay, Lavinia Greenlaw (chair), 'Exchange: the Female Artist', Aldeburgh Poetry Festival, 2 November 2012.

33. A. Varda on the 'unlivable' conditions provided by this makeshift refuge, in the hand-out leaflet for her installation, a whole booklet with map provided for this whole trip around all installations, see <http://levoyageanantes.fr>. See note 2.
34. Kaja Silverman, *Flesh of My Flesh* (Stanford: Standford University Press, 2009)
35. Wilson, 157.
36. See Jackie Kay, *Darling: New and Selected Poems* (Tarset: Bloodaxe, 2007), a widely gleaned and popular collection celebrated, for instance, by Mallorie Blackman, 'My Life in Verse' <https://gerryco23.wordpress.com/.../malorie-blackman-my-life-in-verse> [accessed 24 September 2015]. See also Bill Manhire, *Lifted* (Manchester: Carcanet: 2007), 79.
37. Sophie Fiennes (director), with Slavoj Žižek (screenplay writer and star), *The Pervert's Guide to Ideology* (Film 4, 2012)
38. See Rip Hopkins's Nantes photo album for further photographic traces of Demy (a striking 'bunny girl' in Demy's favourite faded denim blue, as a sort of Lola call-girl, or a sharp dresser in a meticulously chosen outfit perfectly matching the colour scheme of the background staircase): <http://en.nantes-tourisme.com/brochures/nantes-vu-par-rip-hopkins-17730.html> [accessed 24 September 2015]
39. Sally Mann, *Hold Still: A Memoir with Photographs* (New York: Little, Brown and Company, 2015). See 'the treachery of photography', 'with each photograph I was forgetting', in 'Prologue: The Meuse', pp. ix-xiv, xii, xiii.
40. Kaja Silveman, *The Miracle of Analogy, or the History of Photography, Part 1* (Redwood City, CA: Stanford UP, 2015), 12.
41. See Preface, A. Varda , 'Préambule en bulles', 3.
42. Michel Foucault: 'From the idea that the self is not given to us, I think that there is only one practical consequence: we have to create ourselves as a work of art', in 'On the Genealogy of Ethics: An Overview of Work in Progress,' *Ethics: Subjectivity and Truth*, ed. by P. Rabinow, trans. by R. Hurley and others (Allen Lane, London: Penguin Press, 1997), 262; first published in H. Dreyfus and P. Rabinow, *Michel Foucault: Beyond Structuralism and Hermeneutics*, 2nd ed., 1983, 237 [French version: 'À propos de la généalogique de l'éthique: un aperçu d'un travail en cours' (1983), *Dits et écrits: 1954–1988, IV: 1980–1988* (Paris: Gallimard, 1994), 392].
43. Susan Bright, *Art Photography Now* (London: Thames and Hudson, 2005), 19.
44. <http://www.kisskissbankbank.com/av-et-jr-deux-artistes-en-goguette> [accessed 24 July 2015].
45. See n. 45, and widely diverse responses posted on the site, ranging from warm support to harsh criticism for this call to help with such a 'film produced by the people, a film for the people', *ibid.*
46. See also Nicholas Mirzoeff, *How to see the World* (London: Pelican, 2015) on how selfies and online videos of the 'Snapchat' generation has reimagined what visual culture, representation, access and diffusion, could look like, (super)imposing individual and global levels.
47. See Preface for more discussions on this debate about 'the crisis of cinema' relaunched by Varda, and n. 49.
48. On Varda's feminist plea and reaction to her lifetime achievement award at the European film awards, in Riga, Latvia, see Hannah Ellis-Petersen, 'Agnès Varda hits out at European cinema's failure to recognise women', *Guardian*, 14 December 2014. See Varda at Cannes film festival about gender inequality for funding and clarification about 'marginal' independent cinema but 'gender blind' talent, 'Women in Motion', 23 May 2015, before receiving her Palme d'honneur, in 'Cannes 2015 — Agnès Varda. I would have liked more money to fund my films than awards'; Laetitia Ratane's full report and links are on <www.allocine.fr>. See radio interview confirming that funding still is a key issue, Le 7/9, Patrick Cohen and Agnès Varda, *France Inter*, 6 June 2015, 'I was never 'bankable'. I never made enough money' [my translation]. See facts and figures regarding funding for latest project and her answers to criticism as seen in *Libération* about her public appeal with the artist JR on kisskissbankbank. As she explains, 300,000 euros would barely cover the 'simple' budget of shooting a 26-minute documentary film, without all the fees for post-production, distribution, staff salaries, etc. <https://en-gb.facebook.com/agnesvarda> [accessed 24 September 2015]. See 'Varda et JR comptent sur votre générosité pour partir en goguette', 15 June 2015, <http://www.liberation.fr>.
49. See Dave O'Brien and Kate Oakley's report on 'Cultural Value and Inequality: A Critical

Literature review', <https://ahrc.ac.uk/News-and-Events/News/Documents/Cultural.Value-Inequality> [accessed 14 July 2015].

50. See 'Introduction' to 'The Foundation', on <https://foundation.cartier.com> [accessed 21 may 2015].
51. See 'Contemporary Art Conversations', Baltic Centre for Contemporary Art, Gateshead, UK (which hosted the first Turner Prize show outside Tate London and Liverpool in 2011), *Baltic*, 18 (Summer 2015), p. 6.
52. See 'What you may ask yourself: if it involves no discernible craftsmanship or artistic technique, is it art?', *ArtMag*, Scotland and NorthEast England, July/August 2015, 'Art & Travel', 'The Venice Biennale & Grand Canal Art Museums', 18–21, p. 21.
53. Robin Lane Fox, 'Le Nôtre's Anish horribilis', *Financial Times Weekend*, 'House and Home', 11–12 July 2015, p. 1.
54. See Cynthia Freeland, *But Is it Art: An Introduction to Art Theory* (Oxford, OUP, New Ed, 2002).
55. Emma Wilson, *Love, Mortality, and the Moving Image* (London: Palgrave, 2012), p. 37.
56. See <http://www.nottinghamcontemporary.org/art/glenn-ligon>, and 'Black people in post-war America: New exhibition documents an often brutal experience', Zoe Pilger's linked online review of Varda's included film, reflecting on the 'self-defeating' loss in French translation, but how the focus on French Resistance-style berets can also translate as 'the Black Panther aesthetic made radical politics cool' (*The Independent*, 8 April 2015).
57. See LA County Museum of Art, <www.lacma.org>, Glenn Ligon, America, October 23, 2011 and January 22, 2012; *Agnès Varda in Californialand*, 3 November 2013–22 June 22 2014. See Gill Perry's chapter in the present volume about Varda at LACMA.
58. See Preface, n. 8.
59. See n. 3, Nathalie Obadia's presentation of the double style of triptychs, and the 'related' almost clichés, corresponding symbols with twists (i.e. Rosalie Varda-Demy as a pink tinted child looks up and away, holds her black doll which looks at the camera instead; the other young greyish woman holds a turtle dove, appearing like a take on Hans Holbein The Younger's *Lady with a squirrel and a starling*, 1526–28 [London, National Gallery]): 'The *Portraits à volets vidéo* comprise a central image, a photograph, generally in black and white (gelatin silver), printed and hung on the wall, with videos projected on either side. The point is to juxtapose the fascination exerted by still or fixed images at a given moment and the energy exuded by moving images directly linked to the central figure [...] There are other triptych portraits, this time wholly photographic ones, whether in colour or black and white. For these, Varda has conceived metal frames vaguely inspired by the work of Mexican artisans, including the hinges. The photographs in the side panels of each triptych are related to the person in the photograph: *La jeune fille à la tourterelle* (Young Girl with Turtle Dove, 1950)/ *Miquel Barceló* (2011)/ *Rosalie, fille d'Agnès* (Rosalie, Agnès's daughter, 2013)'. See A. Varda's double focus on hands and (artistic/parental) lineage and kinship: 'Rosalie's portrait (my daughter) aged 4 and 54 — it's quite funny because her hands have changed so much, and because I thought of the handmade embossed iron frame for the triptych as a kind of little family icon. It's only a portrait of my daughter, just as all painters and artists have done before me eventually' [my translation], correspondence with the author, 18 July 2014.
60. A. Varda, Conversation with the author, Paris, 16 May 2014.
61. See Varda's analysis in the Preface. See Susan Faludi, *Stiffed: The Betrayal of the American Man* (New York, London: Harper Perennial, (1999), 2000).
62. Julia Kristeva, *Strangers to Ourselves*, trans. by Leon S. Roudiez (New York: Columbia UP, new ed., 1994) [French ed., *Étrangers à nous-mêmes*, Paris: Fayard, 1988].
63. Judith Butler, *Undoing Gender* (London, New York: Routledge, 2004), p. 20.
64. See n. 45.
65. *Sans toit ni loi* is famously dedicated to Nathalie Sarraute, and inspired by her leather-clad profile.

APPENDIX 1

Cléo's 50th Birthday: Questions-Answers

Corinne Marchand (8 September 2012)

Editor's note. All my warmest thanks to Corinne Marchand, who generously and kindly replied to a series of questions pasted on postcards, except question 7 about women's liberation and the Algerian war as key themes inserted in *Cléo de 5 à 7*, which she preferred to set aside as too general and having nothing to do with the film, a point which Agnès Varda will precisely come back to, and comment upon extensively herself in the Q&A included in the present volume. There was another striking element in our correspondence in the autumn of 2012: the most delightful surprise was to receive from Corinne Marchand my annotated questions with keywords highlighted in blue by her (indicated here in capital letters), while her answers were written in black ink as perfect acrostic poems on white pages (my translations lose this 'special effect'). — M.-C. B.

1. Quelle est la PREMIÈRE IMAGE qui vous vient à l'esprit quand on évoque *Cléo de 5 à 7*?

Parc Montsouris
Rendez-vous très tôt le matin
Eblouissement total devant cette nature enrobée de rosée
Marche tranquille dans les sentiers sinueux ombragés
Infinie douceur du temps qui passé
Et ce beau militaire
Rêveur, poète, raccommodeur de porcelaine
Et ce sentiment de virage que Cléo aborde avec sérénité

Il y a assurément en plein Paris
Malgré le béton et les bruits
A un endroit niche dans le 14ème
Grand comme un mouchoir de poche
Encore aujourd'hui: un coin de paradis

2. Comment avez-vous appris que vous aviez été CHOISIE pour le role de Cléo? Vous aviez fait un entretien et un essai avec Agnès V.?

Concours de circonstances
Hé! Vous là-bas vous êtes prête?
Oui! J'ai été meneuse de revue
Il fallait savoir danser, chanter, se faire belle!
Si cela vous convient? Jacques Demy me fait tourner dans Lola
Il invite Agnès Varda à Nantes sur le plateau du tournage
Et elle me regarde intensément et s'exclame : voilà ma Cléo!

3. Humeur vagabonde peut-être...: quelle est pour vous l'ATMOSPHÈRE dominante du film? L'atmosphère du tournage, différences ou nuances?

A coup sûr dans le film
Tout converge vers la douceur, les demi-teintes, le romantisme
Malgré quelques images insolites,
Outrancières même comme le cracheur de grenouilles ou les étudiants grimaçants
Sans prétention ni crainte Cléo navigue entre ciel et eau tel un oiseau
Parfois capricieuse mais pas méchante
Hésitant dans le choix d'un chapeau
Etonnée du monde qui l'entoure
Rien n'est grave
Elle vit sur une musique tendre dans un ton mineur

4. La couleur qui vous vient à l'esprit? Si *Cléo de 5 à 7* était une COULEUR? Nous voyons le film (après le tout début) en noir et blanc, mais vous?

Ce que mes yeux voient dans Cléo
Outre les pois noirs de sa robe
Une volonté précise d'Agnès de faire un film en noir et blanc
Les bonnes sœurs, l'enterrement,
Et autres plans sombres en témoignent
Une chose est sûre: l'image de cette petite chanteuse interpelle
Rien ne peut empêcher son rayonnement couleur arc-en-ciel

5. Le temps retrouvé, au fil rouge du temps. Avez-vous un MOMENT précis, mémorable, ancré dans votre esprit, à propos du tournage à Paris, ou de Cannes?

Milieu du film
On tourne la chanson 'Sans toi'
Michel Legrand au piano, Serge Korbier à ses côtés
Environnement blanc intense
Nul ne bouge, Cléo chante,
Toute l'équipe pleure!

6. La PEUR est aussi au cœur du film. Avez-vous eu un moment de peur au moment du tournage, de qui et de quoi? Les spectateurs s'en rendent-ils compte, pensez-vous?

Pourquoi avoir peur?
Entrer à fond dans un personnage
Utiliser pleinement sa possibilité et faire confiance aux collaborateurs du film
Rester dans cette bulle merveilleuse que vous offre un tournage jusqu'à s'y noyer de bonheur! Pourquoi avoir peur!

7. Cléo 1961–1962, les reflets d'une société et de son temps: la Libération des femmes, la guerre d'Algérie. Qu'est-ce qui vous a marquée le plus, et personnellement, parmi tous ces thèmes clefs qu'Agnès glisse avec subtilité dans tous ses plans à elle?

[vu comme hors-sujet, pas de réponse]

8. Les COSTUMES! Une actrice se déguise, on s'en doute. Mais comment vous êtes-vous glissée dans la peau, les habits de Cléo? Est-ce que le costume contraint ou libère?

C'est à mon avis très important un costume.
On est obligé selon les styles et les époques à faire un choix
S'adapter ensuite à cette nouvelle tenue
Telle guêpière, tel jogging
Uniforme, bottes ou talons aiguilles
Manifestement maintien et démarche en dépendent
Et c'est ainsi que dans la peau et les nippes du personnage
Se laisser aller avec gourmandise permet peut-être un miracle

9. Bel avenir, bel hasard? Ce film tourne avec brio autour des thèmes conjugués du hasard (des rencontres), de l'avenir (hasardeux). En quoi CLEO a-t-elle, ou non, provoqué des suites et des rebonds dans votre parcours d'actrice? Dans votre vie?

Ce fut une aventure merveilleuse
La carte de visite idéale pour le public et les gens du spectacle
Encore aujourd'hui malgré mon âge
On se souvient avec tendresse de ce personnage mythique.

Translations

1. FIRST IMAGE: What is the first image that comes into your mind when someone mentions Cléo from 5 to 7*?*

Parc Montsouris
Early morning meeting
Marvelling at the dewy setting
Walking quietly in the sinuous shaded footpaths
Infinite softness of time passing
The handsome soldier
Dreamer, poet and mender of fragile objects
And this feeling of change that Cléo embraces serenely

There is for sure, in the heart of Paris,
Despite the blocks of flats and noise
Hidden somewhere in the 14th arrondissement,
No bigger than a handkerchief,
And still there today: a little bit of paradise.

2. CHOSEN: How did you find out that you had been chosen for the role? Did you have a meeting and a screen test with Agnès V.?

Lucky circumstances
Hey you, are you ready?
Yes! I had been a show girl!
You had to know how to dance, sing, make yourself pretty!
Did that suit me? Jacques Demy had me work in Lola
He invites Agnès Varda to Nantes while shooting
And she gazes at me, an intense gaze followed by her exclamation: Here's my Cléo!

3. Perhaps a certain mood permeates the film... How would you define the MOOD in the film and during its shooting? Did they differ in any way?

Surely in the film everything tends to converge
Towards softness, shaded colours, a romantic mood
Despite some quite unusual images
Like the outrageous man spitting frogs, students making ugly faces.
Without any pretention or fear, Cléo wanders
Half-way between the sky and the water, like a bird
She may be whimsical but not nasty
She hesitates about choosing a hat
She's all in a wonder about the world around her
Nothing is serious
She lives wrapped in tender music, on a minor key.

4. The film is in black and white after the first few minutes, but when you were playing your character and when you look back at the film now, what if I said to you: If Cléo was a COLOUR...

What my eyes can see in Cléo
After the black polka dots of the dress
Agnès's precise intention to make a black and white film
The nuns, the mourning procession
Many scenes testify to that desire.
One thing definitely stands out: the image of this little singer makes you think
Nothing, it seems, can prevent her solar radiance, she's all rainbow colours.

5. Time regained. Is there a particularly memorable MOMENT fixed in your mind relating to the filming in Paris or the opening at Cannes?

Half-way through the film
We're filming the song 'Sans toi/Without You'
Michel Legrand at the piano, with Serge Korber at his side,
Dazzling white background
No one moves, Cléo sings.
The film crew, all in tears!

6. FEAR is also at the heart of the film. Were you afraid yourself at one point while filming, and what about or whom? Do you think the audience would notice?

Why be scared?
Embrace your character
Exploit all potentials to the maximum and trust all people working on the set
To stay inside that wonderful bubble that surrounds you while filming. Better lose oneself and swoon with utter delight, why be scared?

7. Cléo 1961–1962, inscribing reflections upon/of a society and its times: Women's Liberation, the Algerian war. What affected you and had the stronger impact, would you say, between these key issues that Agnès addresses with great subtlety in her different sequences?

N/A

8. COSTUMES! An actress has to dress up, we all know that. But how did you get under the skin of your character, in Cléo's clothes? Is a costume a constraining or liberating tool?

To me, the choice of a costume is paramount.
Styles and periods, all dictate the selection of certain items of clothing.
One has to grow accustomed to one's costume thereafter,
Adapt to the corset, the sweat pants,

The uniform, tall boots or high heels surely
Are part of the way you basically walk and carry yourself.
That's why if you relish letting your hair down, loosen the old frocks of the character
Get it all under your skin, who knows, what wonders!

9. Cléo from 5 to 7 ***revolves around the themes of chance (meetings) and the (uncertain) future. What was the effect of*** **CLÉO** ***on your career as an actress, and on your life?***

It was a wonderful adventure
The ideal 'calling card' for the public and in show business
Still today, in spite of all the time that has passed,
We remember this mythical character with tenderness.

APPENDIX 2

Agnès Varda's Interview: Verbal Ping-Pong and Matching Points

Agnès Varda (Tyneside Cinema, 24 November 2012)

Editor's note. I would like to express my deep gratitude to the outstanding team at Tyneside Cinema and to the marvellously inquisitive audience at the event 'Agnès, Cléo, Varda, Etcetera: Happy Birthday *Cléo de 5 à 7*', who most enthusiastically and brilliantly contributed to the invitation to take part in our verbal volleyball after a celebratory viewing of *Cléo* 50 years after its initial release. They demonstrated that a keen interest in Varda's work is still pronounced, resolute, thankfully diverse and wonderfully warm. I want to underline that it is their invaluable input that simply made it happen, made possible such an inspired and engaging exchange of questions/answers. With all our thanks, again and always, to the bright star who stole the show, Agnès Varda. — M.-C. B.

On Corinne Marchand's recollections and impressions of Cléo from 5 to 7 *50 years on, and regarding her own take on the creative process and intentions behind the scenes*

It's interesting that Corinne Marchand has such a vivid impression of something that was so important in her life, which it was also in mine, and I've been lucky to find a woman, an actress, who could really embody this, [by] the fact that she's supposed to be a very beautiful body, so to speak, but she's supposed to change — which she understood very well — so that little by little, something in her gets her out of her *coquetterie* (vanity) and selfishness. Everybody looks at her as a little star in her little world, and then, because she opens her eyes by fear, by shock, whatever it is, she starts to look at other people. There's the fact she then goes into cafés and nobody listens to her song, and she starts seeing people making money in the street, strange things like swallowing frogs (yes!); she looks at her friend Dorothée, who is a simple, beautiful character as a very nice person, very simple and very pure about what it is to be alive in a body, and the whole thing changes. She did this in a very refined style, I helped her by doing the film in the order of the screenplay, which is very rare, but because it makes sense. I'd say, okay, we'll do 2 days, all the things in the apartment while we go there, it's much more easy for the planning of the film, so we do the scenes 2 to 5 in the apartment, then we go into the café and do that. I said: 'I think it's so fragile what she has to do, so difficult, so we'll shoot the film in the order of the screenplay', which meant we went to the apartment, then we went out, then she came back, then out; and it helped her really to build a little space in her, something that speaks to her, that makes her change. It seems odd to only have one hour to change in your life, but that was the wager: can we believe that she can change in 90 minutes? And she helped me to make us believe something happened to her, that made her able to meet that soldier, because any other day, she'd just say, come on, let me go, you know, as beautiful women do with people speaking to them, because beauty sometimes puts you in such a loneliness. And because she's open to people, because she's ready to understand something, the fear of that man, this specific situation, make them both suddenly understand each other, even if they don't know each other. So, I'm so glad she succeeded in that, and Antoine [Bourseiller] also, with what she has already been through, suddenly to be able to be with somebody, as if it's not so much in the dialogue but the 'being together thing' that changes her and makes her feel she's through with the panic. She is afraid, well, because when you say 'radiation' and all that, we don't know; but, it's like one moment, 10 minutes, perhaps 15 minutes, of grace that they share together. An artist has to be modest, I'm trying to learn from what I do, and from the reactions of people. When you prepare a screenplay and you prepare a film, you have to imagine what could be the reaction. In French we have a verb, *subodorer* [to detect, to sense], here I'd say 'to imagine'. I have to imagine that if I do this, if she says that, how will it be understood, or not understood, and where are the possibilities for misunderstanding? Because there are always some, in every single conversation, you can slip and go off. So what I try, from *Cléo* onwards, and before, is to say this: what I put in the film is what I'd hoped to put in; but then, the film — the action, the actors, the movement become the film, and maybe they say something different, slightly different from what I thought I was putting in. Then, it's the way it's received that teaches me if I went in the right or wrong direction, to make believe this or that. I was very much asked, very often, 'why is the beginning in colour?' And I don't know if it's illogical: in the superstition, it's one thing, the life, the fate told by the card reader, it's fake in a way, as if she sees the illness in her; and in a way, she sees the truth, Cléo meets the man. Then, we see her tell her husband 'I saw death', and we're supposed to be afraid that Cléo is in big danger, but again, it's fiction, the cards, it is fiction. So I thought, the minute we'll see the card reader say 'are you sick?' it becomes reality. But you know it's a circle in orbit, a film, as much as you can believe, you can step in a reality that anyone can believe in, but anyway, it's a film, so I was trying to get enough movement and details in that specific time that I spoke about, so that people would really follow her, be with her, and that's why I did the setting with one scene after another. It's also logical for the money spent on a film, you have to be logical and organised. But it's also for the story, I thought the movement, the evolution, the screenplay should be respected to help her to act, to help me too to be as refined as possible, so that people would go from the impression that she's a beautiful woman, with her big *déshabillé* [negligee], and her lover is so chic but doesn't look at her, and nobody believes she's sick; so we have to make her lonely, and more lonely, even if everybody makes compliments. That was something very difficult, and I did it the way I thought it should be. We had little money but we had time, that's precious. At the time, we had, I think, 300 000 francs, ridiculously low, but the producer said, when I told him the plot, 'Don't say the word cancer, it's bad luck'; but I said, it's about cancer, what do we do? So he said, I allow you to say it once; so she just said it then in the garden: 'What are you afraid of?' he [the soldier] asks, she says 'Well, death, cancer maybe'. I was not allowed to say it twice! The money factor? That's why I made the film too. Because we had little money, we couldn't travel, go to different places, we couldn't do a film over 2 months because you'd have to change places, costumes; so, by making it so 'narrow' in a way, in little time, we were saving money — because that's what the producer wanted — but it helped me to concentrate. Instead of thinking about 'we don't have money', to say 'what can we do with the money we have?' That's why Cléo is in Paris, in a very strict time, and I knew the places because I live around there: near le Dôme, near Parc Montsouris, that's where I brought the children to learn how to walk. I knew all these places so well that I was in a very simple setting, I didn't have to look for something specially beautiful, specially Parisian, I just went to the places I knew very well to help me to be with the film, and to help Corinne to be in it.

On timing. About feature films versus short films

Normally, it's true, what is expected is 90 to 100 minutes, but a film requires and asks for a certain length. You have to say something in 2 hours or 12 minutes. I made *Cléo from 5 to 7* but stopped at 6:30 PM because it was too much, 6:30 was enough. We all need to have a strong feeling about what is needed, in order to do a film; I don't do a film to fulfil a programme, I do a film the way I feel it should be made, the length it requires to be made.

On choosing mirrors and names, or chance

Using mirrors in *Cléo* is for all the *coquettes* [vain], beautiful women who look at themselves a lot, because they like themselves or whatever. But I use mirrors in a very different way at the beginning of *Les Plages d'Agnès*, since it was a self-portrait, as everybody does, like painters who look at themselves and paint. I thought I should take a mirror, which is the tool of the self-portrait, and turn it back like this, back to the people, the people surrounding me, the people who help me, the people I met in my life, so the mirror can be used in different ways.

How do I pick names? Cléo Victoire Florence, the pop singer. Cléo because of Cléopâtre, and she says her middle name is Florence. The soldier then talks about Flore, but he makes a mistake. He says you can think about the goddess of summer, it's in June, 21st of June is the start of summer, but Flore is the goddess of Spring. Victoire, I don't remember why. I thought it would be her name as a singer, I don't think it's her real name. But I remember too when I look for a name: in *Vagabond* with Sandrine Bonnaire, I had to pick a name for that girl, and I thought she should have a very normal name and a nickname. In France, Monique is a very 'usual' name, not very fancy, and I said from Monique I can make Mona. One day, one of these bright people analyzing films said she [Varda] picked Mona because in Greek 'mono' is one, loneliness, so she picked Mona because she's alone. No, I didn't pick it because of that, but it's okay! She is alone. But you see, sometimes we do things like this, for no special reasons, thinking or organizing what would be the best, it comes as it comes. I follow sometimes, very often, my impressions. I rely on my intuition, on chance; chance brings me a lot, I used to say chance is my first assistant. It brings me things, they come to me; it's not like I go to things, they come to me. Exactly like when I started *The Gleaners and I*, I was following trucks on the second day of shooting. Farmers want to have very formatted potatoes, 3 to 5 centimetres, whenever it's too big or too small, they throw it away. So I thought I should follow these trucks, to see if they bring these potatoes to other people in other villages, and I saw a man say 'it's a monster, like a heart'. I said well, they brought me this on a tray, because that gives me what I should be doing in the film. A potato is the most modest vegetable and cheap, some are big, but this one with the shape of a heart means a lot! That got me the feeling that I should get out of these people why they reject what is not formatted, and what it is, that is warm, and why we should feel warm towards them. The meaning of my whole film came out of the heart shaped potato. They are rejected as monsters, that's what gave me the impulse to go and approach these people, try to be very patient to try to get out of them things they had to say — not only poor people, other people too, but okay, poor people especially, and what they have to say about society, it's interesting. Just going like this, being ready to discover things, that's how and why I work, that helped me, as if I'm helped by chance, and by different things.

To come back to Cléo's choice as a singer: I loved Edith Piaf so much when I was young, and I thought it was a sort of beautiful thing to be a singer, which I couldn't be because I didn't have a voice for singing. I think it's so mysterious that a song comes out of the body. Somebody can learn how to sing but it's like a gift, some people can't sing. I thought if Cléo is a singer, will we be more sad if she's sick? And I can write songs for her, which I loved to do. Is Cléo so alone? A lot of people have no families around them, plus, many times, artists have chosen a way that is not agreeable to their families, so they are more alone than other people. Artists, they're not well seen, I mean sometimes I remember feeling in my own family like a black duck — is that sheep in English? — but I don't feel like a sheep, I'd rather be a duck!

On time in films, friends and films within films

In *Cléo*, the radio news is inserted from that day because it's the Algerian war. I had the idea that the soldier is on leave, in Paris, and he has to go back, take a train to Marseilles, take a boat, and then go to where the war is. Even though I'm so glad that the film is remembered 50 years later, it's interesting to situate a film in a very specific time, on a very specific day. There was that little doggy which was on Sputnik, which at the time was an incredible thing and which now is like a *gag* [a joke], but the war was really there, while some of the news was also about Edith Piaf who was sick. It's nice to situate a film in time, not that I want it to look like the fashion of 1961! I was very careful that it would be out of fashion, as much as possible, so that you can see it today without thinking, ah, ah, that's the way they were dressed; but still, I like the idea, and yes it is a political film we had to do, because it was a terrible war that a lot of people didn't wish for, and thought that Algeria should be free. It was the government that sent young men there, like Americans sent to Vietnam. Everywhere in the countries they send soldiers, they're not too excited about the reasons why they're sent.

I also inserted a film within a film with friends, because I was afraid, when making *Cléo*, that people would get bored because it's a 'thin' subject — as we go along with Cléo, she's afraid, she's afraid — and I thought maybe, they won't be able to stay for 90 minutes! In many films, as you may notice, at the end of the third quarter, there's a little weakness, and I thought I should do something, like a pause, so that's the reason — if I make a pause with something very different, they will come back to Cléo, as if they know her. I decided, because I invented that Dorothée's boyfriend is running the film booth in a cinema, if they go there, and she's very nice, gives him a reel, he could show them something supposedly funny. At that time in 1961, there were not so many funny *burlesque* [slapstick comedy] films, and I decided to make a little short film, very short, in one day, on a bridge — it doesn't exist anymore because we have freeways everywhere. It was the Macdonald bridge, near Parc de la Villette, and it was nice because you could see trains, trucks, I liked the place very much. The subject came — I talked about this in the 'making of' — because we were very good friends, Jacques Demy and I, with Jean-Luc Godard and Anna Karina, his wife at the time. We went out very often and Godard was wearing these black glasses that you could not see his eyes through. It was getting on my nerves all the time because I think people should show their eyes, that's where we share things. If you get glasses, you have to make them slightly clear so that you can see, so I decided, sorry, because of his black glasses, he doesn't see reality, he will be obliged to take them off! As you can see, when he takes them off, he has a beautiful look, like Harry Langdon, he really looked very good; that was my private little joke, to make take off his glasses and he did it because he played the game, he didn't refuse to do it. I invited them all because we knew each other, like old friends, Sami Frey, Eddy Constantine by chance — because I had met him 2 days before so I told him, come along — Jean-Claude Brialy, Danièle Delorrme, Yves Robert, the producer Georges de Beauregard, who played the driver of the hearse and the driver of the ambulance, I invited them all! Nobody was paid. I said, give me one day, half a day, and come on this bridge, and we did it, that fast. I thought that's a reason to make a little pause about being afraid, when she comes out of the house, goes into the steps, breaks a mirror, that's part of the superstition that came from my mother. She was very superstitious, you know, and everything about Tuesday, never putting a hat on a bed and all that, I thought it's funny, but I don't believe it's that funny. And there she goes and breaks her mirror, bad luck like in the superstition, so here's a shock, the little film to start again, stop being afraid, even if I captured the sense of being afraid, then the broken window in the street, and then again, she's in total fear, that's why I made that short film, I thought it was like a pause, a stop.

On cats as unpredicted features, or the quest for la petite musique *rather than love*

Cats are in the film, but it's not only about cats! They are not always part of conscious decisions. Natural things come in a film, and it's not only a set. For me, it's strange when I see the way cinema is, with a lot of action, a lot of chasing and violence. I saw a little bit of an action film while waiting, and think I understood nothing, there's an incredible tension of action, very well done, very tense, with very sharp editing. My mind is different I guess. I was looking at that film like a ballet, I thought I understood nothing, and I think there are so many worlds of cinema so I'm so glad some people love what I do. Because I feel it's so like a little music, you know, which doesn't make a lot of noise. Most of the time, there's good music, and strong music, and I feel mine is like a little song you can capture, and I feel very grateful to audiences.

What about my impression, or my attitude, towards love, since shooting *Cléo*? I don't know what this means, because love is a word which can mean everything; so you say, make love, refined feelings, love for God, love for shoes, but what about love between people? *Cléo* is not about love. Or if it is about love, it's about sharing. It's about feeling for others so strongly that you can be together. It should be called 'love', but it's different. I made a film called *Le Bonheur,* in which love is very different, nice family love; then, the man loves another woman and he feels it's natural, because it's natural; so I make different films, and in each film you need to show feelings, or not, but what kind of feelings? I cannot explain my relation with the feeling of love: I work, it's in my life, but that's not something that can be discussed in any way. Each film brings its own understanding of feelings.

On actors and non-actors

I have a way to see *les vrais gens*, 'real people', because I love to work with non-actors, even if actors have been helping me since *Cléo*, like Michel Piccoli, some people have been, I would say, 'directing actors'. But I love to work with non-actors because sometimes they bring their own mystery, and they are not professional, but I get something out of them that maybe I would not be able to ask of actors. In many films, like *Vagabond*, besides Sandrine — who was a very young actress, she was 17 years old, so she didn't have a lot of film experience — there was Macha Méril, but all the others were in the countryside, peasants, *garagistes* [mechanics], workers. I spent time with them and explained I needed them, and they played the game; the way they do their best brings exactly what I needed. So it's true, I'm more helped by documentaries. I made 2 documentaries which taught me to listen to people, and get what is so specific about each of them, so that I could ask then ask non-actors to enter my fictions. *La Pointe courte*, on the other end, is not a documentary, and it was done in 1954, but don't make me feel I'm the oldest one on the planet. Manoel de Oliveira was 102 when he made a film recently, a good film.*

* Manoel de Oliveira released his first documentary in 1931 and his last in 2014, two years after this interview. He died on 2 April 2015, aged 106.

On feminism, favourite films, and what she really thinks about Corinne's perception of a non-feminist agenda...

I think I was a feminist before I was born. I remain strongly feminist. You don't have to make feminist films all the time, but I really belong to the people who believe it was unfair, and it's still unfair about women. Many things have vaguely changed but there's still a lot to do. In France there's still a lot of feminist activism, a lot of women 'in the resistance', resisting against the system. I made a film called *One sings, the Other doesn't*, about the fight, the struggle in France to get the permission to have contraception, which is some sort of minimum, since abortion is for an accident of contraception, we have to get the right to do it. Those are just basic rights about the body of every woman, but it's still not really well accepted, it's still a struggle because some planning centres helping with abortion are closing down, even in France. Sometimes they reduce funding, especially about that, and we fight. We fight about beaten women, all the things that still exist everywhere, rape, injustice, and I'm still very strongly on the side — not only of women, and it doesn't mean I hate men — but of the general fight for justice, equality specifically for women, we need others to continue the struggle, so I remain a feminist really.

A favourite film of mine, that's a very interesting question! I'm not so proud about all the things I did, but among not so many films — some people do a film a year — over so many years, and I think made 17 or 18 films, and roughly 17 short ones — sometimes it's short! — I love 2 or 3 films. I love very much a film which is 61–65 minutes called *Documenteur*, which is called in English *An Emotion Picture*, that I made in Los Angeles (1981). It's about a woman and her son, trying to find a place; and it's about loneliness and exile, it's a 'little music' special film. And I like very much *Jacquot de Nantes*, which is called *Jacquot*, and is about the childhood of Jacques Demy, that he told me about and I made a film of. *Vagabond, Sans toit ni loi*, I think is the best I did according to my desire for structure, and not falling into sentimentalism, to try to bring out emotion, but not fully to the point of sentimentalism but of something tough, the toughness of loneliness. Being revolted and being furious about it, as if you stop the dialogue, you die yourself. I like the violence of the subject and I was incredibly lucky to have Sandrine Bonnaire, incredibly good, and the excellent music of Joanna Bruzdowicz. A lot of things were helped with music too. I made sure that in my short film, called *L'Opéra Mouffe*, Rue Mouffetard, Georges Delerue made the music. Some of my films I feel good about, because of the subject, the way it was shot, the music, plus the people who helped me to do the image, when it's put together and follows the project. Sometimes I 'slide' a little, I like it less, and I'm not so proud that I wouldn't think I could have done it better.

What about Corinne Marchand's statement that *Cléo* had absolutely nothing to do with feminism? Corinne is very wrong. I always say about *Cléo* that it's a very hidden feminist story. Because the film is exactly 90 minutes, and after 45 minutes, she gets rid of her wig, her bed, she puts on a little dress and goes out: the feminist side starts when a woman goes out on her own, out of her look, her problems, when she turns and looks at other people. The beginning of feminism is to look at other people, including women.

INDEX

Adler, Laure 72, 135
Akerman, Chantal 8, 48
Altman, Rick 63 n. 10
Audé, Françoise 45, 120

Barnes, Julian ix
Barratier, Christophe 48
Barthes, Roland 102, 147, 186
Bastide, Bernard 100, 136–37, 139
Baudelaire, Charles 51–52, 118–19, 120–23
Bellour, Raymond 127, 144, 151–52
Bénezet, Delphine 4
Benjamin, Walter 33, 111–12, 119, 120
Benedetti, Sandra 71
Berger, John 11–12, 22, 111–12, 119
Bíró, Yvette 110
Bishop, Claire 160, 172, 173
Blanck, Dorothée 11–12, 13, 15–17, 18, 22, 23 nn. 1 & 3, 24 n. 13
Bluher, Dominique 175, 181
Blunt, Alison 159, 169 n. 12
Boltanski, Christian 5, 6, 144, 152, 178
Bonnaire, Sandrine 154, 192, 205, 209
Borzello, Frances 19, 24 nn. 8 &10, 25 n. 19
Bourseiller, Antoine ix, 1, 6, 16, 18, 69, 204
Boyle, Claire 172
Boubat, Edouard 24 n. 16
Breton, André 188
Bright, Susan 183, 189
Butler, Judith 14–15, 17, 24 n. 4, 171, 172, 186, 189, 190, 193 n. 2

Cartier-Bresson, Henri 144–45
Chabrol, Claude 97, 98, 106
Chamarette, Jenny 127
Chomsky, Noam 172, 194
Clair, René 47
Colvile, Georgiana 73
Cooper, Sarah 12, 127
Cruickshank, Ruth 131

Dahan, Olivier 48
Dällenbach, Lucien 97, 104
Darke, Chris 71
Demy, Jacques ix, 2, 3, 5, 9 n. 12, 13, 14, 24 n. 16, 47–48, 70, 77, 134, 135, 136, 139, 166, 172, 173–76, 178, 182, 185, 188, 193 n. 10, 194 n. 14, 195 n. 38, 198, 200, 207, 209
Demy, Mathieu 66, 67, 73
DeRoo, Rebecca 48, 50–51, 87, 95 n. 8, 97–98, 102, 104, 105
Derrida, Jacques 95 n. 7
Dowling, Robyn 159, 169 n. 12
Drillon, Jacques 157, 176, 183
Ducastel, Olivier 48

Faludi, Susan 188
Feuer, Jane 63 n. 10
Fiant, Antony 2, 141 n. 12
Flitterman-Lewis, Sandy 29–30, 37, 77, 87, 95 n. 8, 154
Forbes, Jill 73
Ford, Charles 71
Ford, Harrison 134
Ford, John 32
Foucault, Michel 130, 195 n. 42

Giannoli, Xavier 48
Godard, Jean-Luc 28–29, 42 n. 66, 47, 97, 98, 207
Gorbman, Claudia 30, 69, 70

Hambling, Maggi 172, 181
Hamery, Roxane 2, 141 n. 12
Higonnet, Anne 111
Himid, Lubaina 164–66, 170 nn. 33 & 35
Holbein, Hans 196 n. 59
Honoré, Christophe 48
Hopkins, Rip 195 n. 38
Horn, Rebecca 187
Hottell, Ruth 51, 87, 88, 89, 95 n. 4
Hutcheon, Linda 104, 105

JR 2, 183–84, 192, 195 n. 48

Kapoor, Anish 185
Kay, Jackie 172, 182, 195 n. 36
Kaufmann, Stanley 127
Klein, Naomi 172, 190
Kline, Franz 186
Knelman, Martin 67
Kristeva, Julia 189

Lautréamont 81, 188

Le Corbusier 145, 157, 158, 159, 161, 169 n. 10
Ligon, Glenn 186

Mann, Sally 172, 182, 195 n. 39
Mapplethorpe, Robert 187
Marker, Chris 70, 72, 86 n. 9
Marks, Laura U. 32, 147
Martineau, Jacques 48
Mayer, Sophie 127
McKim, Kristi 127
Meskimmon, Marsha 167, 170 n. 44 & 46
Miller, Henry 166
Miller, Philippe 48
Mirzoeff, Nicholas 195 n. 46
Moseley, Roger 65, 66, 72, 76, 81, 82
Mulvey, Laura 151
Musil, Robert 109

Nancy, Jean-Luc 33, 39–40
Nelson, Roy Jay 29, 30, 40
Nora, Pierre 4

Oakley, Kate 195 n. 49
O'Brien, Dave 195 n. 49
Offenbach 118–20, 123
Olin, Margaret 149, 153
Oliviera, Manoel de 193
Oukrate, Françoise 45–46
Ozon, François 47, 87, 141 n. 19, 176

Païni, Dominique 176
Prelorenzo, Claude 169 n. 9

Renoir, Jean 23 n. 3, 67, 91, 93, 94, 95 n. 9, 100–01
Renoir, Pierre-Auguste 6, 113
Resnais, Alain 16, 17, 24 n. 13, 47
Riffaterre, Michael 100, 106 n. 19
Rollet, Brigitte 77
Rosello, Mireille 71
Rounding, Virginia 122

Sarraute, Nathalie 192, 196 n. 65
Sayad, Cecilia 127, 141 n. 15
Shields, Rob 130
Silverman, Kaja 172, 182, 187, 189
Siri, Florent Emilio 48
Smith, Alison 5, 47, 53, 58, 100, 105, 138
Sobchack, Vivian 31

Thouvenel, Éric 2, 141 n. 12
Todorov, Tzvetan 153
Toubiana, Serge 175
Tyrer, Ben 129

Ungar, Steven 19, 25 n. 20, 29, 38
Urbain, Jean –Didier 129–30

Vallaux, Christophe 67
Varda, Agnès:
exhibitions:
Agnès Varda in Californialand 2, 3, 170 n. 40
Dépot de la cabane de pêcheur 167–68
La Cabane de cinéma 157–61
La Cabane de plage 158, 160–63
La Cabane aux Portraits 158, 160–61
La Mer Méditerranée, avec deux r et un n, entre Sète et Agde 161, 168
Le Voyage à Nantes : 'Des Chambres en ville et des téléviseurs', 'La Chambre occupée, paroles de squatteurs' 171, 182, 189
Hommage aux Justes de France 2, 149, 150, 152, 153
L'Île et Elle 2, 24 n. 11, 67, 86 n. 12, 134, 143, 161
Patatutopia 2, 67, 86 n. 4, 144
Plages et pages chinoises 2
Portraits brisés 147, 155 n. 12
Triptyques atypiques 67, 72, 144, 154, 186–87
Triptyque de Noirmoutier 143
Varda/Cuba 9
Y'a pas que la mer 144
films:
7 p., cuis., s. de b. 68–69, 111
Agnès de ci de là Varda 4, 5, 7, 66, 70, 72, 82, 144–45, 155 n. 12, 186, 193 & n. 10
Black Panthers 3, 186, 189
Cléo de 5 à 7 ix, 1, 11–25, 27–43, 50, 56, 58, 64 n. 13, 64 n. 16, 69, 77, 97, 110, 133, 134, 197–202, 203–09
Daguerréotypes 110
Du Côté de la côte 132
Documenteur 3, 24 n. 11, 111, 209
Jane B. par Agnès V. 12, 24 nn. 7 & 11, 67
Jacquot de Nantes 70, 135, 175, 193 n. 10, 194 n. 17, 209
Kung-fu Master 66, 72–76, 82
Le Bonheur 83, 87–95, 97–107, 208
Les Créatures 66, 68, 76–82
Les Dites Cariatides 24 n. 5, 64 n. 20, 109–25
Les Glaneurs et la glaneuse 3, 64 n. 13, 70, 71, 86 n. 4, 110, 128, 129, 131, 186
Les Glaneurs et la glaneuse: deux ans après 56, 86 n. 4, 131, 194 n. 28
L'Opéra Mouffe 11, 13, 14, 15, 17, 18, 19, 21, 22, 23 nn. 1 & 3, 24 n. 15, 110, 179, 189, 209
Les Plages d'Agnès 24 n. 6, 56, 66, 71, 73, 83, 110, 127–42, 146–47, 152, 157–70, 172, 178, 205
La Pointe-courte 77
L'Une chante, l'autre pas 25 n. 18, 45–64
Mur murs 3, 175
Oncle Yanco 137, 166, 170 n. 38
Ô saisons, ô châteaux 25 n. 18
Salut les Cubains 9, 145
Sans toit ni loi 7, 56, 58, 68, 136, 154, 179, 187, 190, 192, 196 n. 65, 209

Tout(e) Varda 3
Ulysse 147–48, 149, 155 n. 13
writings:
Regards sur l'exposition (*L'Île et Elle*) 194 n. 20
Varda par Agnès 5, 11, 21, 23 n. 2, 46, 67, 71, 72, 109
Zoetrope: All-Story 7

Varda-Demy, Rosalie 3, 89, 135, 187, 196 n. 59
Velazquez 16

Woolf, Virginia 11, 13, 23 n. 2, 173

Žižek, Slavoj 172, 182

Lightning Source UK Ltd.
Milton Keynes UK
UKHW051918171119
353714UK00010B/273/P